CAMBRIDGE LIBRARY COLLECTION

Books of enduring scholarly value

Classics

From the Renaissance to the nineteenth century, Latin and Greek were compulsory subjects in almost all European universities, and most early modern scholars published their research and conducted international correspondence in Latin. Latin had continued in use in Western Europe long after the fall of the Roman empire as the lingua franca of the educated classes and of law, diplomacy, religion and university teaching. The flight of Greek scholars to the West after the fall of Constantinople in 1453 gave impetus to the study of ancient Greek literature and the Greek New Testament. Eventually, just as nineteenth-century reforms of university curricula were beginning to erode this ascendancy, developments in textual criticism and linguistic analysis, and new ways of studying ancient societies, especially archaeology, led to renewed enthusiasm for the Classics. This collection offers works of criticism, interpretation and synthesis by the outstanding scholars of the nineteenth century.

The Euthydemus of Plato

Headmaster of King Edward's School in Birmingham for fourteen years, Edwin Hamilton Gifford (1820–1905) also held a number of ecclesiastical posts, including select preacher at both Cambridge and Oxford. Better known for his biblical and patristic scholarship, he also prepared this edition of the *Euthydemus*, Plato's most comical dialogue. Thought to be an early work, depicting a discussion between Socrates and two sophists trained in *eristic* (argument for the sake of conflict), it is among the earliest-known treatises on logic, satirising various fallacies that were subsequently categorised by Aristotle. Published in 1905, a generation after Jowett's standard translation, this edition was intended for university and advanced school students. A thorough introduction is given in English, followed by the Greek text, extensive notes, and indexes of vocabulary and names. As such, this reissue illuminates the educational preoccupations of both early twentieth-century England and classical Athens.

Cambridge University Press has long been a pioneer in the reissuing of out-of-print titles from its own backlist, producing digital reprints of books that are still sought after by scholars and students but could not be reprinted economically using traditional technology. The Cambridge Library Collection extends this activity to a wider range of books which are still of importance to researchers and professionals, either for the source material they contain, or as landmarks in the history of their academic discipline.

Drawing from the world-renowned collections in the Cambridge University Library and other partner libraries, and guided by the advice of experts in each subject area, Cambridge University Press is using state-of-the-art scanning machines in its own Printing House to capture the content of each book selected for inclusion. The files are processed to give a consistently clear, crisp image, and the books finished to the high quality standard for which the Press is recognised around the world. The latest print-on-demand technology ensures that the books will remain available indefinitely, and that orders for single or multiple copies can quickly be supplied.

The Cambridge Library Collection brings back to life books of enduring scholarly value (including out-of-copyright works originally issued by other publishers) across a wide range of disciplines in the humanities and social sciences and in science and technology.

The Euthydemus of Plato

*With Revised Text,
Introduction, Notes and Indices*

EDITED BY
EDWIN HAMILTON GIFFORD

CAMBRIDGE
UNIVERSITY PRESS

CAMBRIDGE
UNIVERSITY PRESS

University Printing House, Cambridge, CB2 8BS, United Kingdom

Published in the United States of America by Cambridge University Press, New York

Cambridge University Press is part of the University of Cambridge.
It furthers the University's mission by disseminating knowledge in the pursuit of
education, learning and research at the highest international levels of excellence.

www.cambridge.org
Information on this title: www.cambridge.org/9781108059930

© in this compilation Cambridge University Press 2013

This edition first published 1905
This digitally printed version 2013

ISBN 978-1-108-05993-0 Paperback

THE EUTHYDEMUS
OF PLATO

HENRY FROWDE, M.A.

PUBLISHER TO THE UNIVERSITY OF OXFORD

LONDON, EDINBURGH

NEW YORK

THE EUTHYDEMUS
OF PLATO

WITH REVISED TEXT
INTRODUCTION, NOTES, AND INDICES

BY

EDWIN HAMILTON GIFFORD, D.D.

HONORARY FELLOW OF ST. JOHN'S COLLEGE, CAMBRIDGE,
AND FORMERLY ARCHDEACON OF LONDON

OXFORD
AT THE CLARENDON PRESS
1905

OXFORD
PRINTED AT THE CLARENDON PRESS
BY HORACE HART, M.A.
PRINTER TO THE UNIVERSITY

TO

THE MASTER AND FELLOWS

OF

ST. JOHN'S COLLEGE, CAMBRIDGE

THIS LITTLE VOLUME IS INSCRIBED
IN GRATEFUL REMEMBRANCE
OF THE MANY PRIVILEGES ENJOYED
BY THE EDITOR
DURING SIXTY-FIVE YEARS
AS SCHOLAR FELLOW
AND HONORARY FELLOW
OF THE COLLEGE

PREFACE

This edition of the *Euthydemus* is intended for the use of University Students and the Higher Forms of Public Schools. To such readers there will be little force in the objection made by some critics of a sterner mood that the dialogue is too amusing, too full of satirical humour and even broad comedy, to be worthy of so great a philosopher as Plato. On this character of the 'Literary Form' of the dialogue see the Introduction, § ii.

In revising the text I have made no new collation of manuscripts, but have depended on the critical apparatus of Schanz and the revision of the same by Burnet, except as to a few readings for which I have carefully inspected the phototype of the Codex Clarkianus in the Bodleian Library.

The only original emendations which I have ventured to introduce are 271 c 7 καθ' ἅ for κατά, and 286 ε 7 Σὺ δ' ἐκέλευες; for οὐδὲ κελεύεις.

In attempting to determine the date of the *Euthydemus* and its relation to the *Phaedrus* I have derived most help from the Introductions to the latter dialogue by Stallbaum and Thompson, and from Lutoslawski's *Origin and Growth of Plato's Logic*.

My best thanks are due to the Delegates of the Clarendon Press for allowing the work to be published under their auspices, and to the Secretary and other officials for much valuable assistance and unfailing kindness during the passage of the volume through the press.

OXFORD:
November, 1904.

CONTENTS

INTRODUCTION

I. CONTENTS.

THE *Euthydemus* is a conversation between Socrates and his old friend Crito, consisting chiefly of a highly dramatized narrative of a discussion in which Socrates himself had played a principal part, the other chief actor being the Sophist from whose name the dialogue takes its title.

The other persons taking part in the action are Dionysodorus, the elder brother of Euthydemus; Cleinias, an ingenuous and handsome youth of noble birth, first cousin to the famous Alcibiades; and Ctesiphon, an enthusiastic admirer of Cleinias, a high-spirited young gentleman of irascible temper and rough and ready speech, who has been previously introduced in the *Lysis* (204 C, 205 A, 206 C, D) as rallying his sentimental friend Hippothales with a boisterous kind of wit.

There are also present many pupils and admirers of the two Sophists, and on the other hand many young friends of Cleinias.

i. In the opening scene Socrates gives an account to Crito of the two Sophists with whom he had held a discussion in the Lyceum on the previous day. They were natives of Chios, who had migrated to Thurii, and being banished thence had spent many years in various parts of Greece, and had recently come to Athens as professional teachers of wisdom and virtue. The varied accomplishments which they had displayed on a former visit are extolled by Socrates with playful irony. He had never understood before what true pancratiasts were; but these men were perfect in every kind of combat. They could teach men to fight in heavy armour with the weapons of actual war, or to arm themselves with speeches for the harder conflicts of the law-courts. They had now set the crown upon pancratiastic art by making themselves masters of the 'eristic philosophy,' an irresistible method of disputation by which every statement, true and false alike, could be refuted with equal certainty. Let Crito come with Socrates to be taught these noble arts; it was not too late to learn, for the teachers themselves were old men, and had only learned this new system last year. If Socrates and Crito took their sons with them, they would, no doubt, be admitted as fellow pupils (271 A–272 D).

As Crito wishes to know what sort of wisdom he is to be taught, Socrates proceeds to describe what had occurred in the Lyceum. He had been sitting alone in the apodyterium, and was just rising up to go away when he was forbidden by the usual sign (τὸ δαιμόνιον) to leave his seat. The two Sophists presently enter and walk up and down in the colonnade, followed by an admiring crowd of pupils. Cleinias, accompanied by Ctesippus and other friends, comes in and sits beside Socrates. On seeing this the Sophists approach, and seat themselves, Euthydemus beside Cleinias, and Diodorus on the other side of Socrates, who introduces them to Cleinias with high commendation of their military and forensic skill. But the brothers receive these compliments with rude contempt, for they are no longer proud of such minor accomplishments, but make the loftier boast of imparting virtue more perfectly and more quickly than any other men. 'The possessors of such a power, says Socrates, must be divine: forgive my irreverent speeches, and grant us an exhibition of this marvellous wisdom: we are all eager to learn, and let the first experiment be made on Cleinias, for whose advancement in wisdom and virtue we are all most anxious' (272 D–275 C).

ii. Before attempting to describe the next scene Socrates, like the poets (Hom. *Il.* ii. 484), invokes the Muses and Mnemosyne to aid him in so great a task: cf. *Theaet.* 191 D.

Then comes the wonderful exhibition of the Sophists' skill in teaching virtue.

Euthydemus. Are those who learn the wise or the unwise (οἱ σοφοὶ ἢ οἱ ἀμαθεῖς)?

Cleinias. The wise.

Euthydemus. Do they already know the things which they are learning?

Cleinias. No.

Euthydemus. Then the learners are the unwise (ἀμαθεῖς), not the wise, as you suppose.

I. CONTENTS

The chorus of the Sophists' followers laugh and applaud; and before Cleinias has time to recover breath Dionysodorus takes him in hand.

'Which of the schoolboys learn the dictated lesson, the clever or the stupid (οἱ σοφοὶ ἢ οἱ ἀμαθεῖς)?'—'The clever.'—'Then the wise (οἱ σοφοί) are the learners, not the unwise (οἱ ἀμαθεῖς), and your answer to Euthydemus was wrong.'

Amid shouts of applause Euthydemus returns to the attack.

'Do the boys learn (μανθάνουσιν) what they know (ἐπίστανται), or what they do not know?'—'What they do not know.'—'But they know the letters?'—'Yes.'—'And the letters make up the lesson?'—'Yes.'—'Then they learn what they know, and your answer was wrong.'

Upon this Diodorus again takes up the ball: 'To learn is to receive knowledge: to know is to have knowledge. The learners receive but have not knowledge: therefore they who do not know learn, not those who know' (275 C–277 C).

Cleinias is quite bewildered, and Socrates interposes to shield him from a third attack. The Sophists, he says, are only playing with him, and dancing round him like the Corybantes, and initiating him by these preparatory rites into the Sophistic mysteries. They are tripping him up with their verbal fallacies in order to teach him that a word may be used in more senses than one. But there has been enough of such play: let them now show Cleinias how to improve in wisdom and virtue; he will himself give an example of what he means in his own simple way (277 C–278 D).

All men desire to be happy, in other words to do well (εὖ πράττειν): to this end they count many good things necessary, riches, health, beauty, noble birth, power, honour. To these must be added temperance, justice, fortitude, wisdom, and good fortune. But good fortune is already included in wisdom. In the practice of every art, in playing the flute, in reading and writing, in navigation, in war, in medicine the wise are the fortunate, and he who has wisdom has no further need of fortune.

Moreover all those good things must be used, and used rightly, in order to make men happy; and to use them rightly there must be knowledge for a guide. Without it riches and strength and

3   B 2

INTRODUCTION

power become even worse than useless, as giving wider opportunities for ill doing. In short all such things are in themselves neither good nor bad : wisdom alone is good, and folly bad, therefore get wisdom.

But how to get it ? Can it be taught, or does it come spontaneously? Cleinias replies with youthful confidence, ' In my opinion it can be taught '; and Socrates is delighted to accept so ready a solution of the great question (278 E–282 D).

Socrates now invites either of the Sophists to discuss the same subject more scientifically, or to go on to show whether it is necessary to acquire every kind of knowledge, or only some one science that will suffice to make Cleinias wise and happy. Dionysodorus, after being assured that they truly and earnestly desire to have Cleinias made wise, argues that they wish him to be now what he is not, that is to be no longer what he now is, in fact to be destroyed. Worthy friends, to wish destruction to the boy !

' Destruction on your own head ! ' cries Ctesippus, ' for telling such an impious lie about us.'—' A lie ! ' says Euthydemus. ' Is it possible to tell a lie ? By telling the thing of which you speak you tell a real thing ; and he who tells the real thing tells the truth, and tells no lie. You can do nothing to what is not, you can only speak what is, that is, speak truth.'—' Yes, of course,' says Ctesippus, ' he speaks in a certain way of real things, but not as they really are.' —' What do you mean ? ' says Diodorus. ' Do any speak of things as they are ? '—' Yes, gentlemen, and those who speak the truth.'— ' Do good men then speak badly of what is bad ? '—' Indeed they do speak very badly of bad men, and if you do not take care, they will speak badly of you.'—' And do they speak greatly of the great, and hotly of the hot ? '—' Certainly, and speak frigidly of the frigid and their frigid arguments.'—' You are insolent, Ctesippus, insolent, I say.'—' Not so, but as a friend I advise you never to say so rudely in my presence that I wish destruction to my dearest friends ' (282 D–284 E).

Socrates again interposes to keep the peace : ' Let us not quarrel over a word ; if by " destruction " they mean making foolish and bad men wise and good, let them try the experiment on me, and boil me, if they please, as in Medea's cauldron.'—' Or they may flay me like Marsyas,' said Ctesippus, ' only let them make virtue, not

4

I. CONTENTS

a bottle, out of my hide : but Dionysodorus must not call contradiction insolence.'

'Is contradiction possible?' said the Sophist. 'At all events you could not prove that you ever heard one person contradicting another.'—'That is true; but let us listen now whether I am proving it to you while Ctesippus is contradicting Dionysodorus' (see the note on the passage).

'Would you undertake to argue this? We should not contradict each other at all, if we both knew the right definition (λόγον) of each thing; but when neither knows the right definition, then we should contradict each other, or in this case neither would speak of the thing at all. So when I give the right definition and you some other, you do not speak of the thing itself at all, and, if you do not speak, you cannot contradict' (284 E–286 B).

Ctesippus kept silence, but Socrates said that this argument was as old as Protagoras or older, and had a wonderful way of tripping up the speaker himself as well as others. 'But you can best tell us the truth about it. Is it impossible to speak or even think what is false? Is there no such thing as ignorance, or an ignorant man? Do you really mean this?'—'Refute me if you can,' said Dionysodorus.—'Is refutation possible, if according to your argument no one speaks what is false?'—'No, it is not,' said Euthydemus.— 'Neither then did I bid you refute me,' said Dionysodorus.—'Was it you then that bade me, Euthydemus : for I do not clearly understand these subtleties. However, I am going to ask perhaps a stupid question: If it is impossible to contradict, to speak or even think what is false, to be ignorant or in error, pray what are you come to teach?' (285 A–287 A).

Dionysodorus tries to evade this troublesome question: 'Why go back to former arguments? Can you make nothing of the present?'—'They are very difficult,' says Socrates, 'for what does this last phrase, "make nothing of them," mean (νοεῖ), except that I cannot "refute" them?'

Dionysodorus has heard enough of that word 'refute' (286 E), and insists on passing to a new question: 'Can a mere lifeless word "mean" anything?'—'It was my stupidity,' says Socrates; 'but was I right or wrong? If I was right, you cannot "refute" me: and if I was wrong, you cannot be right in saying that error

5

is impossible (287 A). This is not going back to the past: for your present argument can only trip one up and then itself fall' (287 A-288 A).

Ctesippus begins again to jeer at the Sophists, but is checked by Socrates : 'They are not yet in earnest, but are playing tricks like Proteus, and must be held fast till they show themselves in their true form.' He will give them another example of the sort of teaching which he wishes them to impart, by continuing his argument with Cleinias.

It was agreed (282 D 1) that philosophy or the acquisition of knowledge is necessary to make men happy. But what kind of knowledge? Such as teaches them to make the right use of all other acquirements and advantages. Not the knowledge of healing or money-making, nor even a knowledge that would make us immortal without teaching us to use immortality aright : not the art of the speech-maker, sublime and inspired though it sometimes appears ; for some know not how to use the speeches they have themselves made, and after all it is only a kind of charm for fascinating judges and assemblies. Is it then the strategic art that makes men happy?—No, says Cleinias, that is only a kind of man-hunting ; and hunters and fishermen give over what they catch to cooks, and geometers and astronomers give their discoveries to dialecticians to make use of them.

iii. At this point the narrative of Socrates is interrupted by Crito, who is astonished that one so young as Cleinias should be so wise. A long conversation follows, in which Socrates explains that even the kingly art is found wanting, because it does not impart wisdom or knowledge, and its claim is only an empty boast like ὁ Διὸς Κόρινθος (290 E-293 A).

iv. Socrates being thus unable, as he pretends, to find the kind of knowledge that will make men happy entreats the Sophists to be serious and rescue them from their difficulty. Euthydemus boldly undertakes to prove that Socrates already possesses the knowledge of which he is in search : he knows something, nay many things, therefore he knows everything ; for he cannot be both knowing and not knowing.

'Then you two also,' says Socrates, 'know everything.'—'Yes,' says Dionysodorus, 'and all men know all things, if they know

I. CONTENTS

one.'—' Good heavens!—for now I see you are in earnest—do you really know all things, such as carpentering, shoemaking, astronomy, and the number of the sands?'—' Of course we do.' At this Ctesippus bursts in with an impudent jibe : ' Does each of them know how many teeth the other has?' Some lively bantering follows, and then Euthydemus, still maintaining that Socrates, as well as themselves, knows all things, insists on having his questions answered categorically, 'Yes' or 'No,' without any exception or limitation, and thus proves to his own satisfaction that Socrates knew all things even before he was born or begotten, and before the earth and the heaven were made (293 A–296 D).

Socrates now turns their own mode of argument against them : ' Do I, or do I not, know that the good are unjust?'—'Yes,' says Euthydemus. 'You know that they are not unjust.'—'But that is not what I ask. How do I know that they *are* unjust?'—'You do not know it at all,' says Dionysodorus ; but he is reproved by Euthydemus for spoiling the argument, by admitting that Socrates is at the same time knowing and not knowing.

' Must not your brother, who knows all things, be right?'—'Am I his brother?' says Dionysodorus, trying again to change the argument. To this Socrates replies : ' I cannot fight two at once ; even Hercules called his nephew Iolaus to help him.'—'Was Iolaus any more Hercules' nephew than yours?'—'As you will not let Euthydemus answer my question, I must, I suppose, answer yours : Iolaus was Hercules' nephew, not mine at all, not being the son of my brother Patrocles.'—'Is Patrocles your brother?'—'Yes, on the mother's side, not on the father's.'—'Then he both is and is not your brother.'—'Not on the father's side : Chaeredemus was his father, Sophroniscus mine.'—'Then Chaeredemus, being different from a father, was not a father ; and so Sophroniscus, in like manner being different from a father, was not a father : so you, Socrates, had no father' (296 D–298 B).

This style of argument suits Ctesippus : 'Your father, you say, is also my father, and father of all, both men and beasts ; you therefore are the brother of gudgeons and puppies and little pigs.'— ' So are you,' says Dionysodorus : 'your dog is a father of puppies, and he is yours ; therefore he is your father, and you are the puppies' brother. When you beat your dog, you beat your own

7

INTRODUCTION

father.'—'I would much rather beat your father for begetting such wise sons,' replies Ctesippus.

Then follows an argument with Euthydemus about having too much of a good thing : a whole cartload of hellebore would be too much for a sick man, unless he were as big as the statue at Delphi ; but one shield and spear would not be enough for a Geryon or Briareus (298 B–299 C).

Diodorus here comes to his brother's aid : ' Gold you admit is good; then the happiest man must be one who has most gold : gold in his stomach, and skull, and both eyes.'—'Yes, indeed,' said Ctesippus, turning to Euthydemus, 'they say that among the Scythians the happiest and bravest men have much gold in their own skulls, and drink out of their own skulls, and holding their own heads in their hands, see into the inside.'

Euthydemus, catching at the word 'see,' carries on the argument by quibbling about the double meaning of δυνατὰ ὁρᾶν, 'able to see,' or 'able to be seen,' of σιγῶντα λέγειν, and λέγοντα σιγᾶν, until Ctesippus asks, 'Do all things speak, or all keep silence?'— 'Neither and both,' cries Dionysodorus ; and Ctesippus with a loud laugh declares that by this 'both' he has ruined his argument and is beaten and done for (ἀπόλωλε alluding perhaps to 283 D, E).

Cleinias laughs with delight, and Ctesippus swells with pride. 'Why do you laugh,' says Socrates, 'at things so important and beautiful?'—'Are beautiful things different from beauty or the same?' asks Dionysodorus. Socrates pretends to be puzzled and sorry to have spoken, but answers that they are different from beauty itself, though some beauty is present with each.—'Then if an ox be present with you, you are an ox, and because I am present with you now, you are Dionysodorus?'—'Heaven forbid,' said Socrates.—'But in what way must one thing be present to another in order that this other may be other (than it was)?'— 'Do you doubt about that?'—'Of course I doubt about what is not possible.'—'Is not the same same, and the other other? Even a child could not doubt that the other is other.' (Socrates here confounds the Sophist by his own device of using 'other' in different senses ; see the note on 301 B 1). 'This point, Dionysodorus, you missed on purpose, but in other respects your dialectic is excellent.'

8

I. CONTENTS

Thus encouraged Dionysodorus proceeds in his own fashion to prove the propriety of boiling the cook, smiting the smith, and making pots of the potter. Further he makes Socrates admit that he may give, or sell, or slay his own animals, and that since his gods Zeus, Apollo, or Athene having souls are animals, he may give, sell, or slay them. Socrates is struck dumb, but Ctesippus cries ' Bravo Hercules, what a fine argument ! ' ' Is " Bravo Hercules," or " Hercules Bravo " ? '—' O Poseidon, what clever arguments ! I give up,' says Ctesippus ; ' they are irresistible.'

Not only are the admirers of Euthydemus bursting with delight, but the very columns of the portico seem to ring with laughter and applause. Socrates, as if enchanted by the Sophists' wisdom, extols ironically their utter disregard of other men's opinions, who would be ashamed to conquer by such arguments, and slyly adds that by denying all predication (301 B 3), and declaring that nothing is either beautiful, or good, or white, they sew up other men's mouths and their own also, a delightful result that does away all offence. But the most marvellous thing is that they can teach others so quickly, as was seen when Ctesippus beat them with their own weapons. So they must not exhibit their skill in public, but only argue with each other alone, or with those who will pay them : such rare wisdom is of too great price to be made as common as water ; but he begs them to receive him and Cleinias as pupils (303 B–304 B).

v. Having ended his narrative of the discussion with the Sophists Socrates playfully invites Crito to become his fellow-pupil. But Crito declines the proposal, and tells how he had met a certain person who had heard the discussion, and criticized it as an unworthy fuss about worthless matters. Philosophy itself he said was good for nothing, and Crito would have been ashamed if he had heard how Socrates gave himself up to the Sophists. Socrates ascertains that the critic was no orator, but one of the speech-writers who being neither philosophers nor statesmen, but halfway between the two, tried to disparage real philosophers as their only rivals in wisdom, and shrank from all personal discussion lest they might be worsted by the fallacious tricks of the Sophists, which they supposed to be practised by the philosophers also. Crito might well be afraid of entrusting the education of his sons to

INTRODUCTION

impostors such as the Sophists, but let him satisfy himself as to the value of true philosophy, and then both study and practise it himself, and encourage his sons to do the same (304 B-307 C).

II. THE LITERARY FORM.

In the foregoing sketch of the contents of the dialogue we see that its general form and arrangement are clearly marked.

The main subject is the narration by Socrates of a discussion between himself and the Sophists ; but this is set in the frame of a conversation between Socrates and Crito, which both forms the introduction (271 A-272 D), and is resumed in the middle (290 E-293 A) and at the end of the discussion (304 B-the end).

Apart from this conversation the narrative of the discussion itself may be regarded as a drama in five scenes distinguished by the different characters who speak in each. Cf. Bonitz, *Platonische Studien*, ii. p. 258.

Sc. 1. Euthydemus, Dionysodorus, Cleinias, Socrates (272 E-277 C).

Sc. 2. Socrates, Cleinias (277 D-282 E).

Sc. 3. Dionysodorus, Socrates, Ctesippus, Euthydemus (283 A-288 B).

Sc. 4. Socrates, Cleinias (288 B-290 D).

Sc. 5. Euthydemus, Socrates, Dionysodorus, Ctesippus (293 D-304 B).

This dramatic form is more prominent in the Euthydemus than in any other of the Platonic dialogues, and from the allusions to a chorus and choric dancing in 276 B and 277 D we may infer that it was consciously adopted by Plato in order to give the most vivid expression to the contrast between the methods of argument practised by Socrates and the Sophists. This peculiar character of the dialogue has been noticed by nearly every critic, and particularly by Archer Butler, *Lectures on Ancient Philosophy*, ii. 24 : ' We can never rightly estimate the labours of Plato unless we regard his writings as themselves works of art no less than transcripts of doctrine. His versatility in the dramatic representation of character has made some of his dialogues far more resemble what we should call " Genteel Comedy " than a philosophical exposition. Thus the entire *Euthydemus* is nothing

II. LITERARY FORM

less than a *dramatic satire*, of boundless humour and variety, upon the follies of the Sophistic professors, and assuredly lies much nearer to Aristophanes than to Aristotle.'

But it is strange, as Schleiermacher remarks in his Introduction, 'that attention has always been exclusively given to this sophistical dramatizing, when to every reader the dialogue presents more important matter, a general philosophical bearing, and a visible reference to other Platonic writings.' It is not in the depth of the arguments employed, but in the liveliness of the action and the incisive force of the satire that the excellence of Plato's work is in this case to be recognized.

If therefore we ever find the *Euthydemus* regarded as little better than a farce and quite unworthy of the genius of Plato, we may wonder whether the critic has quite appreciated the subtle irony, and detected the important truths that underlie the playful language. Socrates is in fact represented throughout as giving full play to his satirical humour, and fooling the Sophists to the top of their bent by pretending to be overpowered by their arguments, to marvel at their supernatural wisdom, and even to address them as absolutely divine (273 E, 296 D). As Euthydemus and his brother are represented in the dialogue as old men, it is not likely that they were still living at the time when Plato wrote ; but it is evident that they were men of a very inferior stamp, both socially and mentally, to the greater Sophists such as Protagoras or Gorgias, and were chosen to represent the degenerate class on whom the magnificent Isocrates pours such unmitigated contempt in his oration *Against the Sophists*, 291 D. It was thus easier for Plato to make the contrast between them and Socrates the more striking. Dionysodorus in particular is represented as even more shallow and ignorant than his brother (297 A) : his coarse insolence and stupid attempts at wit (283 D, 297 D) serve to justify the introduction on the other side of such a character as Ctesippus. Thus the anger of Plato, guided by his dramatic instinct, finds an outlet in the quarrels of these minor characters for the unsparing sarcasm and vehement reproaches which serve as a foil to the delicate satire and ironical compliments of Socrates. We can hardly fail to be reminded how often the broadest farce is allowed to alternate with the most tragic and pathetic scenes in Shakespeare.

INTRODUCTION

III. THE GENERAL PURPOSE.

It is evident from the foregoing sketch of the contents, and is in fact universally admitted, that the main purpose of the *Euthydemus* is 'to represent the opposition of Socratic and Sophistic views with regard to their value in the training and education of youth' (Zeller, *Plato*, ch. ii, note 94).

'The peculiar point of view of the *Euthydemus* was long since rightly indicated by Welcker. . . . If we assume that Plato is here . . . attacking a corrupt kind of education, which though essentially worthless is yet through the approval of the multitude not unimportant for the moment, and that its chief excellence is therefore to be looked for not in the depth of the counter arguments but in the vigour of the action and satirical description, all agrees well under this point of view' (Bonitz, *Platon. Stud.* ii. 278). 'The vocation of philosophy to be the true educator of youth is vindicated in opposition to sophistry (" Scheinweisheit ") which would usurp its place, and this through the representation of each in action' (ibid. 276 fin.).

This purpose is clearly indicated in the case of Cleinias by the desire of his friends that he should be persuaded to pursue the study of philosophy and of virtue (275 A 6), and again at the end of the dialogue in the anxiety of Crito about the education of his sons (306 D 2).

The professed aim of the two systems of education thus contrasted is the same, namely to promote the study of wisdom and virtue in all men, and especially in the young (273 D 8, 275 A 1, 278 D 3, 282 D 3). But in the *methods* adopted on either side, and in the *results* attained, there is the most striking contrast.

The Sophists employ the commonest logical fallacies and the most trifling verbal quibbles (275 D 3–277 C 7), and the result is that they fully succeed in reducing the mind of an intelligent and ingenuous youth to utter confusion, and expose him to the vulgar ridicule of their own disciples (276 B, D), while Ctesippus in revenge turns their own weapons against them with well-deserved flouts and jeers (284 E, 288 B).

In the strongest possible contrast to this exhibition of Sophistic folly Plato presents an example of true Socratic teaching.

III. THE GENERAL PURPOSE

Its aim is to guide and encourage Cleinias in the pursuit of wisdom and virtue (278 D). The method adopted is to propose for consideration a serious and important subject, the universal desire for happiness. First there is an enumeration of the good things on which happiness is supposed to depend, and then it is shown by a scientific process of analysis—the division of concepts —that these things contribute to happiness only when rightly used under the guidance of knowledge, which does not come to a man by nature or accident, but by teaching and careful study (282 D).

In continuation (288 D) several kinds of special knowledge, rhetoric, strategy, and government, are found incapable of making men virtuous and happy, the result, so far as Cleinias is concerned, being that he takes part in the discussion with a growing intelligence that excites the admiration of Crito (290 E), while the general inference that philosophy alone can make men wise and good, though clearly indicated, is not expressed in this dialogue but left for further consideration (292 E).

In the renewal of the discussion the contrast between this example of Socratic teaching and that of the Sophists is made more glaring by a series of captious questions, quibbling answers, fallacies and paradoxes, which will be noticed more fully in a later section. Meanwhile it will be sufficient to quote an admirable description of the 'Eristic' art of disputation as practised by the Sophists, and illustrated in the *Euthydemus*, from Zeller's *Pre-Socratic Philosophy*, ii. 462, Eng. Tr.: 'We get a vivid picture of the Sophistic art of disputation, as it was constituted in later times, in Plato's dialogue of Euthydemus, and in Aristotle's Treatise on Fallacies; and though we must not forget that the one is a satire written with all poetic freedom, and the other a universal theory which there is no reason to restrict to the Sophists in the narrower sense or to anything historical, yet the harmony of these descriptions one with the other, and with other accounts, shows that we are justified in applying them in all their essential features to the Sophistic teaching. What they tell us is certainly not much to its advantage. The Eristics were not concerned about any scientific result; their object was to involve their adversary or interlocutor in confusion and difficulties from which he could find no way of escape, so that every answer that he gave seemed incorrect': ibid.

INTRODUCTION

NOTE. 'The ἄφυκτα ἐρωτήματα of which the Sophist boasts, *Euthyd.* 275 E, 276 E.'

Ibid. 463. ' If a discussion is uncomfortable to the Sophist, he evades it[1]; if an answer is desired of him, he insists on asking questions[2]; if any one tries to escape from ambiguous questions by closer definition, he demands "Yes" or "No"[3]; if he thinks his adversary knows of an answer, he begins by deprecating all that can possibly be said on that side[4]; if he is accused of contradicting himself, he protests against bringing forward things that are done with long ago[5]. If he has no other resource, he stupefies his adversary with speeches the absurdity of which precludes any reply[6].'

IV. THE SPECIAL OCCASION.

Besides the general purpose of vindicating the claims of true science in the education of the young, and of distinguishing the Socratic teaching from that of the Sophists, there is a certain character of the dialogue that calls for further explanation. It is evident from the whole tone and temper of the discussion, and especially of the final conversation between Socrates and Crito, that it was written in a mood of unusual irritation due to some more personal cause than the standing opposition between Plato and the Sophists. It is generally supposed that this angry feeling had been roused by the envious attacks of rival teachers, and many attempts have been made to identify the persons whose doctrines are criticized or caricatured both in the body of the dialogue and in the portrait of the λογογράφος in 305 C.

The name of Lysias is naturally one of the first to occur to any one who thinks of the unfriendly feeling between him and Plato. Athenaeus, in one of his bitter attacks upon Plato (xiii. 611), quotes part of a speech of Lysias in order to take down 'the arrogance (βρένθος) of the philosophers.' The speech was written for the

---

[1] *Euthyd.* 287 B sqq., 297 B, 299 A, etc.
[2] 287 B sq., 295 B sqq.
[3] 295 E sq., 297 D sqq.
[4] Thrasymachus in Plato, *Rep.* i. 336 C, 337 A.
[5] This is done with the most delightful *naïveté* in *Euthyd.* 287 B.
[6] *Euthyd.* 293 D, 298 D, 303 A.

IV. THE SPECIAL OCCASION

prosecution of Aeschines Socraticus, whom Lysias charges with crimes especially disgraceful to one ' who had been a disciple of Socrates, and talked so finely about justice and virtue.' Cf. Ast. *Lex. Plat.* ' Σοφιστής a Lysia dictus est Plato una cum Aeschine Socratico, ap. Aristid. c. Plat. ii.' In the oration of Aristides, p. 192, he speaks of Plato as τῶν Ῥητόρων πατέρα καὶ διδάσκαλον (Fabric. *Bibl. Gr.* vol. iv. 386).

Plato's feeling towards Lysias is sufficiently evident in the *Phaedrus* ; but in the description of the λογογράφος at the end of the *Euthydemus* there is one feature which shows that it cannot be meant for him. For ' Lysias did on one memorable occasion plead his own cause. The excellent speech Κατὰ 'Ερατοσθένους was delivered by him during his brief tenure of the Athenian franchise' (Thompson, *Phaedrus*, 181, n. 8) : cf. K. O. Müller, *Lit. of Ancient Greece*, 496.

Schleiermacher, in his introduction to the dialogue, suggests that Antisthenes was one of the persons whom Plato assails under the names of the less important Sophists Euthydemus and Diony-sodorus.

Antisthenes (*circ.* 445–371 B.C.) was at first a pupil of Gorgias, but afterwards a devoted disciple and friend of Socrates, at whose death he was present (*Phaed.* 59 B). In imitation of the self-denial and patient endurance of Socrates, Antisthenes became the founder of the Cynic sect (Diog. Laert. vi. 2). The many anec-dotes recorded of him contain abundant evidence of the ill-feeling which existed between him and Plato. Having been told that Plato spoke ill of him, ' It is a kinglike fate,' he said, 'to do good and to be evil spoken of.' On meeting Plato, who had been sick, ' I see,' said Antisthenes, ' you have got rid of your bile, but not of your conceit.'

Another anecdote preserved by Diogenes Laertius (iii. 35) not only suggests a cause for this ill-will, but also indicates a direct connexion between Antisthenes and a passage in our dialogue. Plato being once invited by Antisthenes to hear him read a philo-sophic treatise inquired what the subject was to be, and, when told that it was an argument to prove the non-existence of contradiction (περὶ τοῦ μὴ εἶναι ἀντιλέγειν), replied, ' How then do you write about it, since it is non-existent ? ' The argument, as Plato showed, can

15

INTRODUCTION

be turned round (περιτρέπεται), for μὴ εἶναι is itself a contradiction. Hereupon Antisthenes wrote a dialogue against Plato, merely changing the name to Satho.

In *Euthydemus* 285 D 7–286 B 6 there is an unmistakable allusion to this paradoxical doctrine of Antisthenes, which is also mentioned by Aristotle, *Top.* i. 11, 4, and again *Metaph.* iv. 29, 4 Ὁ δὲ ψευδὴς λόγος οὐδενός ἐστιν ἁπλῶς λόγος. Διὸ Ἀντισθένης ᾤετο εὐήθως μηθὲν ἀξιῶν λέγεσθαι πλὴν τῷ οἰκείῳ λόγῳ ἓν ἐφ' ἑνός· ἐξ ὧν συνέβαινε μὴ εἶναι ἀντιλέγειν, σχεδὸν δὲ μηδὲ ψεύδεσθαι. The meaning of Aristotle in this passage is well explained by Zeller (Part i, *Outlines*, Eng. Tr. p. 118): 'In passionate contradiction to the Platonic ideas he (Antisthenes) allowed the individual being only to exist, and hence demanded that everything should receive its own name (the οἰκεῖος λόγος) and no other. From this he deduced the conclusion (apparently after the pattern of Gorgias) that no subject can receive a predicate of a different nature. He rejected, therefore, definition by characteristic marks; only for what was composite would he allow an enumeration of its constituent parts. What was simple might be explained by comparison with something else, but it could not be defined. With Protagoras he maintained that no man could contradict himself, for if he said what was different, he was speaking of different things. Thus he gave a thoroughly Sophistic turn to the Socratic philosophy of concepts.' Compare Zeller, *Socrates*, chap. xiii Cynic Logic ; Bonitz, *Platon. Stud.* 284, who argues that the opposition between the doctrines of Antisthenes and Plato, the paradoxical form and inconsistency (' Erfolglosigkeit ') in the philosophy of Antisthenes, and the ludicrous applications which might be made of his dogmas, render it quite conceivable that Plato reckoned him among the Sophists, and that he actually did so is placed beyond doubt by such passages as 283 E, 285 E.

The same opinion is expressed by Zeller (*Plato*, p. 84, note 94), who writes that in the exposition of his subject ' Plato had to do, not merely with the views of the elder Sophists and their later developments, but also . . . with Antisthenes, who seemed to him in true Sophistic fashion to destroy all possibility of cognition, to confuse Socratic with Sophistic views and thereby spoil them.'

We can well believe therefore that the satire of the *Euthydemus* was in certain passages directed against Antisthenes ; but his

16

IV. THE SPECIAL OCCASION

character does not so fully correspond to the particular description in 304 D as to justify the opinion that he was the rhetorician and speech-writer there described. Winckelmann (*Proleg.* xxxiv) thinks that the description of the λογογράφος is intended for Thrasymachus of Chalcedon, the Sophist who argues so vehemently against Socrates on the nature of justice in the first book of the Republic. In the *Phaedrus* he is mentioned (261 C) as a leading Sophist with Gorgias and Theodorus, and in 266 C as a teacher of rhetoric to all who would pay for it (οἳ ἂν δωροφορεῖν αὐτοῖς ὡς βασιλεῦσιν ἐθέλωσιν). Again in *Phaedr.* 267 C he is described as a master of the art of pathetic commonplace: for 'the "sorrows of a poor old man" no one is better than the Chalcedonian giant' (Jowett). In the same passage the words immediately following, ὀργίσαι τε αὖ πολλοὺς ἅμα δεινὸς ἀνὴρ γέγονεν, καὶ πάλιν ὠργισμένοις ἐπᾴδων κηλεῖν, ὡς ἔφη, evidently point to some boastful expressions of Thrasymachus, to which there seems to be an allusion in *Euthydem.* 290 A ἡ μὲν γὰρ τῶν ἐπῳδῶν (τέχνη), ἐχεών τε . . . καὶ νόσων κήλησίς ἐστιν, ἡ δὲ δικαστῶν τε καὶ ἐκκλησιαστικῶι καὶ τῶν ἄλλων ὄχλων κήλησίς τε καὶ παραμυθία τυγχάνει οὖσα. Not less striking is the similarity between the preceding passage of *Euthydemus* and Plat. *Pol.* 358 B Θρασύμαχος γάρ μοι φαίνεται πρῳαίτερον τοῦ δέοντος ὑπὸ σοῦ ὥσπερ ὄφις κηληθῆναι.

It thus seems highly probable that Thrasymachus is alluded to in *Euthydem.* 290 A ; but when Winckelmann tries to prove that he is the λογογράφος referred to in the close of the dialogue, we find that the testimony to which he appeals is quite inadequate to the conclusion. In Cic., *De Orat.* iii. 16, Thrasymachus is named among the rhetoricians ' qui minus ipsi in republica versarentur, sed huius tamen eiusdem sapientiae doctores essent, ut Gorgias, Thrasymachus, Isocrates.' Neither here nor in Quintilian, *Inst. Orator.* iii 1 ' Communes locos tractasse dicuntur Protagoras, Gorgias, Prodicus et Thrasymachus,' is there the slightest indication of his having written speeches for others to deliver in the law-courts, and the absence of a feature which is so prominent in the description in 304 D, 305 B, C, makes it impossible to suppose that he is the person meant.

We have therefore still to inquire who is the individual, if any, there described. In the statement of Crito, 304 E 5, that he is quoting the very words this person used (οὑτωσὶ γάρ πως καὶ εἶπε

INTRODUCTION

τοῖς ὀνόμασι) there is 'an intimation,' says Thompson, p. 181, 'that some one in particular is meant.' And the παρονομασία, ἀξίων ἀναξίαν, and general style of the quotation, may probably be meant to imitate the affected language of Isocrates. Certainly the description which follows seems to correspond with his character as clearly displayed in his writings.

(i) It is almost impossible to open any page of his extant orations without finding abundant evidence that he was ἀνὴρ οἰόμενος πάνυ εἶναι σοφός (*Euthyd.* 304 D), one of those who οἴονται εἶναι πάντων σοφώτατοι ἀνθρώπων, πρὸς δὲ τῷ εἶναι καὶ δοκεῖν πάνυ παρὰ πολλοῖς (305 C). A single example must suffice, taken from the *Panegyrica* (43 D), an oration published in 380 B.C., when Isocrates was fifty-five years old: Ἐγὼ δ' ἦν μὴ καὶ τοῦ πράγματος ἀξίως εἴπω καὶ τῆς δόξης τῆς ἐμαυτοῦ καὶ τοῦ χρόνου μὴ μόνον τοῦ περὶ τὸν λόγον ἡμῖν διατριφθέντος ἀλλὰ καὶ σύμπαντος οὗ βεβίωκα, παρακελεύομαι μηδεμίαν μοι συγγνώμην ἔχειν, ἀλλὰ καταγελᾶν καὶ καταφρονεῖν· οὐδὲν γὰρ ὅ τι τῶν τοιούτων οὐκ ἄξιός εἰμι πάσχειν, εἴπερ μηδὲν τῶν ἄλλων διαφέρων οὕτω μεγάλας ποιοῦμαι τὰς ὑποσχέσεις.

(ii) The next trait, τούτων τις τῶν περὶ τοὺς λόγους τοὺς εἰς τὰ δικαστήρια δεινῶν (304 D, 305 B), is proved to be true of Isocrates by the fact that several of such speeches are included in his remaining works. But in his latter years he was very sore at being reminded of his former occupation: 'For I know that some of the Sophists speak ill of my occupation, and say that it has to do with writing speeches for the law-courts, and in this they act just as if one should dare to call Pheidias who built the temple of Athena a doll-maker (κοροπλάθον), or say that Zeuxis and Parrhasius practised the same art as the sign-painters: nevertheless I have never yet taken revenge for this their detraction' (*Antidosis*, 310 B).

(iii) The sentence ῥήτωρ τις, ἢ τῶν τοὺς τοιούτους εἰσπεμπόντων, ποιητὴς τῶν λόγων οἷς οἱ ῥήτορες ἀγωνίζονται; and Ἥκιστα νὴ τὸν Δία, ῥήτωρ, οὐδὲ οἶμαι πώποτ' αὐτὸν ἐπὶ δικαστήριον ἀναβεβηκέναι (*Euthyd.* 305 B–C) point evidently at Isocrates, who from timidity and weakness of health always shrank from appearing in person in any public assembly or court (Isocr. *Panathen.* 234 D). Cf. *Antid.* 318 A Ἐμὲ δ' οὐδεὶς πώποθ' ἑώρακεν οὔτ' ἐν τοῖς συνεδρίοις οὔτε περὶ τὰς ἀνακρίσεις οὔτ' ἐπὶ τοῖς δικαστηρίοις οὔτε πρὸς τοῖς διαιτηταῖς, ἀλλ' οὕτως ἀπέχομαι τούτων ἁπάντων ὡς οὐδεὶς ἄλλος τῶν πολιτῶν.

IV. THE SPECIAL OCCASION

Plutarch in the *Life of Isocrates, Mor.* 837 A, says that the only speech he ever delivered in public was this, the *De Antidosi*, which we know was not composed till 355 B.C., when he was in his eighty-second year, long after the incident to which it refers: in fact Isocrates himself explains that it was only intended to show what his manner of life had been, and how he might have pleaded in excusing himself from undertaking the trierarchy, which he had actually accepted.

(iv) The next feature in the description of the unnamed writer of speeches is thoroughly characteristic of Isocrates. Οὗτοι γάρ εἰσι μέν, ὦ Κρίτων, οὓς ἔφη Πρόδικος μεθόρια φιλοσόφου τε ἀνδρὸς καὶ πολιτικοῦ (*Euthyd.* 305 C). Σοφοὶ δὲ ἡγοῦνται εἶναι πάνυ εἰκότως· μετρίως μὲν γὰρ φιλοσοφίας ἔχειν, μετρίως δὲ πολιτικῶν, πάνυ ἐξ εἰκότος λόγου· μετέχειν γὰρ ἀμφοτέρων ὅσον ἔδει (ibid. 305 D).

In these passages ' we are inevitably reminded of the description of Isocrates in the *Phaedrus*, as one in whose genius ἔνεστί τις φιλοσοφία ' (Thompson, *Phaedrus*, p. 181).

We may add that the two passages exactly summarize the meaning of a long passage in the *De Antidosi*, 276–290, in which Isocrates, after protesting against the Platonic philosophy (τὴν καλουμένην ὑπό τινων φιλοσοφίαν οὐκ εἶναι φημί) proceeds to say σοφοὺς μὲν νομίζω τοὺς ταῖς δόξαις ἐπιτυγχάνειν ὡς ἐπὶ τὸ πολὺ τοῦ βελτίστου δυναμένους, φιλοσόφους δὲ τοὺς ἐν τούτοις διατρίβοντας ἐξ ὧν τάχιστα λήψονται τὴν τοιαύτην φρόνησιν.

'The finishing touch in the picture—(v) ἐκτὸς δὲ ὄντες κινδύνων καὶ ἀγώνων καρποῦσθαι τὴν σοφίαν—agrees perfectly with the account of himself and his own way of life, which is given by Isocrates with no little self-gratulation in the *Antidosis* ' (Thompson, ibid.). See especially *Antid.* 162 τὴν μὲν ἡσυχίαν καὶ τὴν ἀπραγμοσύνην ἀγαπῶν . . . ἔπειτα τὸν βίον ἡδίω νομίσας εἶναι τοῦτον ἢ τὸν τῶν πολλὰ πραττόντων. The expression καρποῦσθαι τὴν σοφίαν and the synonymous phrase ἀπολέλαυκα τοῦ πράγματος (*Antid.* 208) both refer to the enormous payments which Isocrates received for his teaching and his speeches. That he was the person to whom this description was meant to apply will be made even more evident when we come to examine a passage in which he is mentioned by name at the close of the *Phaedrus*. ' In fact the combination of a smattering of philosophy, a measure of political knowledge, great talent as

INTRODUCTION

a writer of forensic speeches, and a boundless and intolerant vanity, is one which we find in the writings of Isocrates and in no others of that epoch' (Thompson, p. 182).

' No one will doubt any more that the episode at the end of the dialogue is aimed against Isocrates ' (Sudhaus, *Rhein. Mus.* xliv. 52). ' Hunc (Isocratem) esse anonymum de quo ibi sermo est, hodie inter omnes constat' (F. Susemihl, *De Plat. Phaedro* et *Isocr. c. Sophistas oratione,* p. xi).

V. DATE OF THE DIALOGUE.

' The date of the *Euthydemus* we have absolutely no means of determining, and, if we set aside tradition, that of the *Phaedrus* may be said perhaps to be equally uncertain ' (Thompson, *Phaedrus,* Appendix ii. 183).

After such a pronouncement from the late Master of Trinity it may appear presumptuous even to try to determine the approximate dates of the two dialogues, and their mutual relation. But the attempt, I believe, is not hopeless, and in any case can hardly fail to be instructive. Several of Dr. Thompson's own remarks seem to point to what we believe to be the right conclusion.

We have seen reason to believe that Isocrates, though not mentioned by name in the *Euthydemus,* is the person indicated by the description of the clever speech-writer (λογογράφος) at the end of the dialogue.

In the *Phaedrus* Isocrates is mentioned by name in a passage which we shall have to examine carefully in its bearing upon the connexion between the two Platonic dialogues and the relation of each to the oration of Isocrates *Against the Sophists.* Before entering upon this inquiry it is desirable to draw particular attention to the fact that the three works are all concerned with the merits and faults of rival methods of education as practised by the teachers of rhetoric, by the Sophists, and by Socrates and his followers.

We begin with the *Phaedrus.*

The question concerning the date of this dialogue is difficult and much disputed. The oldest opinion, dating from the third century after Christ, is the tradition mentioned by Diogenes Laertius in the *Life of Plato,* iii. 25 λόγος δὲ πρῶτον γράψαι αὐτὸν τὸν Φαῖδρον· καὶ γὰρ ἔχει μειρακιῶδές τι τὸ πρόβλημα. From the first scholion on

V. DATE OF THE DIALOGUE

the *Phaedrus* we learn that the tradition was repeated in the fifth century by Olympiodorus, the master of Proclus: the notion that it was founded by Diogenes on the authority of Euphorion (*c.* 240 B.C.), Panaetius (*c.* 143 B.C.) arose from a corrupt reading in Diog. Laer. λόγον, corrected by Cobet to λόγος. Cf. Thompson, *Phaedrus*, xxiii. H. Usener, *Abfassungszeit des platonischen Phaidros*, assigns the dialogue to the first half of 402 B.C., partly, as it seems, on the ground of the tradition, and partly upon the erroneous notion of Spengel, that the Κατὰ τῶν Σοφιστῶν of Isocrates was written as much as fifty years before the 'Αντίδοσις, on which see p. 32 below.

A comparison of the contents and character of the *Phaedrus* with those of the dialogues known to have been written before or soon after the death of Socrates, B.C. 399, shows beyond all question that so mature a work could not possibly have been written by so young a man as Plato was at the still earlier date to which the 'tradition' would assign it. 'When Socrates died, the philosophical education of Plato had but completed its first stage. The acquaintance with other more ambitious systems which his travels enabled him to acquire or to perfect, though it never disturbed his reverence for the teacher of his youth, greatly enlarged his views of philosophy and the philosophic calling' (Thompson, *Phaedrus*, p.154).

On the other hand a very much later date is proposed by Lutoslawski, who adopts (p. 352) a short and easy method of solving the difficulty. ' Thompson has made it evident to the attentive reader of the four dissertations accompanying his edition of the *Phaedrus* (Introduction and three Appendices) that this dialogue was written after the *Panegyricus* of Isocrates, that is after 380; and before the death of Lysias, that is before 378. This is such an exact determination of date as is possible only for a very few Platonic dialogues.'

Every student of Plato would have reason to be grateful indeed to the author of this discovery, if it were true. But unfortunately it is based upon a misapprehension of Dr. Thompson's meaning; in a note on p. 178 of his edition he compares *Phaedr.* 167 A with Isocr. *Panegyricus*, § 8, and remarks that 'Plato jeeringly attributes this boast to Tisias and Gorgias: Isocrates adopts it as his own in perfect seriousness. The date of the *Panegyricus* is B.C. 380.' This does not mean that the *Panegyricus* was written before the

INTRODUCTION

Phaedrus, but on the contrary that Isocrates seriously appropriates what Plato has previously held up to ridicule. That Isocrates was quite capable of doing this will appear in another instance presently : see p. 31.

Lutoslawski, however, adds a more important remark: ' The same argument has been independently and with far greater assurance produced by Teichmüller in 1881 (*Literarische Fehden*, vol. i. pp. 57–82), and has never been refuted.'

Teichmüller's long argument on *The Phaedrus of Plato and the Panegyricus of Isocrates* (*Lit. Fehd.* i. 3) is summarized by Lutoslawski, p. 348. It is based upon several fundamental errors.

(1) He misunderstands the ironical nature of the prophecy concerning Isocrates in *Phaedrus* 279, on which see p. 26 below.

(2) In particular he misapplies the words τοὺς λόγους οἷς νῦν ἐπι-χειρεῖ, referring them to the time at which Plato wrote instead of the *scenic date* at which Socrates speaks.

(3) He makes the same mistake as Lutoslawski on the relation between the parallel passages *Phaedr.* 167 A and *Panegyr.* § 8.

(4) He fails to notice the statement in the *Life of Isocrates* (Plut. ii. 837 F), that ' in composing the *Panegyricus* he spent ten years, and some say fifteen.' Cf. Quintil. *Inst. Orator.* x. 5 : ' Panegyricum Isocratis, qui parcissime, decem annis dicunt elaboratum.'

If we adopt this ' most moderate' statement, it is still evident that the passage *Paneg.* § 8 may have been written at any time between 390 and 380 B.C., the date of publication, and could therefore afford no closer criterion of the relative date of the passage in the *Phaedrus*.

For more trustworthy evidence we must have recourse to an examination of the contents and purpose of the *Phaedrus* itself, and of any apparent allusions to it in other dialogues of Plato or Isocrates.

During the ten or eleven years that followed the death of Socrates (399 B.C.) Plato had written and studied and taught and travelled much. In the course of his travels there had been many opportunities for personal intercourse with the leaders of the chief schools of philosophy ; at Megara with Eucleides, at Cyrene with Aristippus, at Tarentum with Archytas and other Pythagoreans, at Velia with the Eleatics, and in Sicily with the Sophistical rhetoricians of the school of Corax, Tisias, and Gorgias.

V. DATE OF THE DIALOGUE

On his return to Athens in 388 B.C. with this enlarged knowledge of the existing schools of philosophy, and with the principles of his own system more clearly defined and confirmed by comparison with others, Plato was fully prepared to take a leading part in education as a public teacher of philosophy. Accordingly in the year 387 B.C. he opened his famous school in the Academy.

In Athens at this time the field of education was chiefly occupied by two classes of teachers, both as bitterly opposed to Plato as they were to each other. His old enemies the Eristic Sophists had sunk to the lowest depths of chicanery and imposture, 'their only care being to make money from the young,' Isocr. *Hel. Encom.* 209 B, while 'they put so low a value on all the virtue and happiness which they professed to impart, that they were not ashamed to accept so little as three or four minae in payment,' *Adv. Sophist.* 291 D.

Isocrates himself was not less eager to make money, but on a far grander scale, and by more magnificent professions. From the time of Pericles oratory had been the ruling power in the state, and though its influence over the passions of the democracy had too often led to crime and disaster, it was still the favourite study of all young men whose wealth and ambition prompted them to seek power and fame in the arena of politics. Isocrates was their most popular and successful teacher: in politics his only moral standard was utility, and persuasion, not truth, the end and aim of his rhetorical art.

With the Sophists Plato had already dealt in several of his earlier dialogues, and was to deal with them again even more severely at a later period. His present purpose, carried out in the *Phaedrus*, was to expose the faults of the popular system of education founded upon a shallow rhetoric, and to show the superiority of a new dialectic based upon truer principles both of science and morality. The scene was laid in the lifetime of Socrates, and was to be the mouthpiece of a philosophy which, however enlarged and ennobled by the genius of Plato, was still faithful to the teaching of his master.

'For the purpose of a discussion on rhetoric as an instrument of education, Plato had to select a speech as an example to illustrate his views' (Lutosl. p. 327). At the date when the discourse between Socrates and Phaedrus was supposed to be held, Isocrates was too young to be introduced as the most eminent rhetorician of the day. An older man must be taken, and it was natural to select the orator Lysias who had long enjoyed the highest reputation as a writer of speeches intended for the law-courts (*Phaedr.* 228 A, 257 B.C.). Before he became famous by his accusation of Eratosthenes (403 B.C.) he had been a teacher of rhetoric, and the written essay ascribed to him in the *Phaedrus* was probably a school-exercise of that earlier period. Cf. Lutosl. p. 327.

He is severely and justly censured by Socrates, first for the choice of such a subject, the essay being one of those ἐρωτικοὶ λόγοι of which Lysias is said to have been the first author : cf. Thompson, *Phaedr.* pp. 82, 102. When Socrates consents to show how the same subject might have been more ably and more modestly treated, he says, ' I will put a veil over my face and run through the discourse as fast as I can, lest if I look at you I should not know what to say for shame.' But the criticism of Socrates is directed chiefly against the rhetorical faults in the essay of Lysias, who ' seemed to have said the same things two or three times over, like one too barren of matter to be able to say many things on one subject . . . Also he appeared to me to make an ostentatious display of his skill in two different ways, both equally excellent as he flattered himself' (*Phaedr.* 235 A, Thompson). Again the arguments used by Lysias are described as mere commonplace platitudes, which even the worst of writers could not fail to use: they may be allowed and excused ; there is no merit in inventing them, but only in the arrangement (236 A). Then after showing in an extemporary speech how the same subject might have been treated more skilfully and more effectively even on the principles of the rhetoric then in vogue, Socrates continues his criticism : ' It was a dreadful argument, Phaedrus, that of the speech which you brought with you, and of that which you made me utter . . . Silly and somewhat impious, and nothing could be worse than that. For if Love be something divine, he cannot be evil, though that was what both our speeches said of him. Their simplicity also was quite amusing, that having no truth nor honesty in them they made a solemn pretence of importance, in the hope of deceiving a few mannikins, and being admired by them ' (243 A).

The censure was severe, and was as applicable to Isocrates as to Lysias; but Plato's purpose required yet more: it was neces-

V. DATE OF THE DIALOGUE

sary not only to criticize the defects of the fashionable rhetoric, but also to prove the superiority of his own.

Socrates therefore proceeds (244 A) to give a definition of love as a species of divine madness. The soul, he argues, both divine and human, is immortal : its proper food is beauty, wisdom, and goodness, and its triple form—desire, energy (θυμικόν), and reason—may be described under the image of a charioteer borne upward by winged steeds. Then in an allegory unrivalled even in Plato for brilliancy of imagination, glowing splendour of language, and sublime speculation, he shows how by the aid of philosophy the love of beauty may rise as in that winged car to a realm beyond the bounds of matter and space and time, even to the heaven of heavens where justice, temperance, and knowledge absolute dwell ever unseen by mortal eye.

At the close of his second speech Socrates offers a prayer to Eros to forgive the faults of the two former speeches, laying the blame upon Lysias for choosing such a subject, instead of studying philosophy like his brother Polemarchus (257 A, B).

In the remainder of the dialogue Socrates proposes a scheme of rhetoric founded on true principles of science and morality (259 E, 260 A).

Among the essential requirements are (1) accurate knowledge, and observance of truth and justice (260 C) ; (2) clear definition (265 B); (3) organic arrangement (264 D); (4) generalization by concepts (265 D) ; (5) classification or division into species (265 E).

'Dialectic' thus described is then contrasted with the barren technicalities of the popular rhetoric (266 D–267 E), such as we see exposed in the *Euthydemus*.

Further, the 'dialectician' must understand the motives and principles of human action, and the 'varieties of human character, upon which he has to work in producing that " Persuasion " which is acknowledged to be the final cause of his art' (271 A–272 B ; Thompson, Introduction, p. xiv). In short, true rhetoric must be based upon philosophy and morality. It is thus apparent that the *Phaedrus* is throughout a severe criticism of the kind of rhetoric of which Lysias and Isocrates were the most eminent professors : and 'if no names of contemporaries had been mentioned, it would not have been unreasonable to suspect that he (Isocrates) and not

INTRODUCTION

Lysias was the orator at whom Plato's censures were principally aimed' (Thompson, p. 178). In the conclusion of the dialogue they are both brought forward by name. Lysias is to be told that ' He who cannot rise above his own compilations and compositions, which he has been long turning and twisting this way and that, combining or separating one part and another, may be called poet or speech-maker, or writer of laws,' 278 E. Here the words ἄνω κάτω στρέφων ἐν χρόνῳ, πρὸς ἄλληλα κολλῶν τε καὶ ἀφαιρῶν, ' long patching and piecing ' (Jowett), though addressed to Lysias are far more applicable to Isocrates, who was said to have spent ten or even fifteen years over his Panegyric oration, and was so long in composing a letter in the name of the Athenian state to persuade Philip to make peace, that peace was made long before the letter was ready.

In 278 E Phaedrus asks, ' What message will you send to Isocrates the fair ? ' and the answer is, ' Isocrates is still young, Phaedrus ; but I am willing to tell you what I prophesy concerning him. I think he has a genius which rises above the orations of Lysias, and a moral character of finer mould. So I should not wonder if, as he grows older, he should both surpass all rivals in his present occupation of writing speeches, and becoming dissatisfied with this should be led on to higher things by some diviner impulse : for there is by nature a sort of philosophy in the man's intellect.'

At the time when Plato wrote, this pretended prophecy had been in part fulfilled, and in part already falsified : Isocrates had become the most eminent of rhetoricians, and the bitterest enemy of what Plato taught as the only true philosophy. What then are we to think of this apparent compliment ? Was it sincere or ironical ? Or partly ironical and partly sincere ? The date to be assigned to the *Phaedrus,* and its relation to the fragmentary oration of Isocrates *Against the Sophists,* depend in great measure on the answers to be given to these questions.

Cicero, a professed admirer of Isocrates, says that with this testimony of Plato in his favour he may disregard all other criticism (*Orator* xiii. 40). Then, after translating the passage of the *Phaedrus,* Cicero adds (42) 'Haec de adolescente Socrates auguratur : at ea de seniore scribit Plato et scribit aequalis, et quidem exagitator omnium rhetorum hunc miratur unum. Me autem qui

V. DATE OF THE DIALOGUE

Isocratem non diligunt una cum Socrate et cum Platone errare patiantur.'

Diogenes Laertius in his *Life of Plato* (iii. 9) says that he was a friend of Isocrates, resting his statement on no better reason than the fact that Praxiphanes the Peripatetic wrote a dialogue in which Plato and Isocrates were represented as holding a discussion on the Poets, the scene being laid in Plato's country house.

In recent times the question before us has been much discussed by German scholars, and by none more fully than by Eugen Holzner, *Plato's Phaedrus und die Sophistenrede des Isokrates*, Prag, 1894. He writes thus (p. 5) : ' In an unprejudiced view there can be no doubt of one thing, that in those words Plato bestows real praise upon Isocrates ; hereby the prophecy gains literary importance : for it must be compared with the fact that Plato and Isocrates were at open enmity. This points out the proper path of inquiry, for the business now is to seek in the works of both writers for the evidence of that former agreement of sentiment.'

Holzner then proceeds to compare the *Phaedrus* and the Κατὰ τῶν Σοφιστῶν not with an unprejudiced mind but with the preconceived idea that 'if in the *Phaedrus* Plato appropriated thoughts of Iso-crates, it will be easier to understand that he wished to speak of him in eulogistic terms in the conclusion of the work.'

This notion that Plato had borrowed his ideas from Isocrates is directly contrary to the judgement of some of the ablest students of Plato.

' Usener asserts (*Rhein. Mus.* xxxi. p. 21) that in the Κατὰ τῶν Σοφιστῶν there is a distinct borrowing, sometimes even word for word, from the *Phaedrus*.' To this Holzner can only oppose the very feeble objection that ' Usener has omitted to prove that the relation which he establishes from the passages themselves is the only one possible.'

The passages chiefly discussed and compared are the follow-ing :—

Phaedrus 269 D.	Isocr. *Or.* xiii. § 20.
Τὸ μὲν δύνασθαι, ὦ Φαῖδρε, ὥστε ἀγωνιστὴν τέλεον γενέσθαι, εἰκός,	δεῖν τὸν μὲν μαθητὴν πρὸς τῷ τὴν φύσιν ἔχειν οἵαν χρὴ τὰ μὲν

27

INTRODUCTION

ἴσως δὲ καὶ ἀναγκαῖον, ἔχειν ὥσπερ
τἆλλα. Εἰ μέν σοι ὑπάρχει φύσει
ῥητορικῷ εἶναι, ἔσει ῥήτωρ ἐλλόγι-
μος προσλαβὼν ἐπιστήμην τε καὶ
μελέτην, ὅτου δ᾽ ἂν ἐλλίπῃς τούτων, ταύτῃ ἀτελὴς ἔσει. Ὅσον δὲ
αὐτοῦ τέχνη, οὐχ ᾗ Λυσίας τε καὶ
Θρασύμαχος πορεύεται δοκεῖ μοι
φαίνεσθαι ἡ μέθοδος.

εἴδη τὰ τῶν λόγων μαθεῖν, περὶ δὲ
τὰς χρήσεις αὐτῶν γυμνασθῆναι...,
καὶ τούτων μὲν ἁπάντων συμπεσόν-
των τελείως ἕξουσιν οἱ φιλοσο-
φοῦντες. Καθ᾽ ὃ δ᾽ ἂν ἐλλειφθῇ τι
τῶν εἰρημένων, ἀνάγκη ταύτῃ χεῖρον
διακεῖσθαι τοὺς πλησιάζοντας.

According to Plato the power of becoming a perfect orator
depends upon the possession of three necessary qualifications,
i. A natural faculty for speaking, ii. Knowledge (ἐπιστήμη), iii. Careful
practice.

These are all indispensable : if either be wanting, the man will
be in this respect imperfect. ' But so far as it is technical (αὐτοῦ=
τοῦ δύνασθαι ὥστε ἀγωνιστὴν τέλεον γενέσθαι), the true method is not
shown, I think, in the way by which Lysias and Thrasymachus
proceed.'

Both Lysias and Thrasymachus had published manuals of the
art of Rhetoric (τέχνη ῥητορική), but these technical rules are
expressly rejected by Plato both here and in other passages of the
dialogue ; cf. Phaedr. 269 B τὰ πρὸ τῆς τέχνης ἀναγκαῖα μαθήματα
ἔχοντες ῥητορικὴν ᾠήθησαν ηὑρηκέναι : 271 C οἱ νῦν γράφοντες, ὧν σὺ
ἀκήκοας, τέχνας λόγων πανοῦργοί εἰσι : 266 D where the usual contents of such manuals are described : see also Aristot. Soph.
Elench. xxxiii. οὐ γὰρ τέχνην ἀλλὰ τὰ ἀπὸ τῆς τέχνης διδόντες παιδεύειν
ὑπελάμβανον.

The real art is described by Socrates, Phaedr. 271 D, and consists of (1) 'a dialectical training enabling the man to "divide"
and to "collect," and (2) the power of applying his science to
human nature and its varieties ' (Thompson) : compare with this
the description of a true scheme of rhetoric on p. 25 of this Introduction.

Against this usual and natural interpretation of the passage
Holzner argues that ' If ἐπιστήμη in 269 D already meant that later
Dialectic and Psychology, it would be inconceivable that Plato in
the words ὅσον δὲ αὐτοῦ τέχνη denies to this orator any participa-
tion in the art. But Plato, as I believe, shows clearly enough

28

V. DATE OF THE DIALOGUE

what he understands by ἐπιστήμη, *the mechanical instrument of Rhetoric.*'

On this paradoxical interpretation Lutoslawski justly remarks (341, note)—' Strangely enough this knowledge (ἐπιστήμη, 262 D) has been misunderstood by many interpreters, as if it meant knowledge of the rules of rhetoric. Even E. Holzner, who corrects the error of those who identified this ἐπιστήμη with the following τέχνη, falls into an almost worse error in asserting the identity of ἐπιστήμη in this passage with τὰ πρὸ τῆς τέχνης ἀναγκαῖα μαθήματα 269 B.'

In the two passages thus compared it is, I think, evident that Isocrates is commenting on Plato, and adopting his thoughts so far as they can be fitted to his own more meagre art of Rhetoric. There is then no evidence, so far, that Plato having borrowed from Isocrates was anxious to propitiate him by a compliment in the close of the dialogue.

In passing to the examination of that passage we must first consider the previous state of feeling between Plato and Isocrates. There had been an enmity of long standing between the rhetoricians and Socrates and his followers. They had their representative at his trial, one of the three accusers being the orator Lycon. ' Socrates had offended them by his incessant censure of those who exercised professions of the principles of which they could give no intelligent account ' (Riddell, *Apology*, x) ; and this ' enmity of the rhetoricians extended itself after Socrates' death to the Socratists ' (ibid. p. xii, note). Of Plato's bitter resentment and continued censure there is abundant evidence in his earlier dialogues. Thus in the *Gorgias*, 503 A, Socrates describes two kinds of rhetoric, 'the one a trick of flattery and a base kind of popular declaration, the other noble, being the attempt to improve to the utmost the souls of the citizens, and the earnest striving to say what is best, whether that will prove more or less agreeable to the audience.' ' But such rhetoric as this,' says Socrates, 'you never yet saw ; or if you have any one of this sort to point out among the orators, let me know at once who he is.' ' No, by my faith,' Callicles answers, ' I cannot name you any one, at any rate of the orators of the present day.'

Again, *Gorg.* 520 A, ' The Sophist and the rhetorician are the same thing, or as nearly as possible alike, as I said to Polus : but you for want of knowledge think the one, rhetoric, a very fine thing, and the other you despise. Whereas in truth sophistic is a finer thing than rhetoric.

Having thus ascertained the previous state of Plato's feeling towards Isocrates, we may now proceed to consider the exact meaning of the supposed compliment.

We notice first the manner in which the name of Isocrates is introduced: it shows that, though he had not been hitherto mentioned in the dialogue, its criticisms had been intended for him as well as for Lysias.

'*Soc.* Go then and tell this to your companion.

Phaedr. But what are you going to do yourself? For your own companion must by no means be passed over.

Soc. Whom do you mean?

Phaedr. The fair Isocrates. What message will you carry to him? What shall we say of him?

Soc. Isocrates is still young, Phaedrus. I am willing, however, to tell you what I prophesy of him.'

At the *scenic* date of this conversation Isocrates was barely thirty, and being twenty-two years junior to Lysias is naturally described as still young. Socrates of course speaks of him as a former companion with all kindness and courtesy, and goes on to recognize his undoubted merits, as compared with Lysias, his superior genius and finer temperament. So far all is sincere praise, undeniably true, and expressed without a touch of irony. The expectation of Socrates that as years went on he would far surpass all competitors in the kind of speeches on which he was at that time engaged, had been amply fulfilled, and Plato does not fail to recognize fully the great ability and success of Isocrates. And yet his praise would not be altogether welcome. The speeches on which he had been engaged in the lifetime of Socrates might not altogether satisfy him. This also had come to pass; but it was a sore subject with Isocrates, as we have seen above in the passage of the *Antidosis* 310 B quoted above on p. 18, and Plato's allusion to it could hardly be felt as a sincere compliment.

In further fulfilment of the prophecy Isocrates had become dissatisfied with writing forensic speeches (δικογραφία), and adopted a style of oratory as far superior to that as the work of Pheidias to that of a doll-maker.

V. DATE OF THE DIALOGUE

Finally Socrates expresses a hope that he may be attracted to philosophy for which he showed a natural capacity : and in fact, Isocrates was fond of dignifying his new style of oratory with the name of philosophy, though fully conscious that it was something totally different from what Socrates and Plato meant by philosophy, and that the modified admission ἔνεστί τις φιλοσοφία was not altogether complimentary. On the whole it seems impossible to doubt that while the pretended prophecy acknowledges the real merits of Isocrates, its praises are not unmixed with a delicate vein of satire which Isocrates could not fail to recognize.

If we now turn to the fragmentary oration of Isocrates Κατὰ τῶν Σοφιστῶν, we find that in the very first words (291 A) he finds fault with the large professions of persons ' undertaking the work of education,' as Plato we know was, and especially condemns the pretension to prophesy, which had been made by some rival teacher : ' For it is evident, I suppose, to all that foreknowledge of the future is not within the power of our nature . . . and this is one of the things impossible to man.' Then a little farther on, c. Soph. 293 B (a passage which has received less notice than it deserves), he clearly refers again to the prophecy concerning himself in the *Phaedrus*, and tries to appropriate the ambiguous compliment, as if it were in fact well deserved : ' I should have thought it a priceless gain if there had been in philosophy so great a power as these men say ; for I perhaps should not have been the hindmost therein, nor would my share have been the smallest.'

It seems impossible to doubt that in these passages there is a direct answer to the prophecy in the *Phaedrus*, and this conclusion will be confirmed by the comparison in parallel columns of the original words of these and other passages of the two dialogues, which will be found at the end of this section of the Introduction, p. 33.

We therefore agree with Zeller (*Plato*, 132, note 94) that ' Spengel is certainly right in believing that the *Phaedrus* must have been written before the speech of Isocrates *Against the Sophists*.'

Spengel's conclusion is contained in his article *Isokrates und Plato* in the *Abh. d. Akad. d. Wissenschaften zu München*, vol. vii. pp. 729–769. His argument is founded on the statements of Isocrates in the speech *De Antidosi* written in the year 355 B.C., when Isocrates was eighty-two years of age, as he is careful to mention, § 312 A :

INTRODUCTION

ἔγραφον τὸν λόγον τοῦτον οὐκ ἀκμάζων ἀλλ' ἔτη γεγονὼς δύο καὶ ὀγδοήκοντα. In this same speech, § 207, the latter half of the speech *Against the Sophists* was recited by Isocrates 'in more elegant language, but with the same meaning as before,' οὐ γὰρ ὅτε μὲν ἦν νεώτερος ἀλαζονευόμενος φαίνομαι καὶ μεγάλας τὰς ὑποσχέσεις ποιούμενος, ἐπειδὴ δ' ἀπολέλαυκαι τοῦ πράγματος καὶ πρεσβύτερος γέγονα, τηνικαῦτα ταπεινὴν ποιῶ τὴν φιλοσοφίαν, ἀλλὰ τοῖς αὐτοῖς λόγοις χρώμενος ἀκμάζων καὶ παυόμενος αὐτῆς (v. l. ἀκμῆς).

From the words ὅτε νεώτερος ἦν and ἀκμάζων Spengel argues (p. 751) that the speech *Against the Sophists* must have been written fifty years before the *De Antidosi*, i. e. about the year 405 B.C., six years before the death of Socrates, and when Plato was about twenty-three years old.

This palpable mistake is due to a misunderstanding of the words νεώτερος and ἀκμάζων. Aristotle says that the soul is at its prime about the age of forty-nine years (*Rhet.* ii. 14, 4). Now, when an old man of eighty-two speaks of what he has done when he was 'younger' and 'in his prime,' adding that he is no longer 'in his prime,' but 'declining from it,' he does not mean to speak of a time fifty years ago, but thirty or five-and-thirty at most, i. e. between B. C. 390 (the date supposed by Lutoslawski) and B. C. 385. In this interval, namely in B.C. 388 or 387, Plato began to teach in the Academy. Stallbaum in his Prolegomena to the *Phaedrus* has shown, I think, good reason for believing that it was written at this time, and Zeller is of the same opinion. If this view be accepted, the order of the three works in question will be as follows :

(1) Plato, *Phaedrus*, (2) Isocrates, *Against the Sophists*, (3) Plato, *Euthydemus*. The three dialogues will thus have been all published within two or three years after B.C. 388, in which year Plato was forty-one and Isocrates forty-eight years old.

'There is no contradiction,' writes Lutoslawski (p. 211), 'from the standpoint either of logical or of stylistic development in admitting the close relation between the *Euthydemus* and Isocrates' discourse *Against the Sophists*. This relation, first noticed by Spengel and Thompson, has been since investigated by Teichmüller, Sudhaus, Dümmler, and recognized by Zeller and Susemihl, without any noteworthy opposition. According to these investigations the

32

V. DATE OF THE DIALOGUE

Euthydemus must have been published not before 390 and probably not much later.'

That Isocrates in the oration *Against the Sophists* is referring to Plato's *Phaedrus* will, I think, be placed beyond doubt if we set a few selected passages opposite to each other in parallel columns.

I. ON PROPHESYING.

Phaedr. 278 E Νέος ἔτι, ὦ Φαῖδρε, 'Ισοκράτης· ὃ μέντοι μαντεύομαι κατ' αὐτοῦ, λέγειν ἐθέλω. 242 C εἰμὶ δὴ οὖν μάντις. 244 C τῇ καλλίστῃ τέχνῃ, ᾗ τὸ μέλλον κρίνεται.

Isocr. 291 B εὐθὺς δ' ἐν ἀρχῇ τῶν ἐπαγγελμάτων ψευδῆ λέγειν ἐπιχειροῦσιν· οἶμαι γὰρ ἅπασιν εἶναι φανερὸν ὅτι τὰ μέλλοντα προγιγνώσκειν οὐ τῆς ἡμετέρας φύσεως ἐστίν. 292 C περὶ μὲν τῶν μελλόντων εἰδέναι προσποιουμένους.

II. ON THE RELATION OF ISOCRATES HIMSELF TO PHILOSOPHY.

Phaedr. 279 A φύσει γάρ, ὦ φίλε, ἔνεστί τις φιλοσοφία τῇ τοῦ ἀνδρὸς διανοίᾳ.

Isocr. 293 B 'Εγὼ δὲ πρὸ πολλῶν μὲν ἂν χρημάτων ἐτιμησάμην τηλικοῦτον δύνασθαι τὴν φιλοσοφίαν, ὅσον οὗτοι λέγουσιν· ἴσως γὰρ οὐκ ἂν ἡμεῖς πλεῖστον ἀπελείφθημεν, οὐδ' ἂν ἐλάχιστον μέρος ἀπελαύσαμεν αὐτῆς. id. *De Antidosi* 289 τὴν καλουμένην ὑπό τινων φιλοσοφίαν οὐκ εἶναι φημί.

III. ON THE INFERIORITY OF OPINION (δόξα) TO KNOWLEDGE (ἐπιστήμη).

Phaedr. 248 B ἀτελεῖς τῆς τοῦ ὄντος θέας ἀπέρχονται (αἱ ψυχαί), καὶ ἀπελθοῦσαι τροφῇ δοξαστῇ χρῶνται, 'feed on the chaff and husks of opinion' (Thompson). 260 C ὅταν οὖν ὁ ῥητορικὸς ἀγνοῶν ἀγαθὸν καὶ κακὸν ... δόξας δὲ πλήθους μεμελετηκὼς πείσῃ

Isocr. 292 C 'Επειδὰν κατίδωσι ... μᾶλλον ὁμονοοῦντας καὶ πλείω κατορθοῦντας τοὺς ταῖς δόξαις χρωμένους ἢ τοὺς τὴν ἐπιστήμην ἔχειν ἐπαγγελλομένους κτλ. 294 D ταῦτα δὲ πολλῆς ἐπιμελείας δεῖσθαι καὶ ψυχῆς ἀνδρικῆς καὶ δοξαστικῆς ἔργον εἶναι.

κακὰ πράττειν ἀντ' ἀγαθῶν, ποῖόν
τιν' ἂν οἴει μετὰ ταῦτα τὴν ῥητορικὴν καρπὸν ὃν ἔσπειρε θερίζειν;
262 B λόγων ἄρα τέχνην, ὦ
ἑταῖρε, ὁ τὴν ἀλήθειαν μὴ εἰδώς,
δόξας δὲ τεθηρευκώς, γελοίαν τινά,
ὡς ἔοικε, καὶ ἄτεχνον παρέξεται.

[That this was the fixed
opinion of Isocrates is seen in
a later dialogue *Panathenaicus*
234 D, where he describes his
own genius as πρὸς τοὺς λόγους
οὐ τελείαν οὔτε πανταχῇ χρησίμην,
ἀλλὰ δοξάσαι μὲν περὶ ἑκάστου
τὴν ἀλήθειαν μᾶλλον δυναμένην τῶν
εἰδέναι φασκόντων.]
291 B προσποιοῦνται μὲν τὴν
ἀλήθειαν ζητεῖν.

IV. ON THE COMPARATIVE MERITS OF WRITTEN AND
ORAL DISCOURSE.

Phaedr. 275 A καὶ νῦν σύ,
πατὴρ ὢν γραμμάτων, δι' εὔνοιαν
τοὐναντίον εἶπες ἢ δύναται. τοῦτο
γὰρ τῶν μαθόντων λήθην μὲν ἐν
ψυχαῖς παρέξει μνήμης ἀμελετησίᾳ,
ἅτε διὰ πίστιν γραφῆς ἔξωθεν ὑπ'
ἀλλοτρίων τύπων, οὐκ ἔνδον αὐτοὺς
ὑφ' αὑτῶν ἀναμιμνησκομένους. Οὔκουν μνήμης ἀλλ' ὑπομνήσεως φάρμακον εὗρες· σοφίας δὲ τοῖς μαθηταῖς δόξαν οὐκ ἀλήθειαν πορίζεις.

275 D Οὐκοῦν ὁ τέχνην οἰόμενος
ἐν γράμμασι καταλιπεῖν καὶ αὖ ὁ
παραδεχόμενος ὥς τι σαφὲς καὶ
βέβαιον ἐκ γραμμάτων ἐσόμενον
πολλῆς ἂν εὐηθείας γέμοι.

278 A ἐν δὲ τοῖς διδασκομένοις
καὶ μαθήσεως χάριν λεγομένοις καὶ
τῷ ὄντι γραφομένοις ἐν ψυχῇ περὶ
δικαίων τε καὶ καλῶν καὶ ἀγαθῶν
ἐν μόνοις ⟨τούτοις⟩ τό τε ἐναργὲς
εἶναι καὶ τέλεον καὶ ἄξιον σπουδῆς.

ISOCR. 293 C Θαυμάζω δ' ὅταν
ἴδω τούτους μαθητῶν ἀξιουμένους,
οἳ ποιητικοῦ πράγματος τεταγμένην
τέχνην παράδειγμα φέροντες λελή-
θασι σφᾶς αὐτούς. τίς γὰρ οὐκ
οἶδε πλὴν τούτων ὅτι τὸ μὲν τῶν
γραμμάτων ἀκινήτως ἔχει καὶ μένει
κατὰ ταὐτόν, ὥστε τοῖς αὐτοῖς ἀεὶ
περὶ τῶν αὐτῶν χρώμενοι διατελοῦ-
μεν, τὸ δὲ τῶν λόγων πᾶν τοὐναντίον
πέπονθεν.

293 E τοῖς δὲ γράμμασιν οὐδενὸς τούτων προσεδέησεν· ὥσθ' οἱ
χρώμενοι τοῖς τοιούτοις παραδείγ-
μασι πολὺ ἂν δικαιότερον ἀποτίνοιεν
ἢ λαμβάνοιεν ἀργύριον, ὅτι πολλῆς
ἐπιμελείας αὐτοὶ δεόμενοι παιδεύειν
τοὺς ἄλλους ἐπιχειροῦσιν.

In these two passages Isocrates treats the opinion expressed in the *Phaedrus* as a
mere platitude known to every
body, and proving its author to
be unfit for a teacher.

VI. LOGICAL PRINCIPLES AND FALLACIES

V. On the Importance of Philosophy.

239 B πολλῶν μὲν ἄλλων συνου-
σιῶν ἀπείργοντα καὶ ὠφελίμων ὅθεν
ἂν μάλιστ' ἀνὴρ γίγνοιτο, μεγάλης
αἴτιον εἶναι βλάβης, μεγίστης δὲ τῆς
ὅθεν ἂν φρονιμώτατος εἴη· τοῦτο
δὲ ἡ θεία φιλοσοφία τυγχάνει ὄν.

Isocr. 294 A ἡγοῦμαι πάντας ἂν
μοι τοὺς εὖ φρονοῦντας συνειπεῖν
ὅτι πολλοὶ μὲν τῶν φιλοσοφησάν-
των ἰδιῶται διετέλεσαν ὄντες, ἄλλοι
δέ τινες οὐδενὶ πώποτε συγγενό-
μενοι τῶν σοφιστῶν καὶ λέγειν καὶ
πολιτεύεσθαι δεινοὶ γεγόνασιν.

VI. LOGICAL PRINCIPLES AND FALLACIES.

The chief instrument employed by the Sophists in their discussions was the 'Sophistical Elenchus,' a seeming but not real refutation of the opponent's statement. The various forms of this device are fully described in a treatise ascribed to Aristotle and entitled *De Sophisticis Elenchis*. ' Of confutation there are two kinds ; for some depend on the language, and others are independent of the language. The causes dependent on language which produce the false appearance of reasoning are six in number' (*Soph. El.* iv. 525). These are 'Equivocation' the ambiguity of a term (ὁμωνυμία), the ambiguity of a proposition (ἀμφιβολία), false composition (σύνθεσις), false disjunction (διαίρεσις), wrong accentuation (προσῳδία), formation of words (σχῆμα λέξεως).

This arrangement was retained by subsequent writers on Logic, as for instance by Aldrich, whose explanation of the several fallacies will be found in Mansel's *Artis Logicae Rudimenta*, Appendix, pp. 133 ff.

In the *Euthydemus* we have first several examples of the fallacy of *Equivocation*.

(i) 275 D 3 πότεροί εἰσι τῶν ἀνθρώπων οἱ μανθάνοντες, οἱ σοφοὶ ἢ οἱ ἀμαθεῖς;

(ii) 276 D 7 Πότερον γὰρ οἱ μανθάνοντες μανθάνουσιν ἃ ἐπίστανται ἢ ἃ μὴ ἐπίστανται;

The explanation is given by Plato himself in 277 E, where Socrates comforts Cleinias by telling him that the Sophists wish to teach him first the right use of words, that μανθάνω may mean

INTRODUCTION

either to acquire knowledge of something previously unknown, or to examine and understand (συνιέναι) it by the use of such knowledge. The same explanation is given in Aristot. *Soph. El.* iv. 1 Εἰσὶ δὲ παρὰ μὲν τὴν ὁμωνυμίαν οἱ τοιοίδε τῶν λόγων, οἷον ὅτι μανθάνουσιν οἱ ἐπιστάμενοι . . . τὸ γὰρ μανθάνειν ὁμώνυμον, τό τε ξυνιέναι χρώμενον τῇ ἐπιστήμῃ καὶ τὸ λαμβάνειν τὴν ἐπιστήμην.

We observe also that the words σοφοί, ἀμαθεῖς, and ἐπίσταμαι are all used equivocally in the discussion of these two questions.

(iii) 283 D Οὐκοῦν ὃς μὲν οὐκ ἔστιν, βούλεσθε αὐτὸν γενέσθαι, ὃς δ' ἔστι νῦν, μηκέτι εἶναι. The pronoun ὅς is here equivocal, being used both in its proper sense as referring to a person and in an adjectival sense like οἷος.

(iv) 283 E 9 Πότερον λέγοντα τὸ πρᾶγμα περὶ οὗ ἂν ὁ λόγος ᾖ, ἢ μὴ λέγοντα; Here also λέγειν is used in two different senses, either ' to speak of a thing,' or to ' speak (i. e. utter) a word.' ' Scilicet is qui loquitur, *loquitur de re aliqua*, nec nisi improprie dicitur *rem loqui*. Verba igitur, quae faciat loquens, omnino exsistunt et vere sunt; sed nisi res exsistant et eundem ad modum quo verba prae se ferunt ea non sunt vera ' (Routh).

The original question out of which this equivocation arises, ἢ δοκεῖ σοι οἷόν τ' εἶναι ψεύδεσθαι, is discussed at great length in *Cratyl.* 385 B, and again *Soph.* 236 E–246 A, where after examining the many difficulties involved in the dogma of Parmenides ' that not-being is ' Plato comes to the conclusion that the nature of ' being ' is quite as difficult to define as that of ' not-being ' (ὅτι τὸ ὂν τοῦ μὴ ὄντος οὐδὲν εὐπορώτερον εἰπεῖν ὅ τι ποτ' ἔστιν).

(v) 284 C 2 οὐκ ἄρα τά γε μὴ ὄντα, ἔφη, λέγει οὐδείς. Again the fallacy lies in the assumption that to speak or think of *a thing* is the same as *doing* something to the thing itself, thereby making it a *real object* (ὥστε καὶ εἶναι ποιήσειεν ἂν καὶ ὁστισοῦν τὰ μηδαμοῦ ὄντα;) 284 B 6.

I do not understand how Bonitz explains this and the two preceding fallacies as dependent upon the identification of subject and predicate, i. e. that the λόγος τοῦ πράγματος is the same as the thing itself.

(vi) 284 D 1 εἰσὶ γάρ τινες οἳ λέγουσι τὰ πράγματα ὡς ἔχει; As used by Ctesippus ὡς ἔχει refers only to the true relation between

36

VI. LOGICAL PRINCIPLES AND FALLACIES

subject and predicate, as in *Cratyl.* 385 B Ἆρ' οὖν οὗτος, ὃς ἂν τὰ ὄντα λέγῃ ὡς ἔστιν, ἀληθής· ὃς δ' ἂν ὡς οὐκ ἔστιν, ψευδής; but Dionysodorus makes ὡς ἔχει refer to the conditions or qualities of the subject, and afterwards seeks refuge from the sarcasm of Ctesippus, 284 D 2, in the ambiguous use of κακῶς λέγειν, a fallacy παρ' ἀμφιβολίαν: *Sophist. El.* iv. 4.

(vii) 285 D 7 Ὡς ὄντος, ἔφη, τοῦ ἀντιλέγειν . . . ποιεῖ τοὺς λόγους; Every thing has its own proper definition. If two men give the proper definition (λόγον), there is no contradiction. If they give different definitions, they are not speaking of the same thing, and again there is no contradiction.

This rests on the assumption that the definition given, i. e. the predicate, is identical with the subject (Bonitz).

(viii) 287 C 1 τί . . . νοεῖ τοῦτο τὸ ῥῆμα; Here νοεῖ is applied metaphorically to a thing without life, and the Sophist immediately seizes on the ambiguous use of the word: cf. 305 A παντὸς δὲ ῥήματος ἀντέχονται. This is an example of the second kind of ambiguity, in the use of a word in a sense which is customary but not proper (ὅταν εἰωθότες ὦμεν οὗτω λέγειν, *Soph. El.* iv. 4). Socrates is willing to admit his error, only it had been argued (287 A) that to err is impossible.

(ix) 293 C 4 οὐκ ἀνάγκη σε ἔχει πάντα ἐπίστασθαι ἐπιστήμονά γε ὄντα; This and several following arguments of the Sophists are examples of the fallacy 'a dicto secundum quid ad dictum simpliciter,' which is described in Aristot. *Soph. El.* iv. 10 τὸ ἁπλῶς, ἢ μὴ ἁπλῶς ἀλλὰ πῇ ἢ ποῦ ἢ ποτὲ ἢ πρός τι λέγεσθαι.

(x) 295 E 4 πότερον ἐπίστασαί τῳ ἃ ἐπίστασαι ἢ οὔ; The Sophist proceeds to argue that since Socrates 'knows all things (that he knows) always (by the same faculty),' therefore 'he knows all things always,' the limitations being disregarded. This argument is closed by a *reductio ad absurdum*, when Socrates asks (296 E 4), 'Do I know that the good are unjust?' Dionysodorus admits that Socrates does not know this, and so does not know all things.

The only resource left to the Sophists is to refuse to answer the questions of Socrates, and to insist on his answering a series of captious quibbles which they hang upon any convenient word that is casually employed by him. This neglect of methodical arrange-

37

INTRODUCTION

ment, far from being a fault, is part of Plato's artistic imitation of the eristic mode of argument, while he yet 'allows a definite order to peep out in this seemingly arbitrary irregularity' (Bonitz, 259, note 7).

(xi) Thus 297 E 5 Patrocles the half-brother of Socrates both *is* and *is not* his brother. Chaeredemus the father of Patrocles not being Sophroniscus the father of Socrates both is and is not a father, and Sophroniscus being different from a father (Chaeredemus) is not a father, and Socrates had no father.

(xii) 298 C 2 ἢ οἴει τὸν αὐτὸν πατέρα ὄντα οὐ πατέρα εἶναι; Hence a father of one is a father of all, and the father and mother of Euthydemus are father and mother of all kinds of animals, and Euthydemus brother of puppies and little pigs.

(xiii) 298 E 3. The dog is *yours*, Ctesippus, and he is the *father* of puppies, therefore he is *your father*, and you the puppies brother. Cf. *Soph. El.* xxiv. 2 Ἆρ' ὁ ἀνδριὰς σόν ἐστιν ἔργον, ἢ σὸς ὁ κύων πατήρ; ibid. 4 οἷον εἰ ὅδε ἐστὶ πατήρ, ἔστι δὲ σός. Cf. 298 C 4.

(xiv) 299 A 6. That no one wants good things in great quantities, being proved in the case of medicine, is assumed to be true universally.

Thus in the group ix–xiv the arguments of the Sophists all involve the fallacy of omitting all limitations, and passing arbitrarily 'a dicto secundum quid ad dictum simpliciter.'

(xv) 300 A 4 δυνατὰ οὖν ὁρᾶν ἐστὶ ταῦτα. Cf. *Soph. El.* iv. 527 καὶ ἆρα ὃ ὁρᾷ τις, τοῦτο ὁρᾷ; ὁρᾷ δὲ τὸν κίονα, ὥστε ὁρᾷ ὁ κίων. Here τοῦτο is ambiguous; it may mean either τὸν κίονα or ὁ κίων. Cf. Poste, *Soph. El.* p. 105. Cf. 300 A 2, note.

(xvi) 300 B 1 ἢ γὰρ οὐχ οἷόν τε σιγῶντα λέγειν; Cf. *Soph. El.* iv. 523 καὶ ἄρ' ἔστι σιγῶντα λέγειν; διττὸν γὰρ καὶ τὸ σιγῶντα λέγειν, τό τε τὸν λέγοντα σιγᾶν καὶ τὸ τὰ λεγόμενα, ibid. x. 558. See notes on 300 B.

(xvii) 300 B 2 ἆρ' οὐδὲ λέγοντα σιγᾶν; The fallacy is the same as in xvi, for λέγοντα σιγᾶν may mean either 'a speaker's silence,' or 'silence about a speaker.'

(xviii) 301 A 6 καὶ ὅτι νῦν ἐγώ σοι πάρειμι, Διονυσόδωρος εἶ; The sense of πάρειμι here is different from that of πάρεστι in A 4 πάρεστιν μέντοι ἑκάστῳ αὐτῶν κάλλος τι. The fallacy therefore is παρ' ὁμωνυ-

38

VI. LOGICAL PRINCIPLES AND FALLACIES

μίαν, πάρεστι being changed from its meaning as a philosophical term to its common sense of local proximity.

(xix) 301 D 3 τὸν μάγειρον κατακόπτειν. Another example of the fallacy παρ' ἀμφιβολίαν, as μάγειρον may be either subject or object of κατακόπτειν.

(xx) 303 A 1 ἆρα ἔξεστί σοι αὐτοὺς (τοὺς θεοὺς) ἀποδόσθαι; This final paradox is the result of a whole series of fallacies. 'For θεός the universal ζῷον is substituted, the possessive σός is applied to ζῷον and to θεός in different senses, and then what is true only of a particular class of ζῷα is predicated of ζῷα universally and so of θεός' (Bonitz, p. 263). Cf. Soph. El. v. 533 ὅταν τὸ ἐν μέρει λεγόμενον ὡς ἁπλῶς εἰρημένον ληφθῇ.

(xxi) 303 A 7 Πότερον οὖν, ἔφη, ὁ Ἡρακλῆς πυππάξ ἐστιν, κτλ.; Dionysodorus pretends to understand the exclamation πυππάξ as a proper name, and besides this silly grammatical joke assumes that if two words stand side by side they must be in apposition.

On the fallacies thus enumerated compare Bonitz, *Platonische Studien*, ii. 266. We may add to the series the example of *Fallacia Accidentis*, 298 B 2 ἕτερος ὢν πατρὸς οὐ πατήρ ἐστιν, and the *Fallacia Plurium Interrogationum*, 300 C 7, where Ctesippus insists on a categorical answer 'Yes' or 'No' to his question, 'Do all things keep silence or speak?' See the notes on these passages. Notice also that in 301 C 1 ὡς οὐ τὸ ἕτερον ἕτερόν ἐστιν Socrates himself adopts the fallacy of equivocation, turning it against the Sophists.

Besides the long series of fallacies thus exposed, there are more important logical principles to be noticed in the dialogue.

In *Euthyd*. 301 A 'Beautiful things are not the same as absolute beauty, but some beauty is present with each of them,' we have an example of the process of *generalization by concepts* which had been already fully described in the *Meno*, 75 A ζητῶ τὸ ἐπὶ πᾶσι τούτοις ταὐτόν, κτλ. On the importance of the discovery see Lotze, *Microcosm*. ii. 319, 320: 'Long as it was since language had begun to indicate in words the general concepts of things ... consciousness had still continued unaware of what it was about; and even for the contemporaries of Socrates it was hard to see that the convenience of using a common name for different things arose from their dependence upon something which was common to them all, and in all self-identical.'

INTRODUCTION

Of *Definition*, which follows immediately from the doctrine of *General Concepts*, we have a brief statement in *Euthyd.* 285 E 9 εἰσὶν ἑκάστῳ τῶν ὄντων λόγοι, κτλ., where right definition is shown to be necessary as the means of avoiding contradiction. This subject also had been fully treated in *Meno* 72-76.

Not less important is the question of *Predication*, and the denial of any proper union between *Subject* and *Predicate* implied but not explained in *Euthyd.* 300 E 3, where Dionysodorus asks Σὺ γὰρ ἤδη τι πώποτ' εἶδες, ὦ Σώκρατες, καλὸν πρᾶγμα; The denial began with Antisthenes the Cynic, and was adopted by Stilpo the Megarian, of whom Zeller writes, *Socrates*, p. 277 : ' He rejected, as did Antisthenes, every combination of subject and predicate, since the conception of the one is different from the conception of the other, and two things with different conceptions can never be declared to be the same.'

That predication does not necessarily imply the identity of subject and predicate is shown by Plato in the *Sophist* 251 A : ' Let us inquire then how we come to predicate many names of the same thing... And thus we provide a rich feast for tiros, whether young or old; for there is nothing easier than to argue that the one cannot be many, or the many one ; and great is their delight in denying that man is good; but man, they insist, is man, and good is good ' (Jowett).

The term *Not-Being* (τὸ μὴ ὄν, τὰ μὴ ὄντα), which occurs several times in the *Euthydemus*, does not there receive its true explanation. The Sophists maintain, in accordance with the doctrine of Parmenides, that τὸ μὴ ὄν can never be the object of thought or speech or any kind of action (*Euthyd.* 284 B, 286 A). The question is treated in the same manner in the *Republic* 477 A, 478 B. The true explanation of the difficulty is first reached in the *Sophist* 237 B-238 D, where the doctrine of Parmenides is formally discussed, and in 257 B it is explained that ' *Not-Being* means only different *Being*, and denotes the relation of notions which do not agree with each other ' (Ὁπόταν τὸ μὴ ὄν λέγωμεν, ὡς ἔοικεν, οὐκ ἐναντίον τι λέγομεν τοῦ ὄντος ἀλλ' ἕτερον μόνον). Cf. Zeller, *Pre-Socr. Philos.* I. 606 ; Lutoslawski, p. 228.

VII. THE SOPHISTS

The term Σοφιστής denoted in its earliest use an eminent master of some liberal art.

Thus in Pindar, *Isthm.* iv. (v.) 28 it means 'poets':

μελέταν δὲ σοφισταῖς
Διὸς ἕκατι πρόσβαλον.

It is applied to 'musicians' in a fragment of Aeschylus quoted by Athenaeus, xiv. 632 C καὶ πάντας τοὺς χρωμένους τῇ τέχνῃ ταύτῃ (τῇ μουσικῇ) σοφιστὰς ἀπεκάλουν, ὥσπερ καὶ Αἰσχύλος ἐποίησεν·

Εἶτ᾽ οὖν σοφιστὴς καλὰ παραπαίων χέλυν.

Thamyris is described by the same term in Euripides, *Rhes.* 924:

ὅτ᾽ ἤλθομεν . . .
Μοῦσαι μεγίστην εἰς ἔριν μελῳδίας
δεινῷ σοφιστῇ Θρῃκί, κἀτυφλώσαμεν
Θάμυριν.

It is applied by Herodotus, ii. 49, to the priests of the Bacchic mysteries, and (iv. 95) as a title of honour to Pythagoras (Ἑλλήνων οὐ τῷ ἀσθενεστάτῳ σοφιστῇ Πυθαγόρῃ), and to the wise men of Greece including Solon by name (i. 29).

When Herodotus thus wrote the name 'Sophist' had already been assumed in a special sense by one whose arrogant claims to universal knowledge, and acceptance of pecuniary reward, quickly tended to degrade an honourable title into a byword and a reproach. Protagoras first appeared in Athens about the middle of the fifth century B.C.

'It was the time when the controversies which had long been carried on in the ancient schools of philosophy had been succeeded by an interval of general lassitude, despondency, and indifference to philosophical truth, which afforded room for a new class of pretenders to wisdom, who in a sense which they first attached to the word were first called Sophists.

'They professed a science superior to all the elder forms of philosophy, which it balanced against each other with the perfect impartiality of *universal scepticism* ; and an art which treated them all as instruments useless indeed for the discovery of truth, but equally capable of exhibiting a fallacious appearance of it . . .

'As according to this view there was no real difference between

41

INTRODUCTION

truth and falsehood, right and wrong, the proper learning of a statesman consisted in the arts of argument and persuasion by which he might sway the opinions of others on every subject at his pleasure, and these were the arts which they practised and taught' (Thirlwall, *History of Greece*, ch. xxiv).

It will be well to inquire first whether this is a fair representation of Plato's description of the Sophist, and further whether that description is confirmed by other contemporary testimony.

Plat. *Phaed.* 90 B : ' Most especially those who devote themselves to the practice of disputation end, you know, by thinking that they have become the cleverest fellows in the world, and that they alone have discovered that neither in things nor in arguments is there anything sound or sure, but that all existing objects are in a constant flux and reflux, exactly as in the Euripus, and never abide an instant in any state.'

Ibid. 91 A : ' Just at present I fear that on this very subject I am not in a philosophic mood, but, like those vulgar disputants, in a contentious humour. For they whenever they are disputing on a point are utterly regardless of the real truth of the matters in question, but are only anxious to make their own positions seem true to the hearers.'

Ibid. 101 E : ' You would not, like those Eristics (οἱ ἀντιλογικοί), confuse in your argument the first principle and its consequences, that is if you wished to discover any real truth.'

Meno 75 C: ' I should have told him the truth, and if the inquirer were one of those wise and Eristic and antagonistic persons I should say to him, That is what I have to say, and if I am wrong, it is your business to take up the argument and refute me.'

Rep. 454 A : ' Truly, Glaucon, said I, the power of the art of contradiction is a noble one.—Why so?—Because it seems to me that many fall into it even against their will, and think that they are reasoning when they are only disputing, because they cannot examine the question by dividing and classifying, but persist in contradicting the mere words of the argument, and practising disputation not real discussion.'

Sophist. 225 E : ' But who is the other who makes money out of private disputations (ἐριδων)? There is only one true answer: he is the wonderful Sophist, of whom we are in pursuit, and who

42

VII. THE SOPHISTS

re-appears again for the fourth time.—Yes, for he is the money-making species, as it seems, of the Eristic art, that disputations, controversial, pugnacious, combative, acquisitive art, as our argument has now shown, in a word the Sophist.'

The extreme contrast between the stigma thus affixed by Plato to the name ' Sophist ' and its original use as a title of honour is so remarkable, that we cannot wonder if historians of different schools of thought have adopted widely different explanations of so surprising a change. Until the middle of the last century it was generally believed that Plato's descriptions corresponded more or less closely to the real character and practices of the Sophists of his day. But the confidence with which this view was entertained received a sudden shock when Mr. Grote published his famous defence of the Sophists in his *History of Greece*, vol. vii. ch. 67. The effect produced by that brilliant but paradoxical essay was, however, of short duration. More exact and impartial students had no difficulty in showing that the misrepresentations alleged by the modern historian were for the most part based upon his own misinterpretation of the ancient testimony. See especially Cope's excellent article ' The Sophists ' in the *Journal of Classical and Sacred Philology*, No. ii. 1854, and the same scholar's *Gorgias*, Introduction, pp. xxii, xxiii ; Poste, Aristotle's *Sophistical Elenchi*, p. 100 ; Jowett, *Sophist*, Introd. pp. 377–380.

It was alleged by Grote (p. 486) that Plato ' stole the term Sophistes out of general circulation . . . and fastened it upon the eminent teachers of the Socratic age.' That the term was in general circulation, and that it was fastened in an unfavourable sense upon a certain class of teachers of bad eminence in the Socratic age, is easily shown by the testimony of contemporary writers other than Plato.

Thus Lysias says in his *Olympic Oration*, 912 : ' I have not come hither to make petty quibbles nor to dispute about names. For I think that these are the practices of very worthless Sophists in great want of a livelihood.' Only the commencement of this oration is extant, but according to Plutarch, *Life of Lysias, Mor.* 836 D, it was read by him at the Olympic Festival. However this may be, it is certain that the composition could only have been undertaken in the short interval when Lysias was in possession

INTRODUCTION

of the full rights of citizenship, that is, during the Archonship of Eucleides, B.C. 403.

In that same year Thucydides returned from exile to Athens, and was still engaged in the composition of his History: a description of the Athenians which he puts into the mouth of Cleon (iii. 38) shows somewhat of his estimation of the Sophists, and the theatrical character of their public exhibitions : ἁπλῶς τε ἀκοῆς ἡδονῇ ἡσσώμενοι καὶ σοφιστῶν θεαταῖς ἐοικότες καθημένοις μᾶλλον ἢ περὶ πόλεως βουλευομένοις. The Scholiast remarks that σοφιστῶν here means 'those who in customary language are so called, the teachers of rhetorical questions.' Lysias was no friend of Plato, and Thucydides was too grave a writer to give currency to any slanderous gossip, so that their testimony leaves no room to doubt the existence at Athens of a distinct class of Sophists such as Plato describes. We may therefore confidently accept the further descriptions given by Xenophon and Aristotle, without attributing them to the mere prejudice or jealousy of the Socratic School.

Nothing can be more severe than the censure of Socrates himself as recorded in Xen. *Mem.* i. 6. 13 καὶ τὴν σοφίαν ὡσαύτως τοὺς μὲν ἀργυρίου τῷ βουλομένῳ πωλοῦντας σοφιστὰς ὥσπερ πόρνους ἀποκαλοῦσιν. The plural ἀποκαλοῦσιν implies that this was not an uncommon way of speaking of the Sophists. A like evil reputation is indicated in Xenophon, *De Venatione*, xiii. 8, where in a full description of their methods of teaching he adds—οἱ σοφισταὶ δ' ἐπὶ τῷ ἐξαπατᾶν λέγουσι καὶ γράφουσιν ἐπὶ τῷ ἑαυτῶν κέρδει, καὶ οὐδένα οὐδὲν ὠφελοῦσιν· οὐδὲ γὰρ σοφὸς αὐτῶν ἐγένετο οὐδεὶς οὐδ' ἔστιν, ἀλλὰ καὶ ἀρκεῖ ἑκάστῳ σοφιστὴν κληθῆναι, ὅ ἐστιν ὄνειδος παρά γε τοῖς εὖ φρονοῦσι.

Aristotle's opinion of the Sophists is sufficiently shown in a passage of the *Ethics*, ix. 1 : 'In such matters some like the principle of a "stated wage." Those, however, who take the money beforehand, and then do nothing of what they promised, are naturally blamed in consequence of their excessive promises, for they do not fulfil what they agreed. But this course the Sophists are perhaps obliged to adopt, because no one would be likely to give money for the things which they know.' Sir A. Grant remarks on this passage that 'Aristotle contrasts the conduct of Protagoras (of whom he speaks honourably) with that of "the Sophists" after the profession had become regularly settled.'

44

VII. THE SOPHISTS

Compare *Sophistical Elenchi*, c. i : ' Now it answers the purpose of some persons rather to seem to be philosophers and not to be than to be and not to seem : for sophistry is seeming but unreal philosophy, and the Sophist a person who makes money by the semblance of philosophy without the reality ; and for his success it is requisite to seem to perform the function of the philosopher without performing it rather than to perform it without seeming to do so. . . The existence of such a mode of reasoning, and the fact that such a faculty is the aim of the persons we call Sophists, is manifest ' (Poste's translation).

Mr. Poste's own conclusion concerning the Sophists is expressed as follows (p. 100) : ' Did the Sophist ever exist ? Was there ever a class of people who professed to be philosophers and to educate, but, instead of method or a system of reasoned truth, only knew and only taught, under the name of philosophy, the game of eristic ? . . . Grote says, the only reality corresponding to the name are the *disiecti membra sophistae* in all of us, the errors incidental to human frailty in the search after truth.'

On the manner in which Grote tries to disparage the testimony of Aristotle, see Cope, *Journal of Classical and Sacred Philology*, p. 160.

A question was raised by Schleiermacher in his Introduction to the dialogue whether Euthydemus and his brother were real persons and such as Plato describes them. ' Who, then, were these men, Dionysodorus and Euthydemus, to deserve such notice and meet with such treatment ? History is silent respecting them more than any other of the Sophists mentioned by Plato, so that we may certainly conclude that they never formed any kind of school, nay it would even seem that they were not generally men in very great repute.'

We readily agree that these itinerant professors of universal knowledge were men of no great repute ; but they were none the less fit representatives on that account of the low class of Sophists of Plato's day, whom it was part of his purpose to expose. Also the testimony of history is sufficient to show that they were certainly real persons, and in some respects at least such as Plato has described them.

Dionysodorus the elder brother (283 A) is the subject of a whole

INTRODUCTION

chapter in Xenophon, *Mem. Socr.* iii. I. 1-11. He comes to Athens pretending to teach strategy, but actually teaching nothing beyond the merest elementary tactics and those most imperfectly. ' Go back,' says Socrates, ' and ask him again : for if he knows these things and is not a shameless person, he will be ashamed after taking money to send you away untaught.' How exactly this agrees with Plato's description of the two Sophists and their pretensions may be seen by referring to *Euthyd.* 271 D, 273 C, and to the specimens of their actual teaching in the discussions which follow.

Euthydemus is mentioned by name in the *Cratylus* 386 D, where a distinction is drawn between the dogma of Protagoras that ' for every man all things really are such as they appear to him,' and the more extravagant paradox of Euthydemus, that ' all things are alike to all men at the same time and always.' Other passages in which allusions more or less evident are made to Euthydemus and Dionysodorus are *Sophist.* 251 B, C, and *Pol.* 495 C, D. But the independent testimony of Aristotle proves beyond all question both that Euthydemus was a person well known at Athens, and that he used in discussion similar fallacies to those which Plato imputes to him. Cf. Aristot. *Rhetor.* ii. 24 Ἄλλος τὸ διῃρημένον συντιθέντα λέγειν ἢ τὸ συγκείμενον διαιροῦντα· ἐπεὶ γὰρ ταὐτὸν δοκεῖ εἶναι οὐκ ὂν ταὐτὸν πολλάκις, ὁπότερον χρησιμώτερον, τοῦτο δεῖ ποιεῖν. Ἔστι δὲ τοῦτο Εὐθυδήμου λόγος. Οἷον τὸ εἰδέναι ὅτι τριήρης ἐν Πειραιεῖ ἐστίν· ἕκαστον γὰρ οἶδεν. Καὶ τὸν τὰ στοιχεῖα ἐπιστάμενον ὅτι τὸ ἔπος οἶδεν· τὸ γὰρ ἔπος τὸ αὐτό ἐστιν. *Soph. Elench.* xx. Καὶ ὁ Εὐθυδήμου δὲ λόγος, Ἆρ᾽ οἶδας σὺ νῦν οὔσας ἐν Πειραιεῖ τριήρεις ἐν Σικελίᾳ ὤν ; It is needless to quote the words of Sextus Empiricus, *Adv. Mathem.* vii. 13, ibid. 48, 64, as the statements of so late a writer can add no weight to the contemporary testimony of such authors as Xenophon and Aristotle.

On this historical testimony we cannot refuse to believe that Euthydemus and Dionysodorus were real persons well known at Athens at the *scenic* date of the dialogue, and at that time elderly men like Socrates.

But a further question has been raised by Teichmüller, *Litera-rische Fehden*, I. ii, who maintains with much ingenuity that Dionysodorus is intended to represent Lysias. The theory is based upon the points of resemblance which may be traced between them.

46

VII. THE SOPHISTS

(1) Lysias and Dionysodorus each had a younger brother named Euthydemus : the occurrence therefore of this name in the dialogue would at once turn the thoughts of Plato's contemporaries to Lysias and Euthydemus, the well-known sons of Cephalus (Plat. *Rep.* 328 B).

(2) Both pairs of brothers had joined the colony which the Athenians founded at Thurii 444 B.C.

(3) Lysias was not, except for a few months, an Athenian citizen but a ξένος, though ἰσοτελής. The two Sophists were also ξένοι (271 A).

(4) Lysias was at one time a teacher of rhetoric, having been a pupil of Tisias the founder, with Corax, of the Sicilian school of dialectic. This was the same system as that which Diodorus and his brother are described as practising.

(5) Lysias was joint owner with his brother of a shield manufactory in Peiraeus, and had helped Thrasybulus with money, shields, and a band of mercenaries. If, as Teichmüller thinks, Euthydemus the brother of Lysias is the Sophist described by Plato, *Theaet.* 165 D, as πελταστικὸς ἀνὴρ μισθοφόρος ἐν λόγοις, the phrases there applied to him all relate to the art of war, ἐλλοχῶν, ἐμβαλών, χειρωσάμενός τε καὶ ξυνδήσας, ἐλύτρου.

From Xen. *Mem.* iii. 1 we know that Dionysodorus came to Athens as a teacher of the art of strategy, and both brothers are described by Plato as masters of the art of fighting in heavy armour (ὁπλομάχοι).

(6) Lysias was the most successful writer of speeches for the warfare of the law-courts.

In the dialogue (272 A) Dionysodorus and Euthydemus are both described as τὴν ἐν τοῖς δικαστηρίοις μάχην κρατίστω καὶ ἀγωνίσασθαι καὶ ἄλλον διδάξαι λέγειν τε καὶ συγγράφεσθαι λόγους οἵους εἰς τὰ δικαστήρια, and in 273 C as οἵω τε δὲ καὶ ποιῆσαι δυνατὸν εἶναι αὐτὸν αὑτῷ βοηθεῖν ἐν τοῖς δικαστηρίοις, ἄν τις αὐτὸν ἀδικῇ. The description is remarkably applicable to Lysias, who not only wrote speeches and taught others, but had made himself famous by the one excellent speech which he had himself delivered in court against the injuries done to him by Eratosthenes, 403 B.C.

Many other points of resemblance more or less striking are discussed by Teichmüller in a long chapter, but the examples given above are sufficient to show the general nature of his argument. The degree of probability resulting from it is much increased by the consideration that 'Plato in his dialogues does not rehearse old histories, as a chronicler or a novelist ; but contends with living opponents and rival teachers, who disputed with him for influence over the best men of the time and especially over the young, since they professed to teach the same things as he did, only better.'

The theory is very interesting, and by no means improbable : it agrees well with the known relations of Plato and Lysias, and adds to the life and spirit of the dialogue.

VIII. TEXT.

In this edition of the *Euthydemus* the text is based upon the three chief MSS. collated by Schanz.

(1) Codex Clarkianus, n. 39 in the Bodleian Library, Oxford, written in the year 895 B.C. by Johannes Calligraphus for Arethas a Deacon of Patras, afterwards Archbishop of Caesarea in Cappadocia. This excellent MS. is very fully described by Schanz, *Novae Commentationes Platonicae*, 105-118, and by T. W. Allen in the *Preface to the Phototype edition*, 1898. In the MS. as a whole there are many corrections by the hand of the learned Archbishop himself (*Classical Review*, vol. xvi. Nos. 1 and 8). These contemporary corrections (B²) are rightly distinguished by Professor Burnet from later corrections (b). But in the *Euthydemus* there is only one legible note in the margin, and this is in the handwriting of Arethas, and refers to the word σκληφρός, 271 B 4.

(2) T. In the Library of St. Mark's at Venice this MS. is described as 'Append. Class. 4, cod. 1,' and by Bekker as t : it has been shown by Schanz 'to be the source of all MSS. of the second family,' except that which immediately follows.

(3) Vind., or V, distinguished by Burnet as 'W= cod. Vindobonensis 54, suppl. phil. gr. 7 = Stallbaum Vind. 1.' This MS. Schanz considered to be derived not directly from T, but from a common source, which he marked by the letter M.

In choosing between various readings I have preferred those of Cod. B as being by far the oldest and best authority, except where they are evidently corrupt or fail to give any adequate meaning to the passage.

VIII.   TEXT

The text of Plato as represented in the MSS. has been subjected to much alteration by recent critics, among whom Cobet, Badham, and Schanz are especially distinguished for ingenious emendations and brilliant conjectures, often most successful, and, even when unnecessary, very attractive. In Schanz's edition of the *Euthydemus* such alterations and omissions are extremely frequent, and Professor Burnet has done good service to the students of Plato in the Oxford edition by frequently restoring the readings of the chief MSS.

I have acted on the same principle still more frequently, being convinced that it is often easier to alter the words of such an author as Plato than to understand and explain them. It is, however, the duty of an editor not to tamper with a reading authenticated by the best MSS., until he has exhausted all means within his power of elucidating the words ascribed to his author. Wherever I have ventured to differ from recent editors, I have stated my reasons in the notes.

In the matter of orthography I have been unwilling to depart unnecessarily from long-established and almost universal custom.

Thus, for example, I have retained the usual method of printing the pronoun ὅ τι so as to distinguish it from the conjunction ὅτι. The usefulness of the distinction may be seen in such phrases as οὐδ' ἤδη πρὸ τοῦ ὅτι εἶεν οἱ παγκρατιασταί (*Euthyd.* 271 C), ἵνα εἰδῶ ὅτι καὶ μαθησόμεθα (272 D), σοὶ εἰς κεφαλήν, ὅτι μου . . . καταψεύδει (283 E), τὸν ὑμέτερον πατέρ' ἂν τύπτοιμι, ὅτι μαθὼν σοφοὺς υἱεῖς οὕτως φύσει· (29 9 A), οὔπω οἶδα ὅτι μέλλω ἐρεῖν.

Passages thus printed may have no ambiguity for a competent scholar, but they put a needless difficulty in the way of a beginner.

It is more important, however, to consider whether this mode of printing is or is not etymologically correct. The combination ὅς τις, ἥ τις, ὅ τι is made up of two separate words, each of which is separately declined, as *Pol.* 462 C ἐν ᾗ ᾗ τινι δὴ πόλει, where, if we write ᾗτινι as one word, the accent becomes impossible. Cf. Plat. *Epist.* vii. 347 E ὅπῃ τε καὶ ὅπως ἤθελε καὶ οἷς τισι. *Epist.* xi. 359 A ὑπὸ νόμων θέσεως καὶ ὧν τινων. *Legg.* ix. 864 E τὴν βλάβην ἣν ἄν τινα καταβλάψῃ. If therefore we were to be guided by etymology, both the pronoun and the conjunction should be written ὅ τι, but for the

INTRODUCTION

sake of distinguishing them the conjunction is conventionally written as one word ὅτι.

The remarks and practice of Jannaris are inconsistent and misleading: in 610. 3 he prints 'ὅστις, ὅ,τι [1],' and adds in a footnote [1], 'It should be written ὅτι, but ancient grammarians introduced ὅ,τι—for which modern scholars substitute ὅ τι—to distinguish it from the conjunction ὅτι 'that' (79).' But Jannaris himself constantly prints ὅ,τι, as in ὅ,τι μαθών, ὅ,τι παθών: see his Index.

Cf. Kühner-Blass I. i. 353 (§ 93 Diastole) 'ὅ,τι, nicht wie ὅτι.'

We may add that Schanz is mistaken in his critical note on 271 c 6, 'ὅτι BT,' for Cod. B certainly has ὅ τι.

272 A 5 ἐπιτεθείκατον B, ἐπιτεθήκατον. There is apparently no authority in the MSS. for the latter form which is adopted in the Oxford text, 1903.

In Kühner-Blass, *Ausführliche Grammatik*, § 277, p. 186, τέθεικα is described as 'nachklass'; and in § 285, p. 201, on the Doric dialect, we find 'Von τίθημι lautet das Pf. τέθεκα, τέθεμαι, so auf Inschr. ἀνατεθέκαντι.' In this case τέθεκα stood for τέθεικα.

Jannaris is of opinion that the diphthong EI arose from the insertion of a simple vertical stroke (not iota) to mark the metrical quantity of E (App. ii. 9). ' Accordingly, when representing a rhythmical or grammatical length E now begins (sixth century B.C.) to figure in the Attic inscriptions as EI (later on as �ⴱ or H identified with EI) . . . only in sporadic cases, the old orthography . . . remaining in universal practice down to the middle of the fifth century B.C. . . . It is only since the year 403 B.C., under the archonship of Eucleides, (that) the new spelling obtained by a public act official recognition or formal sanction' (ibid. 12). The further inference of Jannaris that 'a new system of orthography was created into which *all previous literary and many inscriptional compositions had to be transliterated*' (the italics are mine) must be regarded as a somewhat doubtful or, at least, exaggerated conjecture. It is, I believe, generally acknowledged that such forms as ἐπιτεθήκατον, and φοβῇ (2nd person *indicative* middle), are unknown to the MSS. of the Attic drama, and it would require much more evidence than has yet been alleged to prove in opposition to all MSS. that so artistic and poetic a writer as Plato at once discarded the style

VIII. TEXT

to which he had been accustomed from childhood to his twenty-fifth or twenty-sixth year in favour of an official novelty.

The Attic inscriptions of the period contained in the *Corpus Graecarum Inscriptionum* are almost exclusively legislative or magisterial decrees and public accounts. In such documents the second person naturally is not used, and there is no evidence of any such change as that of φοβεῖ to φοβῇ. In the accounts ἔθηκαν the aorist only occurs, so that there is no evidence in favour of the change to ἐπιτεθήκατον.

On this subject it may be well to quote an incidental remark of the author of the *New Phrynichus*, who will not be thought too conservative in the matter of orthography. Mr. Rutherford writes (p. 45): 'It is no rare experience to find the most distinguished critics advocating an alteration of all the manuscripts, simply because they have never tried to estimate, as is done in this inquiry, the extraordinary ease with which an Athenian of the best age moved among the various coexistent literary dialects of his time.'

ERRATUM

281 b 1 *before* ἡγουμένη *insert* ⟨ἢ⟩

ΕΥΘΥΔΗΜΟΣ

ΚΡΙΤΩΝ   ΣΩΚΡΑΤΗΣ

ΚΡ. Τίς ἦν, ὦ Σώκρατες, ᾧ χθὲς ἐν Λυκείῳ διελέγου; a
ἢ πολὺς ὑμᾶς ὄχλος περιειστήκει, ὥστ' ἔγωγε βουλόμενος
ἀκούειν προσελθὼν οὐδὲν οἷός τ' ἦ ἀκοῦσαι σαφές· ὑπερκύψας
μέντοι κατεῖδον, καί μοι ἔδοξεν εἶναι ξένος τις ᾧ διελέγου.
τίς ἦν;   5
ΣΩ. Ὁπότερον καὶ ἐρωτᾷς, ὦ Κρίτων; οὐ γὰρ εἷς ἀλλὰ
δύ' ἤστην.
ΚΡ. Ὃν μὲν ἐγὼ λέγω, ἐκ δεξιᾶς τρίτος ἀπὸ σοῦ καθῆστο·
ἐν μέσῳ δ' ὑμῶν τὸ Ἀξιόχου μειράκιον ἦν. καὶ μάλα πολύ, b
ὦ Σώκρατες, ἐπιδεδωκέναι μοι ἔδοξεν, καὶ τοῦ ἡμετέρου οὐ
πολύ τι τὴν ἡλικίαν διαφέρειν Κριτοβούλου. ἀλλ' ἐκεῖνος
μὲν σκληφρός, οὗτος δὲ προφερὴς καὶ καλὸς καὶ ἀγαθὸς τὴν
ὄψιν.   5
ΣΩ. Εὐθύδημος οὗτός ἐστιν, ὦ Κρίτων, ὃν ἐρωτᾷς, ὁ δὲ
παρ' ἐμὲ καθήμενος ἐξ ἀριστερᾶς ἀδελφὸς τούτου, Διονυσό-
δωρος· μετέχει δὲ καὶ οὗτος τῶν λόγων.
ΚΡ. Οὐδέτερον γιγνώσκω, ὦ Σώκρατες. καινοί τινες αὖ
οὗτοι, ὡς ἔοικε, σοφισταί· ποδαποί; καὶ τίς ἡ σοφία;   c
ΣΩ. Οὗτοι τὸ μὲν γένος, ὡς ἐγᾦμαι, ἐντεῦθέν ποθέν
εἰσιν ἐκ Χίου, ἀπῴκησαν δὲ ἐς Θουρίους, φεύγοντες δὲ
ἐκεῖθεν πόλλ' ἤδη ἔτη περὶ τούσδε τοὺς τόπους διατρίβουσιν.
ὃ δὲ σὺ ἐρωτᾷς τὴν σοφίαν αὐτοῖν, θαυμασία, ὦ Κρίτων· 5
πάσσοφοι ἀτεχνῶς τώ γε, οὐδ' ἤδη πρὸ τοῦ ὅ τι εἶεν οἱ
παγκρατιασταί. τούτω γάρ ἐστον κομιδῇ παμμάχω. οὐ ⟨καθ' ἃ⟩

τὼ Ἀκαρνᾶνε ἐγενέσθην τὼ παγκρατιαστὰ ἀδελφώ· ἐκείνω
d μὲν γὰρ τῷ σώματι μόνον οἵω τε μάχεσθαι, τούτω δὲ πρῶτον
μὲν τῷ σώματι δεινοτάτω ἐστὸν καὶ μάχῃ, ᾗ πάντων ἔστι
κρατεῖν—ἐν ὅπλοις γὰρ αὐτώ τε σοφὼ πάνυ μάχεσθαι καὶ
272 ἄλλον, ὃς ἂν διδῷ μισθόν, οἵω τε ποιῆσαι—ἔπειτα τὴν ἐν
τοῖς δικαστηρίοις μάχην κρατίστω καὶ ἀγωνίσασθαι καὶ
ἄλλον διδάξαι λέγειν τε καὶ συγγράφεσθαι λόγους οἵους
εἰς τὰ δικαστήρια. πρὸ τοῦ μὲν οὖν ταῦτα δεινὼ ἤστην
5 μόνον, νῦν δὲ τέλος ἐπιτεθείκατον παγκρατιαστικῇ τέχνῃ. ἣ
γὰρ ἦν λοιπὴ αὐτοῖν μάχη ἀργός, ταύτην νῦν ἐξείργασθον,
ὥστε μηδ' ἂν ἕνα αὐτοῖς οἷόν τ' εἶναι μηδ' ἀνταραι· οὕτω
δεινὼ γεγόνατον ἐν τοῖς λόγοις μάχεσθαί τε καὶ ἐξελέγχειν
b τὸ ἀεὶ λεγόμενον, ὁμοίως ἐάντε ψεῦδος ἐάντε ἀληθὲς ᾖ. ἐγὼ
μὲν οὖν, ὦ Κρίτων, ἐν νῷ ἔχω τοῖν ἀνδροῖν παραδοῦναι
ἐμαυτόν· καὶ γάρ φατον ἐν ὀλίγῳ χρόνῳ ποιῆσαι ἂν καὶ
ἄλλον ὁντινοῦν τὰ αὐτὰ ταῦτα δεινόν.
5 ΚΡ. Τί δέ, ὦ Σώκρατες; οὐ φοβεῖ τὴν ἡλικίαν, μὴ ἤδη
πρεσβύτερος ᾖς;
ΣΩ. Ἥκιστά γε, ὦ Κρίτων, ἱκανὸν τεκμήριον ἔχων καὶ
παραμύθιον τοῦ μὴ φοβεῖσθαι. αὐτὼ γὰρ τούτω, ὡς ἔπος
εἰπεῖν, γέροντε ὄντε ἠρξάσθην ταύτης τῆς σοφίας ἧς ἔγωγε
10 ἐπιθυμῶ, τῆς ἐριστικῆς· πέρυσιν ἢ προπέρυσιν οὐδέπω ἤστην
c σοφώ. ἀλλ' ἐγὼ ἓν μόνον φοβοῦμαι, μὴ αὖ ὄνειδος τοῖν
ξένοιν περιάψω, ὥσπερ Κόννῳ τῷ Μητροβίου, τῷ κιθαριστῇ,
ὃς ἐμὲ διδάσκει ἔτι καὶ νῦν κιθαρίζειν· ὁρῶντες οὖν οἱ παῖδες
οἱ συμφοιτηταί μου ἐμοῦ τε καταγελῶσι καὶ τὸν Κόννον
5 καλοῦσι γεροντοδιδάσκαλον. μὴ οὖν καὶ τοῖν ξένοιν τις
ταὐτὸν τοῦτο ὀνειδίσῃ· οἱ δ' αὐτὸ τοῦτο ἴσως φοβούμενοι
τάχα με οὐκ ἂν ἐθέλοιεν προσδέξασθαι. ἐγὼ δ', ὦ Κρίτων,
ἐκεῖσε μὲν ἄλλους πέπεικα συμμαθητάς μοι φοιτᾶν πρε-
d σβύτας, ἐνταῦθα δέ γε ἑτέρους πειράσομαι πείθειν. καὶ σὺ τί
οὐ συμφοιτᾷς; ὡς δὲ δέλεαρ αὐτοῖς ἄξομεν τοὺς σοὺς υἱεῖς·
ἐφιέμενοι γὰρ ἐκείνων οἶδ' ὅτι καὶ ἡμᾶς παιδεύσουσιν.

ΚΡ. Ἀλλ᾽ οὐδὲν κωλύει, ὦ Σώκρατες, ἐάν γε σοὶ δοκῇ.
πρῶτον δέ μοι διήγησαι τὴν σοφίαν τοῖν ἀνδροῖν τίς ἐστιν, 5
ἵνα εἰδῶ ὅ τι καὶ μαθησόμεθα.

ΣΩ. Οὐκ ἂν φθάνοις ἀκούων· ὡς οὐκ ἂν ἔχοιμί γε εἰπεῖν
ὅτι οὐ προσεῖχον τὸν νοῦν αὐτοῖν, ἀλλὰ πάνυ καὶ προσεῖχον
καὶ μέμνημαι, καί σοι πειράσομαι ἐξ ἀρχῆς ἅπαντα διηγή-
σασθαι. κατὰ θεὸν γάρ τινα ἔτυχον καθήμενος ἐνταῦθα, e
οὗπερ σύ με εἶδες, ἐν τῷ ἀποδυτηρίῳ μόνος, καὶ ἤδη ἐν νῷ
εἶχον ἀναστῆναι· ἀνισταμένου δέ μου ἐγένετο τὸ εἰωθὸς
σημεῖον τὸ δαιμόνιον. πάλιν οὖν ἐκαθεζόμην, καὶ ὀλίγῳ
ὕστερον εἰσέρχεσθον τούτω—ὅ τ᾽ Εὐθύδημος καὶ ὁ Διονυ- 273
σόδωρος—καὶ ἄλλοι μαθηταὶ ἅμα αὖ πολλοὶ ἐμοὶ δοκεῖν·
εἰσελθόντες δὲ περιεπατείτην ἐν τῷ καταστέγῳ δρόμῳ. καὶ
οὔπω τούτω δύ᾽ ἢ τρεῖς δρόμους περιεληλυθότε ἤστην,
καὶ εἰσέρχεται Κλεινίας, ὃν σὺ φῂς πολὺ ἐπιδεδωκέναι, 5
ἀληθῆ λέγων· ὄπισθεν δὲ αὐτοῦ ἐρασταὶ πάνυ πολλοί τε
[καὶ] ἄλλοι καὶ Κτήσιππος, νεανίσκος τις Παιανιεύς, μάλα
καλός τε κἀγαθὸς τὴν φύσιν, ὅσον μὴ ὑβριστὴς [δὲ] διὰ τὸ
νέος εἶναι. ἰδὼν οὖν με ὁ Κλεινίας ἀπὸ τῆς εἰσόδου μόνον b
καθήμενον, ἀντικρὺς ἰὼν παρεκαθέζετο ἐκ δεξιᾶς, ὥσπερ καὶ
σὺ φῄς. ἰδόντε δὲ αὐτὸν ὅ τε Διονυσόδωρος καὶ ὁ Εὐθύδημος πρῶτον μὲν ἐπιστάντε διελεγέσθην ἀλλήλοιν, ἄλλην
καὶ ἄλλην ἀποβλέποντε εἰς ἡμᾶς—καὶ γὰρ πάνυ αὐτοῖν 5
προσεῖχον τὸν νοῦν—ἔπειτα ἰόντε ὁ μὲν παρὰ τὸ μειράκιον
ἐκαθέζετο, ὁ Εὐθύδημος, ὁ δὲ παρ᾽ αὐτὸν ἐμὲ ἐξ ἀριστερᾶς,
οἱ δ᾽ ἄλλοι ὡς ἕκαστος ἐτύγχανεν.

Ἠσπαζόμην οὖν αὐτὼ ἅτε διὰ χρόνου ἑωρακώς· μετὰ δὲ c
τοῦτο εἶπον πρὸς τὸν Κλεινίαν· Ὦ Κλεινία, τώδε μέντοι τὼ
ἄνδρε σοφώ, Εὐθύδημός τε καὶ Διονυσόδωρος, οὐ τὰ σμικρὰ
ἀλλὰ τὰ μεγάλα· τὰ γὰρ περὶ τὸν πόλεμον πάντα ἐπίστασθον, ὅσα δεῖ τὸν μέλλοντα ἀγαθὸν στρατηγὸν ἔσεσθαι, 5
τάς τε τάξεις καὶ τὰς ἡγεμονίας τῶν στρατοπέδων καὶ ὅσα
ἐν ὅπλοις μάχεσθαι διδακτέον· οἵω τε δὲ καὶ ποιῆσαι

δυνατὸν εἶναι αὐτὸν αὐτῷ βοηθεῖν ἐν τοῖς δικαστηρίοις, ἄν
τις αὐτὸν ἀδικῇ.

d   Εἰπὼν οὖν ταῦτα κατεφρονήθην ὑπ' αὐτοῖν· ἐγελασάτην
οὖν ἄμφω βλέψαντες εἰς ἀλλήλους, καὶ ὁ Εὐθύδημος εἶπεν·
Οὗτοι ἔτι ταῦτα, ὦ Σώκρατες, σπουδάζομεν, ἀλλὰ παρέργοις
αὐτοῖς χρώμεθα.

5   Κἀγὼ θαυμάσας εἶπον· Καλὸν ἄν τι τὸ ἔργον ὑμῶν εἴη,
εἰ τηλικαῦτα πράγματα πάρεργα ὑμῖν τυγχάνει ὄντα, καὶ
πρὸς θεῶν εἴπετόν μοι τί ἐστι τοῦτο τὸ καλόν.
     Ἀρετήν, ἔφη, ὦ Σώκρατες, οἰόμεθα οἵω τ' εἶναι παραδοῦναι
κάλλιστ' ἀνθρώπων καὶ τάχιστα.

e   Ὦ Ζεῦ, οἷον, ἦν δ' ἐγώ, λέγετον πρᾶγμα· πόθεν τοῦτο
τὸ ἕρμαιον ηὑρέτην; ἐγὼ δὲ περὶ ὑμῶν διενοούμην ἔτι, ὥσπερ
νυνδὴ ἔλεγον, ὡς τὸ πολὺ τοῦτο δεινοῖν ὄντοιν, ἐν ὅπλοις
μάχεσθαι, καὶ ταῦτα ἔλεγον περὶ σφῷν· ὅτε γὰρ τὸ πρότερον
5 ἐπεδημησάτην, τοῦτο μέμνημαι σφὼ ἐπαγγελλομένω. εἰ
δὲ νῦν ἀληθῶς ταύτην τὴν ἐπιστήμην ἔχετον, ἵλεω εἴητον—
ἀτεχνῶς γὰρ ἔγωγε σφὼ ὥσπερ θεὼ προσαγορεύω, συγ-
274 γνώμην δεόμενος ἔχειν μοι τῶν ἔμπροσθεν εἰρημένων. ἀλλ'
ὁρᾶτον, ὦ Εὐθύδημέ τε καὶ Διονυσόδωρε, εἰ ἀληθῆ λέγετον·
ὑπὸ γὰρ τοῦ μεγέθους τοῦ ἐπαγγέλματος οὐδὲν θαυμαστὸν
ἀπιστεῖν.

5   Ἀλλ' εὖ ἴσθι, ὦ Σώκρατες, ἐφάτην, τοῦτο οὕτως ἔχον.
     Μακαρίζω ἄρ' ὑμᾶς ἔγωγε τοῦ κτήματος πολὺ μᾶλλον ἢ
μέγαν βασιλέα τῆς ἀρχῆς· τοσόνδε δέ μοι εἴπετον, εἰ ἐν νῷ
ἔχετον ἐπιδεικνύναι ταύτην τὴν σοφίαν, ἢ πῶς σφῷν βεβού-
λευται.

10   Ἐπ' αὐτό γε τοῦτο πάρεσμεν, ὦ Σώκρατες, ὡς ἐπιδείξοντε
b καὶ διδάξοντε, ἐάν τις ἐθέλῃ μανθάνειν.
     Ὅτι μὲν ἐθελήσουσιν ἅπαντες οἱ μὴ ἔχοντες, ἐγὼ ὑμῖν
ἐγγυῶμαι, πρῶτος μὲν ἐγώ, ἔπειτα δὲ Κλεινίας οὑτοσί,
πρὸς δ' ἡμῖν Κτήσιππός τε ὅδε καὶ οἱ ἄλλοι οὗτοι, ἦν δ' ἐγὼ
5 δεικνὺς αὐτῷ τοὺς ἐραστὰς τοὺς Κλεινίου· οἱ δὲ ἐτύγχανον

ἡμᾶς ἤδη περιστάμενοι. ὁ γὰρ Κτήσιππος ἔτυχε πόρρω
καθεζόμενος τοῦ Κλεινίου—κἀμοὶ δοκεῖν ὡς ἐτύγχανεν ὁ
Εὐθύδημος ἐμοὶ διαλεγόμενος προνενευκὼς εἰς τὸ πρόσθεν,
ἐν μέσῳ ὄντος ἡμῶν τοῦ Κλεινίου, ἐπεσκότει τῷ Κτησίππῳ c
τῆς θέας—βουλόμενός τε οὖν θεάσασθαι ὁ Κτήσιππος τὰ
παιδικὰ καὶ ἅμα φιλήκοος ὢν ἀναπηδήσας πρῶτος προσέστη
ἡμῖν ἐν τῷ καταντικρύ· οὕτως οὖν καὶ οἱ ἄλλοι ἐκεῖνον
ἰδόντες περιέστησαν ἡμᾶς, οἵ τε τοῦ Κλεινίου ἐρασταὶ καὶ 5
οἱ τοῦ Εὐθυδήμου τε καὶ Διονυσοδώρου ἑταῖροι. τούτους δὴ
ἐγὼ δεικνὺς ἔλεγον τῷ Εὐθυδήμῳ ὅτι πάντες ἕτοιμοι εἶεν
μανθάνειν· ὅ τε οὖν Κτήσιππος συνέφη μάλα προθύμως d
καὶ οἱ ἄλλοι, καὶ ἐκέλευον αὐτὼ κοινῇ πάντες ἐπιδείξασθαι
τὴν δύναμιν τῆς σοφίας.

Εἶπον οὖν ἐγώ· Ὦ Εὐθύδημε καὶ Διονυσόδωρε, πάνυ μὲν
οὖν παντὶ τρόπῳ καὶ τούτοις χαρίσασθον καὶ ἐμοῦ ἕνεκα 5
ἐπιδείξασθον. τὰ μὲν οὖν πλεῖστα δῆλον ὅτι οὐκ ὀλίγου
ἔργον ἐπιδεῖξαι· τόδε δέ μοι εἴπετον, πότερον πεπεισμένον
ἤδη ὡς χρὴ παρ' ὑμῶν μανθάνειν δύναισθ' ἂν ἀγαθὸν ποιῆσαι
ἄνδρα μόνον, ἢ καὶ ἐκεῖνον τὸν μήπω πεπεισμένον διὰ τὸ μὴ e
οἴεσθαι ὅλως τὸ πρᾶγμα τὴν ἀρετὴν μαθητὸν εἶναι ἢ μὴ σφὼ
εἶναι αὐτῆς διδασκάλω; φέρε, καὶ τὸν οὕτως ἔχοντα τῆς
αὐτῆς τέχνης ἔργον πεῖσαι ὡς καὶ διδακτὸν ἡ ἀρετὴ καὶ οὗτοι
ὑμεῖς ἐστὲ παρ' ὧν ἂν κάλλιστά τις αὐτὸ μάθοι, ἢ ἄλλης; 5
Ταύτης μὲν οὖν, ἔφη, τῆς αὐτῆς, ὦ Σώκρατες, ὁ Διονυσόδωρος.

Ὑμεῖς ἄρα, ἦν δ' ἐγώ, ὦ Διονυσόδωρε, τῶν νῦν ἀνθρώπων κάλλιστ' ἂν προτρέψαιτε εἰς φιλοσοφίαν καὶ ἀρετῆς 275
ἐπιμέλειαν;

Οἰόμεθά γε δή, ὦ Σώκρατες.

Τῶν μὲν τοίνυν ἄλλων τὴν ἐπίδειξιν ἡμῖν, ἔφην, εἰς αὖθις
ἀπόθεσθον, τοῦτο δ' αὐτὸ ἐπιδείξασθον· τουτονὶ τὸν νεανίσκον 5
πείσατον ὡς χρὴ φιλοσοφεῖν καὶ ἀρετῆς ἐπιμελεῖσθαι, καὶ
χαριεῖσθον ἐμοί τε καὶ τουτοισὶ πᾶσιν. συμβέβηκεν γάρ τι

τοιοῦτον τῷ μειρακίῳ τούτῳ· ἐγώ τε καὶ οἵδε πάντες τυγχάνομεν ἐπιθυμοῦντες ὡς βέλτιστον αὐτὸν γενέσθαι.

10 ἔστι δὲ οὗτος Ἀξιόχου μὲν υἱὸς τοῦ Ἀλκιβιάδου τοῦ παλαιοῦ, αὐτα-
b νέψιος δὲ τοῦ νῦν ὄντος Ἀλκιβιάδου· ὄνομα δ᾽ αὐτῷ Κλεινίας.

ἔστι δὲ νέος· φοβούμεθα δὴ περὶ αὐτῷ, οἷον εἰκὸς περὶ νέῳ, μή τις φθῇ ἡμᾶς ἐπ᾽ ἄλλο τι ἐπιτήδευμα τρέψας αὐτοῦ τὴν διάνοιαν καὶ διαφθείρῃ. σφὼ οὖν ἥκετον εἰς κάλλιστον·
5 ἀλλ᾽ εἰ μή τι διαφέρει ὑμῖν, λάβετον πεῖραν τοῦ μειρακίου καὶ διαλέχθητον ἐναντίον ἡμῶν.

Εἰπόντος οὖν ἐμοῦ σχεδόν τι αὐτὰ ταῦτα ὁ Εὐθύδημος ἅμα ἀνδρείως τε καὶ θαρραλέως, Ἀλλ᾽ οὐδὲν διαφέρει, ὦ
c Σώκρατες, ἔφη, ἐὰν μόνον ἐθέλῃ ἀποκρίνεσθαι ὁ νεανίσκος.

Ἀλλὰ μὲν δή, ἔφην ἐγώ, τοῦτό γε καὶ εἴθισται· θαμὰ γὰρ αὐτῷ οἵδε προσιόντες πολλὰ ἐρωτῶσίν τε καὶ διαλέγονται, ὥστε ἐπιεικῶς θαρρεῖ τὸ ἀποκρίνασθαι.

5 Τὰ δὴ μετὰ ταῦτα, ὦ Κρίτων, πῶς ἂν καλῶς σοι διηγησαίμην; οὐ γὰρ σμικρὸν τὸ ἔργον δύνασθαι ἀναλαβεῖν διεξιόντα σοφίαν ἀμήχανον ὅσην· ὥστ᾽ ἔγωγε, καθάπερ οἱ
d ποιηταί, δέομαι ἀρχόμενος τῆς διηγήσεως Μούσας τε καὶ Μνήμην ἐπικαλεῖσθαι. ἤρξατο δ᾽ οὖν ἐνθένδε ποθὲν ὁ Εὐθύδημος, ὡς ἐγῷμαι· Ὦ Κλεινία, πότεροί εἰσι τῶν ἀνθρώπων οἱ μανθάνοντες, οἱ σοφοὶ ἢ οἱ ἀμαθεῖς;

5 Καὶ τὸ μειράκιον, ἅτε μεγάλου ὄντος τοῦ ἐρωτήματος, ἠρυθρίασέν τε καὶ ἀπορήσας ἔβλεπεν εἰς ἐμέ· καὶ ἐγὼ γνοὺς αὐτὸν τεθορυβημένον, Θάρρει, ἦν δ᾽ ἐγώ, ὦ Κλεινία,
e καὶ ἀπόκριναι ἀνδρείως, ὁπότερά σοι φαίνεται· ἴσως γάρ τοι ὠφελεῖ τὴν μεγίστην ὠφελίαν.

Καὶ ἐν τούτῳ ὁ Διονυσόδωρος προσκύψας μοι μικρὸν πρὸς τὸ οὖς, πάνυ μειδιάσας τῷ προσώπῳ, Καὶ μήν, ἔφη,
5 σοί, ὦ Σώκρατες, προλέγω ὅτι ὁπότερ᾽ ἂν ἀποκρίνηται τὸ μειράκιον, ἐξελεγχθήσεται.

Καὶ αὐτοῦ μεταξὺ ταῦτα λέγοντος ὁ Κλεινίας ἔτυχεν ἀποκρινάμενος, ὥστε οὐδὲ παρακελεύσασθαί μοι ἐξεγένετο

εὐλαβηθῆναι τῷ μειρακίῳ, ἀλλ᾽ ἀπεκρίνατο ὅτι οἱ σοφοὶ 276
εἶεν οἱ μανθάνοντες. Καὶ ὁ Εὐθύδημος, Καλεῖς δέ τινας, ἔφη, διδασκάλους, ἢ
οὔ;—Ὡμολόγει.—Οὐκοῦν τῶν μανθανόντων οἱ διδάσκαλοι
διδάσκαλοί εἰσιν, ὥσπερ ὁ κιθαριστὴς καὶ ὁ γραμματιστὴς 5
διδάσκαλοι δήπου ἦσαν σοῦ καὶ τῶν ἄλλων παίδων, ὑμεῖς
δὲ μαθηταί;—Συνέφη.—Ἄλλο τι οὖν, ἡνίκα ἐμανθάνετε,
οὔπω ἠπίστασθε ταῦτα ἃ ἐμανθάνετε;—Οὐκ ἔφη.—Ἆρ᾽ οὖν
σοφοὶ ἦτε, ὅτε ταῦτα οὐκ ἠπίστασθε;—Οὐ δῆτα, ἦ δ᾽ ὅς. b
—Οὐκοῦν εἰ μὴ σοφοί, ἀμαθεῖς;—Πάνυ γε.—Ὑμεῖς ἄρα
μανθάνοντες ἃ οὐκ ἠπίστασθε, ἀμαθεῖς ὄντες ἐμανθάνετε.—
Ἐπένευσε τὸ μειράκιον.—Οἱ ἀμαθεῖς ἄρα μανθάνουσιν, ὦ
Κλεινία, ἀλλ᾽ οὐχ οἱ σοφοί, ὡς σὺ οἴει. 5
Ταῦτ᾽ οὖν εἰπόντος αὐτοῦ, ὥσπερ ὑπὸ διδασκάλου χορὸς
ἀποσημήναντος, ἅμα ἀνεθορύβησάν τε καὶ ἐγέλασαν οἱ ἑπό-
μενοι ἐκεῖνοι μετὰ τοῦ Διονυσοδώρου τε καὶ Εὐθυδήμου· καὶ c
πρὶν ἀναπνεῦσαι καλῶς τε καὶ εὖ τὸ μειράκιον, ἐκδεξάμενος
ὁ Διονυσόδωρος, Τί δέ, ὦ Κλεινία, ἔφη, ὁπότε ἀποστοματίζοι
ὑμῖν ὁ γραμματιστής, πότεροι ἐμάνθανον τῶν παίδων τὰ
ἀποστοματιζόμενα, οἱ σοφοὶ ἢ οἱ ἀμαθεῖς;—Οἱ σοφοί, ἔφη 5
ὁ Κλεινίας.—Οἱ σοφοὶ ἄρα μανθάνουσιν ἀλλ᾽ οὐχ οἱ ἀμαθεῖς,
καὶ οὐκ εὖ σὺ ἄρτι Εὐθυδήμῳ ἀπεκρίνω.
Ἐνταῦθα δὴ καὶ πάνυ μέγα ἐγέλασάν τε καὶ ἐθορύβησαν d
οἱ ἐρασταὶ τοῖν ἀνδροῖν, ἀγασθέντες τῆς σοφίας αὐτοῖν· οἱ
δ᾽ ἄλλοι ἡμεῖς ἐκπεπληγμένοι ἐσιωπῶμεν. γνοὺς δὲ ἡμᾶς
ὁ Εὐθύδημος ἐκπεπληγμένους, ἵν᾽ ἔτι μᾶλλον θαυμάζοιμεν
αὐτόν, οὐκ ἀνίει τὸ μειράκιον, ἀλλ᾽ ἠρώτα, καὶ ὥσπερ οἱ 5
ἀγαθοὶ ὀρχησταί, διπλᾶ ἔστρεφε τὰ ἐρωτήματα περὶ τοῦ
αὐτοῦ, καὶ ἔφη· Πότερον γὰρ οἱ μανθάνοντες μανθάνουσιν
ἃ ἐπίστανται ἢ ἃ μὴ ἐπίστανται;
Καὶ ὁ Διονυσόδωρος πάλιν μικρὸν πρός με ψιθυρίσας,
Καὶ τοῦτ᾽, ἔφη, ὦ Σώκρατες, ἕτερον τοιοῦτον οἷον τὸ e
πρότερον.

῍Ω Ζεῦ, ἔφην ἐγώ, ἦ μὴν καὶ τὸ πρότερόν γε καλὸν ὑμῖν
ἐφάνη τὸ ἐρώτημα.

5 Πάντ᾽, ἔφη, ὦ Σώκρατες, τοιαῦτα ἡμεῖς ἐρωτῶμεν ἄφυκτα.
Τοιγάρτοι, ἦν δ᾽ ἐγώ, δοκεῖτέ μοι εὐδοκιμεῖν παρὰ τοῖς
μαθηταῖς.

᾽Εν δὲ τούτῳ ὁ μὲν Κλεινίας τῷ Εὐθυδήμῳ ἀπεκρίνατο
ὅτι μανθάνοιεν οἱ μανθάνοντες ἃ οὐκ ἐπίσταιντο· ὁ δὲ ἤρετο
277 αὐτὸν διὰ τῶν αὐτῶν ὦνπερ τὸ πρότερον· Τί δέ; ἦ δ᾽ ὅς, οὐκ
ἐπίστασαι σὺ γράμματα;—Ναί, ἔφη.—Οὐκοῦν ἅπαντα;—
῾Ωμολόγει.—῞Οταν οὖν τις ἀποστοματίζῃ ὁτιοῦν, οὐ γράμματα
ἀποστοματίζει;—῾Ωμολόγει.—Οὐκοῦν ὧν τι σὺ ἐπίστασαι,
5 ἔφη, ἀποστοματίζει, εἴπερ πάντα ἐπίστασαι;—Καὶ τοῦτο
ὡμολόγει.—Τί οὖν; ἦ δ᾽ ὅς, ἆρα σὺ ⟨οὐ⟩ μανθάνεις ἅττ᾽ ἂν
ἀποστοματίζῃ τις, ὁ δὲ μὴ ἐπιστάμενος γράμματα μανθάνει;
—Οὔκ, ἀλλ᾽, ἦ δ᾽ ὅς, μανθάνω.—Οὐκοῦν ἃ ἐπίστασαι, ἦ δ᾽
b ὅς, μανθάνεις, εἴπερ γε ἅπαντα τὰ γράμματα ἐπίστασαι.—
῾Ωμολόγησεν.—Οὐκ ἄρα ὀρθῶς ἀπεκρίνω, ἔφη.

Καὶ οὔπω σφόδρα τι ταῦτα εἴρητο τῷ Εὐθυδήμῳ, καὶ ὁ
Διονυσόδωρος ὥσπερ σφαῖραν ἐκδεξάμενος τὸν λόγον πάλιν
5 ἐστοχάζετο τοῦ μειρακίου, καὶ εἶπεν· ᾽Εξαπατᾷ σε Εὐθύδημος, ὦ Κλεινία. εἰπὲ γάρ μοι, τὸ μανθάνειν οὐκ ἐπιστήμην
ἐστὶ λαμβάνειν τούτου οὗ ἄν τις μανθάνῃ;—῾Ωμολόγει ὁ
Κλεινίας.—Τὸ δ᾽ ἐπίστασθαι, ἦ δ᾽ ὅς, ἄλλο τι ἢ ἔχειν
ἐπιστήμην ἤδη ἐστίν;—Συνέφη.—Τὸ ἄρα μὴ ἐπίστασθαι
c μήπω ἔχειν ἐπιστήμην ἐστίν;—῾Ωμολόγει αὐτῷ.—Πότερον
οὖν εἰσιν οἱ λαμβάνοντες ὁτιοῦν οἱ ἔχοντες ἤδη ἢ οἳ ἂν μὴ
ἔχωσιν;—Οἳ ἂν μή.—Οὐκοῦν ὡμολόγηκας εἶναι τούτων καὶ
τοὺς μὴ ἐπισταμένους, τῶν μὴ ἐχόντων;—Κατένευσε.—
5 Τῶν λαμβανόντων ἄρ᾽ εἰσὶν οἱ μανθάνοντες, ἀλλ᾽ οὐ τῶν
ἐχόντων;—Συνέφη.—Οἱ μὴ ἐπιστάμενοι ἄρα, ἔφη, μανθάνουσιν, ὦ Κλεινία, ἀλλ᾽ οὐχ οἱ ἐπιστάμενοι.

d ῎Ετι δὴ ἐπὶ τὸ τρίτον καταβαλὼν ὥσπερ πάλαισμα ὥρμα
ὁ Εὐθύδημος τὸν νεανίσκον· καὶ ἐγὼ γνοὺς βαπτιζόμενον τὸ

μειράκιον, βουλόμενος ἀναπαῦσαι αὐτό, μὴ ἡμῖν ἀποδειλιά
σειε, παραμυθούμενος εἶπον· Ὦ Κλεινία, μὴ θαύμαζε εἰ
σοι φαίνονται ἀήθεις οἱ λόγοι.   ἴσως γὰρ οὐκ αἰσθάνῃ 5
οἷον ποιεῖτον τὼ ξένω περὶ σέ· ποιεῖτον δὲ ταὐτὸν ὅπερ
οἱ ἐν τῇ τελετῇ τῶν Κορυβάντων, ὅταν τὴν θρόνωσιν
ποιῶσιν περὶ τοῦτον ὃν ἂν μέλλωσι τελεῖν.   καὶ γὰρ ἐκεῖ
χορηγία τίς ἐστι καὶ παιδιά, εἰ ἄρα καὶ τετέλεσαι· καὶ νῦν
τούτω οὐδὲν ἄλλο ἢ χορεύετον περὶ σὲ καὶ οἷον ὀρχεῖσθον e
παίζοντε, ὡς μετὰ τοῦτο τελοῦντε.   νῦν οὖν νόμισον τὰ
πρῶτα τῶν ἱερῶν ἀκούειν τῶν σοφιστικῶν.   πρῶτον γάρ,
ὥς φησι Πρόδικος, περὶ ὀνομάτων ὀρθότητος μαθεῖν δεῖ·
ὃ δὴ καὶ ἐνδείκνυσθόν σοι τὼ ξένω, ὅτι οὐκ ᾔδησθα τὸ 5
μανθάνειν ὅτι οἱ ἄνθρωποι καλοῦσι μὲν ἐπὶ τῷ τοιῷδε, ὅταν
τις ἐξ ἀρχῆς μηδεμίαν ἔχων ἐπιστήμην περὶ πράγματός
τινος ἔπειτα ὕστερον αὐτοῦ λαμβάνῃ τὴν ἐπιστήμην, καλοῦσι 278
δὲ ταὐτὸν τοῦτο καὶ ἐπειδὰν ἔχων ἤδη τὴν ἐπιστήμην ταύτῃ
τῇ ἐπιστήμῃ ταὐτὸν τοῦτο πρᾶγμα ἐπισκοπῇ ἢ πραττόμενον
ἢ λεγόμενον—μᾶλλον μὲν αὐτὸ συνιέναι καλοῦσιν ἢ μαν
θάνειν, ἔστι δ' ὅτε καὶ μανθάνειν—σὲ δὲ τοῦτο, ὡς οὗτοι 5
ἐνδείκνυνται, διαλέληθεν, ταὐτὸν ὄνομα ἐπ' ἀνθρώποις ἐναν
τίως ἔχουσιν κείμενον, τῷ τε εἰδότι καὶ ἐπὶ τῷ μή· παρα
πλήσιον δὲ τούτῳ καὶ τὸ ἐν τῷ δευτέρῳ ἐρωτήματι, ἐν ᾧ
ἠρώτων σε πότερα μανθάνουσιν οἱ ἄνθρωποι ἃ ἐπίστανται b
ἢ ἃ μή.   ταῦτα δὴ τῶν μαθημάτων παιδιά ἐστιν—διὸ καί
φημι ἐγώ σοι τούτους προσπαίζειν—παιδιὰν δὲ λέγω διὰ
ταῦτα, ὅτι, εἰ καὶ πολλά τις ἢ καὶ πάντα τὰ τοιαῦτα μάθοι,
τὰ μὲν πράγματα οὐδὲν ἂν μᾶλλον εἰδείη πῇ ἔχει, προσ- 5
παίζειν δὲ οἷός τ' ἂν εἴη τοῖς ἀνθρώποις διὰ τὴν τῶν ὀνο
μάτων διαφορὰν ὑποσκελίζων καὶ ἀνατρέπων, ὥσπερ οἱ τὰ
σκολύθρια τῶν μελλόντων καθιζήσεσθαι ὑποσπῶντες χαίρουσι
καὶ γελῶσιν, ἐπειδὰν ἴδωσιν ὕπτιον ἀνατετραμμένον.   ταῦτα c
μὲν οὖν σοι παρὰ τούτων νόμιζε παιδιὰν γεγονέναι· τὸ δὲ
μετὰ ταῦτα δῆλον ὅτι τούτω γέ σοι αὐτὼ τὰ σπουδαῖα

ἐνδείξεσθον, καὶ ἐγὼ ὑφηγήσομαι αὐτοῖν ἵνα μοι ὃ ὑπέσχοντο
5 ἀποδῶσιν. ἐφάτην γὰρ ἐπιδείξασθαι τὴν προτρεπτικὴν
σοφίαν· νῦν δέ μοι δοκεῖ δεῖν ᾠηθήτην πρότερον παῖσαι
πρὸς σέ. ταῦτα μὲν οὖν, ὦ Εὐθύδημέ τε καὶ Διονυσόδωρε,
d πεπαίσθω τε ὑμῖν, καὶ ἴσως ἱκανῶς ἔχει· τὸ δὲ δὴ μετὰ
ταῦτα ἐπιδείξατον προτρέποντε τὸ μειράκιον ὅπως χρὴ
σοφίας τε καὶ ἀρετῆς ἐπιμεληθῆναι. πρότερον δ' ἐγὼ σφῷν
ἐνδείξομαι οἷον αὐτὸ ὑπολαμβάνω καὶ οἵου αὐτοῦ ἐπιθυμῶ
5 ἀκοῦσαι. ἐὰν οὖν δόξω ὑμῖν ἰδιωτικῶς τε και γελοίως αὐτὸ
ποιεῖν, μή μου καταγελᾶτε· ὑπὸ προθυμίας γὰρ τοῦ ἀκοῦσαι
τῆς ὑμετέρας σοφίας τολμήσω ἀπαυτοσχεδιάσαι ἐναντίον
e ὑμῶν. ἀνάσχεσθον οὖν ἀγελαστὶ ἀκούοντες αὐτοί τε καὶ
οἱ μαθηταὶ ὑμῶν· σὺ δέ μοι, ὦ παῖ Ἀξιόχου, ἀπόκριναι.
⁹Ἀρά γε πάντες ἄνθρωποι βουλόμεθα εὖ πράττειν; ἢ
τοῦτο μὲν ἐρώτημα ὧν νυνδὴ ἐφοβούμην ἐν τῶν καταγελά-
5 στων; ἀνόητον γὰρ δήπου καὶ τὸ ἐρωτᾶν τὰ τοιαῦτα· τίς γὰρ
οὐ βούλεται ἀνθρώπων εὖ πράττειν;—Οὐδεὶς ὅστις οὔκ, ἔφη
279 ὁ Κλεινίας.—Εἶεν, ἦν δ' ἐγώ· τὸ δὴ μετὰ τοῦτο, ἐπειδὴ βουλόμεθα εὖ πράττειν, πῶς ἂν εὖ πράττοιμεν; ἆρ' ἂν εἰ ἡμῖν
πολλὰ κἀγαθὰ εἴη; ἢ τοῦτο ἐκείνου ἔτι εὐηθέστερον; δῆλον
γάρ που καὶ τοῦτο ὅτι οὕτως ἔχει.—Συνέφη.—Φέρε δή,
5 ἀγαθὰ δὲ ποῖα ἄρα τῶν ὄντων τυγχάνει ἡμῖν ὄντα; ἢ οὐ
χαλεπὸν οὐδὲ σεμνοῦ ἀνδρὸς πάνυ τι οὐδὲ τοῦτο ἔοικεν εἶναι
εὐπορεῖν; πᾶς γὰρ ἂν ἡμῖν εἴποι ὅτι τὸ πλουτεῖν ἀγαθόν·
ἢ γάρ;—Πάνυ γ', ἔφη.—Οὐκοῦν καὶ τὸ ὑγιαίνειν καὶ τὸ
b καλὸν εἶναι καὶ τἆλλα κατὰ τὸ σῶμα ἱκανῶς παρεσκευάσθαι;—Συνεδόκει.—Ἀλλὰ μὴν εὐγένειαί γε καὶ δυνάμεις καὶ
τιμαὶ ἐν τῇ ἑαυτοῦ δῆλά ἐστιν ἀγαθὰ ὄντα.—Ὡμολόγει.—
Τί οὖν, ἔφην, ἔτι ἡμῖν λείπεται τῶν ἀγαθῶν; τί ἄρα ἐστὶν
5 τὸ σώφρονά τε εἶναι καὶ δίκαιον καὶ ἀνδρεῖον; πότερον
πρὸς Διός, ὦ Κλεινία, ἡγῇ σύ, ἐὰν ταῦτα τιθῶμεν ὡς
ἀγαθά, ὀρθῶς ἡμᾶς θήσειν, ἢ ἐὰν μή; ἴσως γὰρ ἄν τις ἡμῖν
ἀμφισβητήσειεν· σοὶ δὲ πῶς δοκεῖ;—Ἀγαθά, ἔφη ὁ Κλει-

νίας.—Εἶεν, ἦν δ᾽ ἐγώ· τὴν δὲ σοφίαν ποῦ χοροῦ τάξομεν; c
ἐν τοῖς ἀγαθοῖς, ἢ πῶς λέγεις;—Ἐν τοῖς ἀγαθοῖς.—Ἐνθυμοῦ δὴ μή τι παραλείπωμεν τῶν ἀγαθῶν, ὅ τι καὶ ἄξιον
λόγου.—Ἀλλά μοι δοκοῦμεν, ἔφη, οὐδέν, ὁ Κλεινίας.—Καὶ
ἐγὼ ἀναμνησθεὶς εἶπον ὅτι Ναὶ μὰ Δία κινδυνεύομέν γε 5
τὸ μέγιστον τῶν ἀγαθῶν παραλιπεῖν.—Τί τοῦτο; ἦ δ᾽ ὅς.
—Τὴν εὐτυχίαν, ὦ Κλεινία· ὃ πάντες φασί, καὶ οἱ πάνυ
φαῦλοι, μέγιστον τῶν ἀγαθῶν εἶναι.—Ἀληθῆ λέγεις, ἔφη.
—Καὶ ἐγὼ αὖ πάλιν μετανοήσας εἶπον ὅτι Ὀλίγου καταγέλαστοι ἐγενόμεθα ὑπὸ τῶν ξένων ἐγώ τε καὶ σύ, ὦ παῖ d
Ἀξιόχου.—Τί δή, ἔφη, τοῦτο;—Ὅτι εὐτυχίαν ἐν τοῖς ἔμπροσθεν θέμενοι νυνδὴ αὖθις περὶ τοῦ αὐτοῦ ἐλέγομεν.—
Τί οὖν δὴ τοῦτο;—Καταγέλαστον δήπου, ὃ πάλαι πρόκειται,
τοῦτο πάλιν προτιθέναι καὶ δὶς ταὐτὰ λέγειν.—Πῶς, ἔφη, 5
τοῦτο λέγεις; —Ἡ σοφία δήπου, ἦν δ᾽ ἐγώ, εὐτυχία ἐστίν·
τοῦτο δὲ κἂν παῖς γνοίη.—Καὶ ὃς ἐθαύμασεν· οὕτως ἔτι νέος
τε καὶ εὐήθης ἐστί.—Κἀγὼ γνοὺς αὐτὸν θαυμάζοντα, Ἆρα
οὐκ οἶσθα, ἔφην, ὦ Κλεινία, ὅτι περὶ αὐλημάτων εὐπραγίαν e
οἱ αὐληταὶ εὐτυχέστατοί εἰσιν;—Συνέφη.—Οὐκοῦν, ἦν δ᾽
ἐγώ, καὶ περὶ γραμμάτων γραφῆς τε καὶ ἀναγνώσεως οἱ
γραμματισταί;—Πάνυ γε.—Τί δέ; πρὸς τοὺς τῆς θαλάττης
κινδύνους μῶν οἴει εὐτυχεστέρους τινὰς εἶναι τῶν σοφῶν 5
κυβερνητῶν, ὡς ἐπὶ πᾶν εἰπεῖν;—Οὐ δῆτα.—Τί δέ; στρα-
τευόμενος μετὰ ποτέρου ἂν ἥδιον τοῦ κινδύνου τε καὶ τῆς
τύχης μετέχοις, μετὰ σοφοῦ στρατηγοῦ ἢ μετὰ ἀμαθοῦς;— 280
Μετὰ σοφοῦ.—Τί δέ; ἀσθενῶν μετὰ ποτέρου ἂν ἡδέως
κινδυνεύοις, μετὰ σοφοῦ ἰατροῦ ἢ μετὰ ἀμαθοῦς;—Μετὰ
σοφοῦ.—Ἆρ᾽ οὐκ, ἦν δ᾽ ἐγώ, ὅτι εὐτυχέστερον ἂν οἴει πράττειν μετὰ σοφοῦ πράττων ἢ μετὰ ἀμαθοῦς;—Συνεχώρει.— 5
Ἡ σοφία ἄρα πανταχοῦ εὐτυχεῖν ποιεῖ τοὺς ἀνθρώπους.
οὐ γὰρ δήπου ἁμαρτάνοι γ᾽ ἄν ποτέ τι σοφία, ἀλλ᾽ ἀνάγκη
ὀρθῶς πράττειν καὶ τυγχάνειν· ἦ γὰρ ἂν οὐκέτι σοφία εἴη.
Συνωμολογησάμεθα τελευτῶντες οὐκ οἶδ᾽ ὅπως ἐν κεφα- b

λαίῳ οὕτω τοῦτο ἔχειν, σοφίας παρούσης, ᾧ ἂν παρῇ μηδὲν
προσδεῖσθαι εὐτυχίας· ἐπειδὴ δὲ τοῦτο συνωμολογησάμεθα,
πάλιν ἐπυνθανόμην αὐτοῦ τὰ πρότερον ὡμολογημένα πῶς
5 ἂν ἡμῖν ἔχοι. Ὡμολογήσαμεν γάρ, ἔφην, εἰ ἡμῖν ἀγαθὰ
πολλὰ παρείη, εὐδαιμονεῖν ἂν καὶ εὖ πράττειν.—Συνέφη.—
Ἆρ᾽ οὖν εὐδαιμονοῖμεν ἂν διὰ τὰ παρόντα ἀγαθά, εἰ μηδὲν
ἡμᾶς ὠφελοῖ ἢ εἰ ὠφελοῖ;—Εἰ ὠφελοῖ, ἔφη.—Ἆρ᾽ οὖν ἄν
c τι ὠφελοῖ, εἰ εἴη μόνον ἡμῖν, χρώμεθα δ᾽ αὐτοῖς μή; οἷον
σιτία εἰ ἡμῖν εἴη πολλά, ἐσθίοιμεν δὲ μή, ἢ ποτόν, πίνοιμεν
δὲ μή, ἔσθ᾽ ὅ τι ὠφελοίμεθ᾽ ἄν;—Οὐ δῆτα, ἔφη.—Τί δέ;
οἱ δημιουργοὶ πάντες, εἰ αὐτοῖς εἴη πάντα τὰ ἐπιτήδεια
5 παρεσκευασμένα ἑκάστῳ εἰς τὸ ἑαυτοῦ ἔργον, χρῷντο δὲ
αὐτοῖς μή, ἆρ᾽ ἂν οὗτοι εὖ πράττοιεν διὰ τὴν κτῆσιν, ὅτι
κεκτημένοι εἶεν πάντα ἃ δεῖ κεκτῆσθαι τὸν δημιουργόν;
οἷον τέκτων, εἰ παρεσκευασμένος εἴη τά τε ὄργανα ἅπαντα
καὶ ξύλα ἱκανά, τεκταίνοιτο δὲ μή, ἔσθ᾽ ὅ τι ὠφελοῖτ᾽ ἂν
d ἀπὸ τῆς κτήσεως;—Οὐδαμῶς, ἔφη.—Τί δέ, εἴ τις κεκτημένος εἴη πλοῦτόν τε καὶ ἃ νυνδὴ ἐλέγομεν πάντα τὰ ἀγαθά,
χρῷτο δὲ αὐτοῖς μή, ἆρ᾽ ἂν εὐδαιμονοῖ διὰ τὴν τούτων
κτῆσιν τῶν ἀγαθῶν;—Οὐ δῆτα, ὦ Σώκρατες.—Δεῖν ἄρα,
5 ἔφην, ὡς ἔοικεν, μὴ μόνον κεκτῆσθαι τὰ τοιαῦτα ἀγαθὰ τὸν
μέλλοντα εὐδαίμονα ἔσεσθαι, ἀλλὰ καὶ χρῆσθαι αὐτοῖς· ὡς
οὐδὲν ὄφελος τῆς κτήσεως γίγνεται.—Ἀληθῆ λέγεις.—Ἆρ᾽
e οὖν, ὦ Κλεινία, ἤδη τοῦτο ἱκανὸν πρὸς τὸ εὐδαίμονα ποιῆσαί
τινα, τό τε κεκτῆσθαι τἀγαθὰ καὶ τὸ χρῆσθαι αὐτοῖς;—
Ἔμοιγε δοκεῖ.—Πότερον, ἦν δ᾽ ἐγώ, ἐὰν ὀρθῶς χρῆταί τις
ἢ καὶ ἐὰν μή;—Ἐὰν ὀρθῶς.—Καλῶς γε, ἦν δ᾽ ἐγώ, λέγεις.
5 πλέον γάρ που οἶμαι θάτερόν ἐστιν, ἐάν τις χρῆται ὁτῳοῦν
μὴ ὀρθῶς πράγματι ἢ ἐὰν ἐᾷ· τὸ μὲν γὰρ κακόν, τὸ δὲ οὔτε
281 κακὸν οὔτε ἀγαθόν. ἢ οὐχ οὕτω φαμέν;—Συνεχώρει.—Τί
οὖν; ἐν τῇ ἐργασίᾳ τε καὶ χρήσει τῇ περὶ τὰ ξύλα μῶν
ἄλλο τί ἐστιν τὸ ἀπεργαζόμενον ὀρθῶς χρῆσθαι ἢ ἐπιστήμη
ἡ τεκτονική;—Οὐ δῆτα, ἔφη.—Ἀλλὰ μήν που καὶ ἐν τῇ

περὶ τὰ σκεύη ἐργασίᾳ τὸ ὀρθῶς ἐπιστήμη ἐστὶν ἡ ἀπεργα- 5
ζομένη.—Συνέφη.—Ἀρ᾽ οὖν, ἦν δ᾽ ἐγώ, καὶ περὶ τὴν χρείαν
ὧν ἐλέγομεν τὸ πρῶτον τῶν ἀγαθῶν, πλούτου τε καὶ ὑγιείας
καὶ κάλλους, τὸ ὀρθῶς πᾶσι τοῖς τοιούτοις χρῆσθαι ἐπιστήμη ἦν ἡγουμένη καὶ κατορθοῦσα τὴν πρᾶξιν, ἢ ἄλλο τι; b
—Ἐπιστήμη, ἦ δ᾽ ὅς.—Οὐ μόνον ἄρα εὐτυχίαν ἀλλὰ καὶ
εὐπραγίαν, ὡς ἔοικεν, ἡ ἐπιστήμη παρέχει τοῖς ἀνθρώποις
ἐν πάσῃ κτήσει τε καὶ πράξει.—Ὡμολόγει.—Ἀρ᾽ οὖν ὦ
πρὸς Διός, ἦν δ᾽ ἐγώ, ὄφελός τι τῶν ἄλλων κτημάτων ἄνευ 5
φρονήσεως καὶ σοφίας; ἆρά γε ἂν ὄναιτο ἄνθρωπος πολλὰ
κεκτημένος καὶ πολλὰ πράττων νοῦν μὴ ἔχων, ἢ μᾶλλον
ὀλίγα [νοῦν ἔχων]; ὧδε δὲ σκόπει· οὐκ ἐλάττω πράττων
ἐλάττω ἂν ἐξαμαρτάνοι, ἐλάττω δὲ ἁμαρτάνων ἧττον ἂν c
κακῶς πράττοι, ἧττον δὲ κακῶς πράττων ἄθλιος ἧττον ἂν
εἴη;—Πάνυ γ᾽, ἔφη.—Πότερον οὖν ἂν μᾶλλον ἐλάττω τις
πράττοι πένης ὢν ἢ πλούσιος;—Πένης, ἔφη.—Πότερον δὲ
ἀσθενὴς ἢ ἰσχυρός;—Ἀσθενής.—Πότερον δὲ ἔντιμος ἢ 5
ἄτιμος;—Ἄτιμος.—Πότερον δὲ ἀνδρεῖος ὢν [καὶ σώφρων]
ἐλάττω ἂν πράττοι ἢ δειλός;—Δειλός.—Οὐκοῦν καὶ ἀργὸς
μᾶλλον ἢ ἐργάτης;—Συνεχώρει.—Καὶ βραδὺς μᾶλλον ἢ
ταχύς, καὶ ἀμβλὺ ὁρῶν καὶ ἀκούων μᾶλλον ἢ ὀξύ;—Πάντα d
τὰ τοιαῦτα συνεχωροῦμεν ἀλλήλοις.—Ἐν κεφαλαίῳ δ᾽, ἔφην,
ὦ Κλεινία, κινδυνεύει σύμπαντα ἃ τὸ πρῶτον ἔφαμεν ἀγαθὰ
εἶναι, οὐ περὶ τούτου ὁ λόγος αὐτοῖς εἶναι, ὅπως αὐτά γε
καθ᾽ αὑτὰ πέφυκεν ἀγαθὰ [εἶναι], ἀλλ᾽ ὡς ἔοικεν ὧδ᾽ ἔχει· 5
ἐὰν μὲν αὐτῶν ἡγῆται ἀμαθία, μείζω κακὰ εἶναι τῶν ἐναν-
τίων, ὅσῳ δυνατώτερα ὑπηρετεῖν τῷ ἡγουμένῳ κακῷ ὄντι,
ἐὰν δὲ φρόνησίς τε καὶ σοφία, μείζω ἀγαθά, αὐτὰ δὲ καθ᾽
αὑτὰ οὐδέτερα αὐτῶν οὐδενὸς ἄξια εἶναι.—Φαίνεται, ἔφη, e
ὡς ἔοικεν, οὕτως, ὡς σὺ λέγεις.—Τί οὖν ἡμῖν συμβαίνει ἐκ
τῶν εἰρημένων; ἄλλο τι ἢ τῶν μὲν ἄλλων οὐδὲν ὂν οὔτε
ἀγαθὸν οὔτε κακόν, τούτοιν δὲ δυοῖν ὄντοιν ἡ μὲν σοφία
ἀγαθόν, ἡ δὲ ἀμαθία κακόν;—Ὡμολόγει. 5

282 Ἔτι τοίνυν, ἔφην, τὸ λοιπὸν ἐπισκεψώμεθα. ἐπειδὴ
εὐδαίμονες μὲν εἶναι προθυμούμεθα πάντες, ἐφάνημεν δὲ
τοιοῦτοι γιγνόμενοι ἐκ τοῦ χρῆσθαί τε τοῖς πράγμασιν καὶ
ὀρθῶς χρῆσθαι, τὴν δὲ ὀρθότητα καὶ εὐτυχίαν ἐπιστήμη
5 ἡ παρέχουσα, δεῖ δή, ὡς ἔοικεν, ἐκ παντὸς τρόπου ἅπαντα
ἄνδρα τοῦτο παρασκευάζεσθαι, ὅπως ὡς σοφώτατος ἔσται·
ἢ οὔ;—Ναί, ἔφη.—Καὶ παρὰ πατρός γε δήπου τοῦτο οἰόμενον δεῖν παραλαμβάνειν πολὺ μᾶλλον ἢ χρήματα, καὶ
b παρ᾽ ἐπιτρόπων καὶ φίλων τῶν τε ἄλλων καὶ τῶν φασκόντων ἐραστῶν εἶναι, καὶ ξένων καὶ πολιτῶν, δεόμενον καὶ
ἱκετεύοντα σοφίας μεταδιδόναι, οὐδὲν αἰσχρόν, ὦ Κλεινία,
οὐδὲ νεμεσητὸν ἕνεκα τούτου ὑπηρετεῖν καὶ δουλεύειν καὶ
5 ἐραστῇ καὶ παντὶ ἀνθρώπῳ, ὁτιοῦν ἐθέλοντα ὑπηρετεῖν τῶν
καλῶν ὑπηρετημάτων, προθυμούμενον σοφὸν γενέσθαι· ἢ οὐ
δοκεῖ σοι, ἔφην ἐγώ, οὕτως;—Πάνυ μὲν οὖν εὖ μοι δοκεῖς
c λέγειν, ἦ δ᾽ ὅς.—Εἰ ἔστι γε, ὦ Κλεινία, ἦν δ᾽ ἐγώ, ἡ σοφία
διδακτόν, ἀλλὰ μὴ ἀπὸ ταὐτομάτου παραγίγνεται τοῖς ἀνθρώ-
ποις· τοῦτο γὰρ ἡμῖν ἔτι ἄσκεπτον καὶ οὔπω διωμολογη-
μένον ἐμοί τε καὶ σοί.—Ἀλλ᾽ ἔμοιγε, ἔφη, ὦ Σώκρατες,
5 διδακτὸν εἶναι δοκεῖ.—Καὶ ἐγὼ ἡσθεὶς εἶπον· Ἦ καλῶς
λέγεις, ὦ ἄριστε ἀνδρῶν, καὶ εὖ ἐποίησας ἀπαλλάξας με
σκέψεως πολλῆς περὶ τούτου αὐτοῦ, πότερον διδακτὸν ἢ οὐ
διδακτὸν ἡ σοφία. νῦν οὖν ἐπειδή σοι καὶ διδακτὸν δοκεῖ
καὶ μόνον τῶν ὄντων εὐδαίμονα καὶ εὐτυχῆ ποιεῖν τὸν
d ἄνθρωπον, ἄλλο τι ἢ φαίης ἂν ἀναγκαῖον εἶναι φιλοσοφεῖν
καὶ αὐτὸς ἐν νῷ ἔχεις αὐτὸ ποιεῖν;—Πάνυ μὲν οὖν, ἔφη,
ὦ Σώκρατες, ὡς οἷόν τε μάλιστα.

Κἀγὼ ταῦτα ἄσμενος ἀκούσας, Τὸ μὲν ἐμόν, ἔφην, παρά-
5 δειγμα, ὦ Διονυσόδωρέ τε καὶ Εὐθύδημε, οἵων ἐπιθυμῶ τῶν
προτρεπτικῶν λόγων εἶναι, τοιοῦτον, ἰδιωτικὸν ἴσως καὶ
μόλις διὰ μακρῶν λεγόμενον· σφῷν δὲ ὁπότερος βούλεται,
ταὐτὸν τοῦτο τέχνῃ πράττων ἐπιδειξάτω ἡμῖν. εἰ δὲ μὴ
e τοῦτο βούλεσθον, ὅθεν ἐγὼ ἀπέλιπον, τὸ ἑξῆς ἐπιδείξατον

τῷ μειρακίῳ, πότερον πᾶσαν ἐπιστήμην δεῖ αὐτὸν κτᾶσθαι, ἢ ἔστι τις μία ἣν δεῖ λαβόντα εὐδαιμονεῖν τε καὶ ἀγαθὸν ἄνδρα εἶναι, καὶ τίς αὕτη. ὥσπερ γὰρ ἔλεγον ἀρχόμενος, περὶ πολλοῦ ἡμῖν τυγχάνει ὂν τόνδε τὸν νεανίσκον σοφόν 5 τε καὶ ἀγαθὸν γενέσθαι.

Ἐγὼ μὲν οὖν ταῦτα εἶπον, ὦ Κρίτων· τῷ δὲ μετὰ τοῦτο 283 ἐσομένῳ πάνυ σφόδρα προσεῖχον τὸν νοῦν, καὶ ἐπεσκόπουν τίνα ποτὲ τρόπον ἅψοιντο τοῦ λόγου καὶ ὁπόθεν ἄρξοιντο παρακελευόμενοι τῷ νεανίσκῳ σοφίαν τε καὶ ἀρετὴν ἀσκεῖν. ὁ οὖν πρεσβύτερος αὐτῶν, ὁ Διονυσόδωρος, πρότερος ἤρχετο 5 τοῦ λόγου, καὶ ἡμεῖς πάντες ἐβλέπομεν πρὸς αὐτὸν ὡς αὐτίκα μάλα ἀκουσόμενοι θαυμασίους τινὰς λόγους. ὅπερ οὖν καὶ συνέβη ἡμῖν· θαυμαστὸν γάρ τινα, ὦ Κρίτων, ἀνὴρ b κατῆρχεν λόγον, οὗ σοὶ ἄξιον ἀκοῦσαι, ὡς παρακελευστικὸς ὁ λόγος ἦν ἐπ' ἀρετήν.

Εἰπέ μοι, ἔφη, ὦ Σώκρατές τε καὶ ὑμεῖς οἱ ἄλλοι, ὅσοι φατὲ ἐπιθυμεῖν τόνδε τὸν νεανίσκον σοφὸν γενέσθαι, πότε- 5 ρον παίζετε ταῦτα λέγοντες ἢ ὡς ἀληθῶς ἐπιθυμεῖτε καὶ σπουδάζετε;

Κἀγὼ διενοήθην ὅτι ᾠηθήτην ἄρα ἡμᾶς τὸ πρότερον παίζειν, ἡνίκα ἐκελεύομεν διαλεχθῆναι τῷ νεανίσκῳ αὐτώ, καὶ διὰ ταῦτα προσεπαισάτην τε καὶ οὐκ ἐσπουδασάτην· 10 ταῦτα οὖν διανοηθεὶς ἔτι μᾶλλον εἶπον ὅτι θαυμαστῶς c σπουδάζοιμεν.

Καὶ ὁ Διονυσόδωρος, Σκόπει μήν, ἔφη, ὦ Σώκρατες, ὅπως μὴ ἔξαρνος ἔσει ἃ νῦν λέγεις.—Ἔσκεμμαι, ἦν δ' ἐγώ· οὐ γὰρ μή ποτ' ἔξαρνος γένωμαι.—Τί οὖν; ἔφη· φατὲ 5 βούλεσθαι αὐτὸν σοφὸν γενέσθαι;—Πάνυ μὲν οὖν.—Νῦν δέ, ἦ δ' ὅς, Κλεινίας πότερον σοφός ἐστιν ἢ οὔ;—Οὔκουν φησί γέ πω· ἔστιν δέ, ἦν δ' ἐγώ, οὐκ ἀλαζών.—Ὑμεῖς δέ, ἔφη, βούλεσθε γενέσθαι αὐτὸν σοφόν, ἀμαθῆ δὲ μὴ εἶναι; d —Ὁμολογοῦμεν.—Οὐκοῦν ὃς μὲν οὐκ ἔστιν, βούλεσθε αὐτὸν γενέσθαι, ὃς δ' ἔστι νῦν, μηκέτι εἶναι.—Καὶ ἐγὼ

ἀκούσας ἐθορυβήθην· ὁ δέ μου θορυβουμένου ὑπολαβών,
5 Ἄλλο τι οὖν, ἔφη, ἐπεὶ βούλεσθε αὐτὸν ὃς νῦν ἐστὶν
μηκέτι εἶναι, βούλεσθε αὐτόν, ὡς ἔοικεν, ἀπολωλέναι; καίτοι
πολλοῦ ἂν ἄξιοι οἱ τοιοῦτοι εἶεν φίλοι τε καὶ ἐρασταί,
οἵτινες τὰ παιδικὰ περὶ παντὸς ἂν ποιήσαιντο ἐξολωλέναι.

e Καὶ ὁ Κτήσιππος ἀκούσας ἠγανάκτησέν τε ὑπὲρ τῶν
παιδικῶν καὶ εἶπεν· Ὦ ξένε Θούριε, εἰ μὴ ἀγροικότερον,
ἔφη, ἦν εἰπεῖν, εἶπον ἄν· " Σοὶ εἰς κεφαλήν," ὅ τι μαθών μου
καὶ τῶν ἄλλων καταψεύδει τοιοῦτον πρᾶγμα, ὃ ἐγὼ οἶμαι
5 οὐδ' ὅσιον εἶναι λέγειν, ὡς ἐγὼ τόνδε βουλοίμην ἂν ἐξολωλέναι.
Τί δέ, ἔφη, ὦ Κτήσιππε, ὁ Εὐθύδημος, ἢ δοκεῖ σοι οἷόν
τ' εἶναι ψεύδεσθαι;—Νὴ Δία, ἔφη, εἰ μὴ μαίνομαί γε.—
Πότερον λέγοντα τὸ πρᾶγμα περὶ οὗ ἂν ὁ λόγος ᾖ, ἢ μὴ
284 λέγοντα;—Λέγοντα, ἔφη.—Οὐκοῦν εἴπερ λέγει αὐτό, οὐκ
ἄλλο λέγει τῶν ὄντων ἢ ἐκεῖνο ὅπερ λέγει;—Πῶς γὰρ ἄν;
ἔφη ὁ Κτήσιππος.—Ἓν μὴν κἀκεῖνό γ' ἐστὶν τῶν ὄντων, ὃ
λέγει, χωρὶς τῶν ἄλλων.—Πάνυ γε.—Οὐκοῦν ὁ ἐκεῖνο
5 λέγων τὸ ὄν, ἔφη, λέγει;—Ναί.—Ἀλλὰ μὴν ὅ γε τὸ ὂν
λέγων καὶ τὰ ὄντα τἀληθῆ λέγει· ὥστε ὁ Διονυσόδωρος,
εἴπερ λέγει τὰ ὄντα, λέγει τἀληθῆ καὶ οὐδὲν κατὰ σοῦ
ψεύδεται.

b Ναί, ἔφη· ἀλλ' ὁ ταῦτα λέγων, ἔφη ὁ Κτήσιππος, ὦ
Εὐθύδημε, οὐ τὰ ὄντα λέγει.
Καὶ ὁ Εὐθύδημος, Τὰ δὲ μὴ ὄντα, ἔφη, ἄλλο τι ἢ οὐκ
ἔστιν;—Οὐκ ἔστιν.—Ἄλλο τι οὖν οὐδαμοῦ τά γε μὴ ὄντα
5 ὄντα ἐστίν;—Οὐδαμοῦ.—Ἔστιν οὖν ὅπως περὶ ταῦτα, τὰ μὴ
ὄντα, πράξειεν ἄν τίς τι, (ὥστε καὶ εἶναι) ποιήσειεν ἂν καὶ
ὁστισοῦν τὰ μηδαμοῦ ὄντα;—Οὐκ ἔμοιγε δοκεῖ, ἔφη ὁ Κτήσιππος.—Τί οὖν; οἱ ῥήτορες ὅταν λέγωσιν ἐν τῷ δήμῳ,
οὐδὲν πράττουσι;—Πράττουσι μὲν οὖν, ἦ δ' ὅς.—Οὐκοῦν
c εἴπερ πράττουσι, καὶ ποιοῦσι;—Ναί.—Τὸ λέγειν ἄρα πράττειν τε καὶ ποιεῖν ἐστιν;—Ὡμολόγησεν.—Οὐκ ἄρα τά

γε μὴ ὄντ᾽, ἔφη, λέγει οὐδείς—ποιοῖ γὰρ ἂν ἤδη τί· σὺ δὲ
ὡμολόγηκας τὸ μὴ ὂν μὴ οἷόν τ᾽ εἶναι μηδένα ποιεῖν—
ὥστε κατὰ τὸν σὸν λόγον οὐδεὶς ψευδῆ λέγει, ἀλλ᾽ εἴπερ 5
λέγει Διονυσόδωρος, τἀληθῆ τε καὶ τὰ ὄντα λέγει.
Νὴ Δία, ἔφη ὁ Κτήσιππος, ὦ Εὐθύδημε· ἀλλὰ τὰ ὄντα
μὲν τρόπον τινὰ λέγει, οὐ μέντοι ὥς γε ἔχει.
Πῶς λέγεις, ἔφη ὁ Διονυσόδωρος, ὦ Κτήσιππε; εἰσὶν
γάρ τινες οἱ λέγουσι τὰ πράγματα ὡς ἔχει;—Εἰσὶν μέντοι, d
ἔφη, οἱ καλοί τε κἀγαθοὶ καὶ οἱ τἀληθῆ λέγοντες.—Τί οὖν;
ἦ δ᾽ ὅς· τἀγαθὰ οὐκ εὖ, ἔφη, ἔχει, τὰ δὲ κακὰ κακῶς;—
Συνεχώρει.—Τοὺς δὲ καλούς τε καὶ ἀγαθοὺς ὁμολογεῖς λέγειν ὡς ἔχει τὰ πράγματα;—Ὁμολογῶ.—Κακῶς ἄρα, ἔφη, 5
λέγουσιν, ὦ Κτήσιππε, οἱ ἀγαθοὶ τὰ κακά, εἴπερ ὡς.ἔχει
λέγουσιν.—Ναὶ μὰ Δία, ἦ δ᾽ ὅς, σφόδρα γε, τοὺς γοῦν
κακοὺς ἀνθρώπους· ὧν σύ, ἐάν μοι πείθῃ, εὐλαβήσῃ εἶναι,
ἵνα μή σε οἱ ἀγαθοὶ κακῶς λέγωσιν. ὡς εὖ ἴσθ᾽ ὅτι κακῶς e
λέγουσιν οἱ ἀγαθοὶ τοὺς κακούς.—Καὶ τοὺς μεγάλους, ἔφη
ὁ Εὐθύδημος, μεγάλως λέγουσι καὶ τοὺς θερμοὺς θερμῶς;—
Μάλιστα δήπου, ἔφη ὁ Κτήσιππος· τοὺς γοῦν ψυχροὺς
ψυχρῶς λέγουσί τε καὶ φασὶν διαλέγεσθαι.—Σὺ μέν, ἔφη ὁ 5
Διονυσόδωρος, λοιδορῇ, ὦ Κτήσιππε, λοιδορῇ.—Μὰ Δί᾽ οὐκ
ἔγωγε, ἦ δ᾽ ὅς, ὦ Διονυσόδωρε, ἐπεὶ φιλῶ σε, ἀλλὰ νου-
θετῶ σε ὡς ἑταῖρον, καὶ πειρῶμαι πείθειν μηδέποτε ἐναντίον
ἐμοῦ οὕτως ἀγροίκως λέγειν ὅτι ἐγὼ τούτους βούλομαι
ἐξολωλέναι, οὓς περὶ πλείστου ποιοῦμαι. 285
Ἐγὼ οὖν, ἐπειδή μοι ἐδόκουν ἀγριωτέρως πρὸς ἀλλήλους
ἔχειν, προσέπαιζόν τε τὸν Κτήσιππον καὶ εἶπον ὅτι Ὦ
Κτήσιππε, ἐμοὶ μὲν δοκεῖ χρῆναι ἡμᾶς παρὰ τῶν ξένων
δέχεσθαι ἃ λέγουσιν, ἐὰν ἐθέλωσι διδόναι, καὶ μὴ ὀνόματι 5
διαφέρεσθαι. εἰ γὰρ ἐπίστανται οὕτως ἐξολλύναι ἀνθρώπους, ὥστ᾽ ἐκ πονηρῶν τε καὶ ἀφρόνων χρηστούς τε καὶ
ἔμφρονας ποιεῖν, καὶ τοῦτο εἴτε αὐτὼ ηὑρήκατον εἴτε καὶ
παρ᾽ ἄλλου του ἐμαθέτην φθόρον τινὰ καὶ ὄλεθρον τοιοῦτον, b

ὥστε ἀπολέσαντες πονηρὸν ὄντα χρηστὸν πάλιν ἀποφῆναι·
εἰ τοῦτο ἐπίστασθον—δῆλον δὲ ὅτι ἐπίστασθον· ἐφάτην
γοῦν τὴν τέχνην σφῶν εἶναι τὴν νεωστὶ ηὑρημένην ἀγαθοὺς
5 ποιεῖν τοὺς ἀνθρώπους ἐκ πονηρῶν—συγχωρήσωμεν οὖν
αὐτοῖν αὐτό· ἀπολεσάντων ἡμῖν τὸ μειράκιον καὶ φρόνιμον
ποιησάντων, καὶ ἅπαντάς γε ἡμᾶς τοὺς ἄλλους. εἰ δὲ ὑμεῖς
c οἱ νέοι φοβεῖσθε, ὥσπερ ἐν Καρὶ ἐν ἐμοὶ ἔστω ὁ κίνδυνος·
ὡς ἐγώ, ἐπειδὴ καὶ πρεσβύτης εἰμί, παρακινδυνεύειν ἕτοι-
μος καὶ παραδίδωμι ἐμαυτὸν Διονυσοδώρῳ τούτῳ ὥσπερ τῇ
Μηδείᾳ τῇ Κόλχῳ. ἀπολλύτω με, καὶ εἰ μὲν βούλεται,
5 ἑψέτω, εἰ δ', ὅ τι βούλεται, τοῦτο ποιείτω· μόνον χρηστὸν
ἀποφηνάτω.

Καὶ ὁ Κτήσιππος, Ἐγὼ μέν, ἔφη, καὶ αὐτός, ὦ Σώκρατες,
ἕτοιμός εἰμι παρέχειν ἐμαυτὸν τοῖς ξένοις, καὶ ἐὰν βούλων-
ται δέρειν ἔτι μᾶλλον ἢ νῦν δέρουσιν, εἴ μοι ἡ δορὰ μὴ εἰς
d ἀσκὸν τελευτήσει, ὥσπερ ἡ τοῦ Μαρσύου, ἀλλ' εἰς ἀρετήν.
καίτοι με οἴεται Διονυσόδωρος οὑτοσὶ χαλεπαίνειν αὐτῷ·
ἐγὼ δὲ οὐ χαλεπαίνω, ἀλλ' ἀντιλέγω πρὸς ταῦτα ἅ μοι
δοκεῖ πρός με μὴ καλῶς λέγειν. ἀλλὰ σὺ τὸ ἀντιλέγειν,
5 ἔφη, ὦ γενναῖε Διονυσόδωρε, μὴ κάλει λοιδορεῖσθαι· ἕτερον
γάρ τί ἐστι τὸ λοιδορεῖσθαι.

Καὶ Διονυσόδωρος, Ὡς ὄντος, ἔφη, τοῦ ἀντιλέγειν, ὦ
Κτήσιππε, ποιῇ τοὺς λόγους;
e Πάντως δήπου, ἔφη, καὶ σφόδρα γε· ἢ σύ, ὦ Διονυσόδωρε, οὐκ οἴει εἶναι ἀντιλέγειν;

Οὔκουν σύ γ' ἄν, ἔφη, ἀποδείξαις πώποτε ἀκούσας οὐδενὸς
ἀντιλέγοντος ἑτέρου ἑτέρῳ.

5 Ἀληθῆ λέγεις, ἔφη· ἀλλὰ ἀκούωμεν νῦν εἴ σοι ἀποδείκνυμι ἀντιλέγοντος Κτησίππου Διονυσοδώρῳ.

Ἦ καὶ ὑπόσχοις ἂν τούτου λόγον;
Πάνυ, ἔφη.

Τί οὖν; ἦ δ' ὅς· εἰσὶν ἑκάστῳ τῶν ὄντων λόγοι;—
10 Πάνυ γε.—Οὐκοῦν ὡς ἔστιν ἕκαστον ἢ ὡς οὐκ ἔστιν;—

Ὡς ἔστιν.—Εἰ γὰρ μέμνησαι, ἔφη, ὦ Κτήσιππε, καὶ ἄρτι 286
ἐπεδείξαμεν μηδένα λέγοντα ὡς οὐκ ἔστι· τὸ γὰρ μὴ ὂν
οὐδεὶς ἐφάνη λέγων.—Τί οὖν δὴ τοῦτο; ἦ δ᾽ ὃς ὁ Κτήσιπ-
πος· ἧττόν τι ἀντιλέγομεν ἐγώ τε καὶ σύ;—Πότερον οὖν,
ἦ δ᾽ ὅς, ἀντιλέγοιμεν ἂν τοῦ αὐτοῦ πράγματος λόγον ἀμφό- 5
τεροι λέγοντες, ἢ οὕτω μὲν ἂν δήπου ταὐτὰ λέγοιμεν;—
Συνεχώρει.—Ἀλλ᾽ ὅταν μηδέτερος, ἔφη, τὸν τοῦ πράγματος
λόγον λέγῃ, τότε ἀντιλέγοιμεν ἄν; ἢ οὕτω γε τὸ παράπαν b
οὐδ᾽ ἂν μεμνημένος εἴη τοῦ πράγματος οὐδέτερος ἡμῶν;—
Καὶ τοῦτο συνωμολόγει.—Ἀλλ᾽ ἄρα, ὅταν ἐγὼ μὲν τὸν τοῦ
πράγματος λόγον λέγω, σὺ δὲ ἄλλου τινὸς ἄλλον, τότε
ἀντιλέγομεν; ἢ ἐγὼ λέγω μὲν τὸ πρᾶγμα, σὺ δὲ οὐδὲ λέγεις 5
τὸ παράπαν; ὁ δὲ μὴ λέγων τῷ λέγοντι πῶς ⟨ἂν⟩ ἀντιλέγοι;
Καὶ ὁ μὲν Κτήσιππος ἐσίγησεν· ἐγὼ δὲ θαυμάσας τὸν
λόγον, Πῶς, ἔφην, ὦ Διονυσόδωρε, λέγεις; οὐ γάρ τοι
ἀλλὰ τοῦτόν γε τὸν λόγον πολλῶν δὴ καὶ πολλάκις ἀκηκοὼς c
ἀεὶ θαυμάζω—καὶ γὰρ οἱ ἀμφὶ Πρωταγόραν σφόδρα ἐχρῶντο
αὐτῷ καὶ οἱ ἔτι παλαιότεροι· ἐμοὶ δὲ ἀεὶ θαυμαστός τις
δοκεῖ εἶναι καὶ τούς τε ἄλλους ἀνατρέπων καὶ αὐτὸς αὑτόν
—οἶμαι δὲ αὐτοῦ τὴν ἀλήθειαν παρὰ σοῦ κάλλιστα πεύ- 5
σεσθαι. ἄλλο τι ψευδῆ λέγειν οὐκ ἔστιν;—τοῦτο γὰρ
δύναται ὁ λόγος· ἢ γάρ;—ἀλλ᾽ ἢ λέγοντ᾽ ἀληθῆ λέγειν ἢ
μὴ λέγειν;
Συνεχώρει.
Πότερον οὖν ψευδῆ μὲν λέγειν οὐκ ἔστι, δοξάζειν μέντοι d
ἔστιν;
Οὐδὲ δοξάζειν, ἔφη.
Οὐδ᾽ ἄρα ψευδής, ἦν δ᾽ ἐγώ, δόξα ἔστι τὸ παράπαν.
Οὐκ ἔφη. 5
Οὐδ᾽ ἄρα ἀμαθία οὐδ᾽ ἀμαθεῖς ἄνθρωποι· ἢ οὐ τοῦτ᾽ ἂν
εἴη ἀμαθία, εἴπερ εἴη, τὸ ψεύδεσθαι τῶν πραγμάτων;
Πάνυ γε, ἔφη.

Ἀλλὰ τοῦτο οὐκ ἔστιν, ἦν δ' ἐγώ.

10 Οὐκ ἔφη.

Λόγου ἕνεκα, ὦ Διονυσόδωρε, λέγεις τὸν λόγον, ἵνα δὴ
ἄτοπον λέγῃς, ἢ ὡς ἀληθῶς δοκεῖ σοι οὐδεὶς εἶναι ἀμαθὴς
ἀνθρώπων;

e Ἀλλὰ σύ, ἔφη, ἔλεγξον.

Ἦ καὶ ἔστι τοῦτο κατὰ τὸν σὸν λόγον, ἐξελέγξαι,
μηδενὸς ψευδομένου;

Οὐκ ἔστιν, ἔφη ὁ Εὐθύδημος.

5 Οὐδ' ἄρα ἐκέλευον, ἔφη, ἐγὼ νυνδή, ὁ Διονυσόδωρος,
ἐξελέγξαι; τὸ γὰρ μὴ ὂν πῶς ἄν τις κελεύσαι;

Σὺ δ' ἐκέλευες; ὅτι, ἦν δ' ἐγώ, ὦ Εὐθύδημε, τὰ σοφὰ
ταῦτα καὶ τὰ εὖ ἔχοντα οὐ πάνυ τι μανθάνω, ἀλλὰ πα-
χέως πως ἐννοῶ. ἴσως μὲν οὖν φορτικώτερόν τι ἐρήσομαι,
287 ἀλλὰ συγγίγνωσκε. ὅρα δέ· εἰ γὰρ μήτε ψεύδεσθαι ἔστιν
μήτε ψευδῆ δοξάζειν μήτε ἀμαθῆ εἶναι, ἄλλο τι οὐδ' ἐξαμαρτάνειν ἔστιν, ὅταν τίς τι πράττῃ; πράττοντα γὰρ οὐκ
ἔστιν ἁμαρτάνειν τούτου ὃ πράττει· οὐχ οὕτω λέγετε;

5 Πάνυ γ', ἔφη.

Τοῦτό ἐστιν ἤδη, ἦν δ' ἐγώ, τὸ φορτικὸν ἐρώτημα. εἰ
γὰρ μὴ ἁμαρτάνομεν μήτε πράττοντες μήτε λέγοντες μήτε
διανοούμενοι, ὑμεῖς, ὦ πρὸς Διός, εἰ ταῦτα οὕτως ἔχει, τίνος
διδάσκαλοι ἥκετε; ἢ οὐκ ἄρτι ἔφατε ἀρετὴν κάλλιστ' ἂν
b παραδοῦναι ἀνθρώπων τῷ ἐθέλοντι μανθάνειν;

Εἶτ', ἔφη, ὦ Σώκρατες, ὁ Διονυσόδωρος ὑπολαβών, οὕτως
εἶ Κρόνος, ὥστε ἃ τὸ πρῶτον εἴπομεν νῦν ἀναμιμνήσκεις, καὶ
εἴ τι πέρυσιν εἶπον, νῦν ἀναμνησθήσει, τοῖς δ' ἐν τῷ παρόντι
5 λεγομένοις οὐχ ἕξεις ὅ τι χρῇ;

Καὶ γάρ, ἔφην ἐγώ, χαλεποί εἰσιν, πάνυ εἰκότως· παρὰ
σοφῶν γὰρ λέγονται—ἐπεὶ καὶ τούτῳ τῷ τελευταίῳ παγ-
χάλεπον χρήσασθαί ἐστιν, ᾧ λέγεις. τὸ γὰρ "Οὐκ ἔχω ὅ τι
χρῶμαι" τί ποτε λέγεις, ὦ Διονυσόδωρε; ἢ δῆλον ὅτι ὡς

οὐκ ἔχω ἐξελέγξαι αὐτόν; ἐπεὶ εἰπέ, τί σοι ἄλλο νοεῖ τοῦτο c
τὸ ῥῆμα, τὸ " Οὐκ ἔχω ὅ τι χρήσωμαι τοῖς λόγοις ";
'Αλλ' ὃ σὺ λέγεις, ἔφη, τούτῳ γ' οὐ πάνυ χαλεπὸν
χρῆσθαι· ἐπεὶ ἀπόκριναι.
Πρὶν σὲ ἀποκρίνασθαι, ἦν δ' ἐγώ, ὦ Διονυσόδωρε; 5
Οὐκ ἀποκρίνῃ; ἔφη.
'Η καὶ δίκαιον;
Δίκαιον μέντοι, ἔφη.

Κατὰ τίνα λόγον; ἦν δ' ἐγώ· ἢ δῆλον ὅτι κατὰ τόνδε,
ὅτι σὺ νῦν πάσσοφός τις ἡμῖν ἀφῖξαι περὶ λόγους, καὶ οἶσθα 10
ὅτε δεῖ ἀποκρίνασθαι καὶ ὅτε μή; καὶ νῦν οὐδ' ἂν ὁτιοῦν d
ἀποκρίνει, ἅτε γιγνώσκων ὅτι οὐ δεῖ;
Λαλεῖς, ἔφη, ἀμελήσας ἀποκρίνασθαι· ἀλλ', ὦγαθέ, πείθου
καὶ ἀπόκρινου, ἐπειδὴ καὶ ὁμολογεῖς με σοφὸν εἶναι.
Πειστέον τοίνυν, ἦν δ' ἐγώ, καὶ ἀνάγκη, ὡς ἔοικεν· σὺ 5
γὰρ ἄρχεις. ἀλλ' ἐρώτα.
Πότερον οὖν ψυχὴν ἔχοντα νοεῖ τὰ νοοῦντα, ἢ καὶ τὰ
ἄψυχα;
Τὰ ψυχὴν ἔχοντα.
Οἶσθα οὖν τι, ἔφη, ῥῆμα ψυχὴν ἔχον; 10
Μὰ Δία οὐκ ἔγωγε.
Τί οὖν ἄρτι ἤρου ὅ τι μοι νοοῖ τὸ ῥῆμα; e
Τί ἄλλο γε, ἦν δ' ἐγώ, ἢ ἐξήμαρτον διὰ τὴν βλακείαν;
ἢ οὐκ ἐξήμαρτον ἀλλὰ καὶ τοῦτο ὀρθῶς εἶπον, εἰπὼν ὅτι
νοεῖ τὰ ῥήματα; πότερα φῂς ἐξαμαρτάνειν με ἢ οὔ; εἰ γὰρ
μὴ ἐξήμαρτον, οὐδὲ σὺ ἐξελέγξεις, καίπερ σοφὸς ὤν, οὐδ' 5
ἔχεις ὅ τι χρῇ τῷ λόγῳ· εἰ δ' ἐξήμαρτον, οὐδ' οὕτως ὀρθῶς
λέγεις, φάσκων οὐκ εἶναι ἐξαμαρτάνειν. καὶ ταῦτα οὐ πρὸς 288
ἃ πέρυσιν ἔλεγες λέγω. ἀλλὰ ἔοικεν, ἔφην ἐγώ, ὦ Διονυσόδωρέ τε καὶ Εὐθύδημε, οὗτος μὲν ὁ λόγος ἐν ταὐτῷ μένειν
καὶ ἔτι ὥσπερ τὸ παλαιὸν καταβαλὼν πίπτειν, καὶ ὥστε
τοῦτο μὴ πάσχειν οὐδ' ὑπὸ τῆς ὑμετέρας πω τέχνης ἐξηυρῆ- 5
σθαι, καὶ ταῦτα οὑτωσὶ θαυμαστῆς οὔσης εἰς ἀκρίβειαν
λόγων.

Καὶ ὁ Κτήσιππος, Θαυμάσιά γε λέγετ', ἔφη, ὦ ἄνδρες
b Θούριοι εἴτε Χῖοι εἴθ' ὁπόθεν καὶ ὅπῃ χαίρετον ὀνομαζόμενοι·
ὡς οὐδὲν ὑμῖν μέλει τοῦ παραληρεῖν.

Καὶ ἐγὼ φοβηθεὶς μὴ λοιδορία γένηται, πάλιν κατεπράϋ-
νον τὸν Κτήσιππον καὶ εἶπον· Ὦ Κτήσιππε, καὶ νυνδὴ ἃ
5 πρὸς Κλεινίαν ἔλεγον, καὶ πρὸς σὲ ταὐτὰ ταῦτα λέγω, ὅτι
οὐ γιγνώσκεις τῶν ξένων τὴν σοφίαν ὅτι θαυμασία ἐστίν.
ἀλλ' οὐκ ἐθέλετον ἡμῖν ἐπιδείξασθαι σπουδάζοντε, ἀλλὰ τὸν
Πρωτέα μιμεῖσθον τὸν Αἰγύπτιον σοφιστὴν γοητεύοντε ἡμᾶς.
c ἡμεῖς οὖν τὸν Μενέλαον μιμώμεθα, καὶ μὴ ἀφιώμεθα τοῖν
ἀνδροῖν ἕως ἂν ἡμῖν ἐκφανῆτον ἐφ' ᾧ αὐτὼ σπουδάζετον·
οἶμαι γάρ τι αὐτοῖν πάγκαλον φανεῖσθαι, ἐπειδὰν ἄρξωνται
σπουδάζειν. ἀλλὰ δεώμεθα καὶ παραμυθώμεθα καὶ προσευχώ-
5 μεθα αὐτοῖν ἐκφανῆναι. ἐγὼ οὖν μοι δοκῶ καὶ αὐτὸς πάλιν
ὑφηγήσασθαι οἵω προσεύχομαι αὐτὼ φανῆναί μοι· ὅθεν γὰρ
d τὸ πρότερον ἀπέλιπον, τὸ ἑξῆς τούτοις πειράσομαι, ὅπως ἂν
δύνωμαι, διελθεῖν, ἐάν πως ἐκκαλέσωμαι καὶ ἐλεήσαντέ
με καὶ οἰκτίραντε συντεταμένον καὶ σπουδάζοντα καὶ αὐτὼ
σπουδάσητον.
5 Σὺ δέ, ὦ Κλεινία, ἔφην, ἀνάμνησόν με πόθεν τότ' ἀπε-
λίπομεν. ὡς μὲν οὖν ἐγᾦμαι, ἐνθένδε ποθέν. φιλοσοφητέον ὡμολογήσαμεν τελευτῶντες· ἢ γάρ;—Ναί, ἦ δ' ὅς.—
Ἡ δέ γε φιλοσοφία κτῆσις ἐπιστήμης· οὐχ οὕτως; ἔφην.
—Ναί, ἔφη.—Τίνα ποτ' οὖν ἂν κτησάμενοι ἐπιστήμην ὀρθῶς
e κτησαίμεθα; ἆρ' οὐ τοῦτο μὲν ἁπλοῦν, ὅτι ταύτην ἥτις ἡμᾶς
ὀνήσει;—Πάνυ γ', ἔφη.—Ἆρ' οὖν ἄν τι ἡμᾶς ὀνήσειεν, εἰ
ἐπισταίμεθα γιγνώσκειν περιιόντες ὅπου τῆς γῆς χρυσίον
πλεῖστον κατορώρυκται;—Ἴσως, ἔφη.—Ἀλλὰ τὸ πρότερον,
5 ἦν δ' ἐγώ, τοῦτό γε ἐξηλέγξαμεν, ὅτι οὐδὲν πλέον, οὐδ' εἰ
ἄνευ πραγμάτων καὶ τοῦ ὀρύττειν τὴν γῆν τὸ πᾶν ἡμῖν
χρυσίον γένοιτο· ὥστε οὐδ' εἰ τὰς πέτρας χρυσᾶς ἐπισταί-
289 μεθα ποιεῖν, οὐδενὸς ἂν ἀξία ἡ ἐπιστήμη εἴη. εἰ γὰρ μὴ καὶ
χρῆσθαι ἐπιστησόμεθα τῷ χρυσίῳ, οὐδὲν ὄφελος αὐτοῦ

ἐφάνη ὄν· ἢ οὐ μέμνησαι; ἔφην ἐγώ.—Πάνυ γ᾽, ἔφη,
μέμνημαι.—Οὐδέ γε, ὡς ἔοικε, τῆς ἄλλης ἐπιστήμης ὄφελος
γίγνεται οὐδέν, οὔτε χρηματιστικῆς οὔτε ἰατρικῆς οὔτε ἄλ- 5
λης οὐδεμιᾶς, ἥτις ποιεῖν τι ἐπίσταται, χρῆσθαι δὲ μὴ ᾧ ἂν
ποιήσῃ· οὐχ οὕτως;—Συνέφη.—Οὐδέ γε εἴ τις ἔστιν ἐπιστήμη ὥστε ἀθανάτους ποιεῖν, ἄνευ τοῦ ἐπίστασθαι τῇ b
ἀθανασίᾳ χρῆσθαι οὐδὲ ταύτης ἔοικεν ὄφελος οὐδέν, εἴ τι
δεῖ τοῖς πρόσθεν ὡμολογημένοις τεκμαίρεσθαι.—Συνεδόκει
ἡμῖν πάντα ταῦτα.—Τοιαύτης τινὸς ἄρα ἡμῖν ἐπιστήμης δεῖ,
ὦ καλὲ παῖ, ἣν δ᾽ ἐγώ, ἐν ᾗ συμπέπτωκεν ἅμα τό τε ποιεῖν 5
καὶ τὸ ἐπίστασθαι χρῆσθαι τούτῳ ὃ ἂν ποιῇ.—Φαίνεται,
ἔφη.—Πολλοῦ ἄρα δεῖ, ὡς ἔοικεν, ἡμᾶς λυροποιοὺς δεῖν
εἶναι καὶ τοιαύτης τινὸς ἐπιστήμης ἐπηβόλους. ἐνταῦθα c
γὰρ δὴ χωρὶς μὲν ἡ ποιοῦσα τέχνη, χωρὶς δὲ ἡ χρωμένη,
διῄρηται δὲ τοῦ αὐτοῦ πέρι· ἡ γὰρ λυροποιικὴ καὶ ἡ κιθαρισ-
τικὴ πολὺ διαφέρετον ἀλλήλοιν. οὐχ οὕτως;—Συνέφη.—
Οὐδὲ μὴν αὐλοποιικῆς γε δῆλον ὅτι δεόμεθα· καὶ γὰρ αὕτη 5
ἑτέρα τοιαύτη.—Συνεδόκει.—Ἀλλὰ πρὸς θεῶν, ἔφην ἐγώ,
εἰ τὴν λογοποιικὴν τέχνην μάθοιμεν, ἆρά ἐστιν αὕτη ἣν ἔδει
κεκτημένους ἡμᾶς εὐδαίμονας εἶναι;—Οὐκ οἶμαι, ἔφη, ἐγώ,
ὁ Κλεινίας ὑπολαβών.

Τίνι τεκμηρίῳ, ἦν δ᾽ ἐγώ, χρῇ;   d
Ὁρῶ, ἔφη, τινὰς λογοποιούς, οἳ τοῖς ἰδίοις λόγοις, οἷς
αὐτοὶ ποιοῦσιν, οὐκ ἐπίστανται χρῆσθαι, ὥσπερ οἱ λυροποιοὶ
ταῖς λύραις, ἀλλὰ καὶ ἐνταῦθα ἄλλοι δυνατοὶ χρῆσθαι οἷς
ἐκεῖνοι εἰργάσαντο, οἱ λογοποιεῖν αὐτοὶ ἀδύνατοι· δῆλον οὖν 5
ὅτι καὶ περὶ λόγους χωρὶς ἡ τοῦ ποιεῖν τέχνη καὶ ἡ τοῦ
χρῆσθαι.

Ἱκανόν μοι δοκεῖς, ἔφην ἐγώ, τεκμήριον λέγειν, ὅτι οὐχ
αὕτη ἐστὶν ἡ τῶν λογοποιῶν τέχνη, ἣν ἂν κτησάμενός τις
εὐδαίμων εἴη. καίτοι ἐγὼ ᾤμην ἐνταῦθά που φανήσεσθαι 10
τὴν ἐπιστήμην ἣν δὴ πάλαι ζητοῦμεν. καὶ γάρ μοι οἵ τε e
ἄνδρες αὐτοὶ οἱ λογοποιοί, ὅταν συγγένωμαι αὐτοῖς, ὑπέρ-

σοφοι, ὦ Κλεινία, δοκοῦσιν εἶναι, καὶ αὐτὴ ἡ τέχνη αὐτῶν
θεσπεσία τις καὶ ὑψηλή. καὶ μέντοι οὐδὲν θαυμαστόν· ἔστι
5 γὰρ τῆς τῶν ἐπῳδῶν τέχνης μόριον μικρῷ τε ἐκείνης ὑπο-
290 δεεστέρα. ἡ μὲν γὰρ τῶν ἐπῳδῶν ἔχεών τε καὶ φαλαγγίων
καὶ σκορπίων καὶ τῶν ἄλλων θηρίων τε καὶ νόσων κήλησίς
ἐστιν, ἡ δὲ δικαστῶν τε καὶ ἐκκλησιαστῶν καὶ τῶν ἄλλων
ὄχλων κήλησίς τε καὶ παραμυθία τυγχάνει οὖσα· ἢ σοί,
5 ἔφην ἐγώ, ἄλλως πως δοκεῖ;
   Οὔκ, ἀλλ᾽ οὕτω μοι φαίνεται, ἔφη, ὡς σὺ λέγεις.
   Ποῖ οὖν, ἔφην ἐγώ, τραποίμεθ᾽ ἂν ἔτι; ἐπὶ ποίαν τέχνην;
'Εγὼ μὲν οὐκ εὐπορῶ, ἔφη.
   'Αλλ᾽, ἦν δ᾽ ἐγώ, ἐμὲ οἶμαι ηὑρηκέναι.
10 Τίνα; ἔφη ὁ Κλεινίας.
b 'Η στρατηγική μοι δοκεῖ, ἔφην ἐγώ, τέχνη παντὸς μᾶλλον
εἶναι ἣν ἄν τις κτησάμενος εὐδαίμων εἴη.
   Οὐκ ἔμοιγε δοκεῖ.
   Πῶς; ἦν δ᾽ ἐγώ.
5 Θηρευτική τις ἥδε γέ ἐστιν τέχνη ἀνθρώπων.
   Τί δὴ οὖν; ἔφην ἐγώ.
   Οὐδεμία, ἔφη, τῆς θηρευτικῆς αὐτῆς ἐπὶ πλέον ἐστὶν ἢ
ὅσον θηρεῦσαι καὶ χειρώσασθαι· ἐπειδὰν δὲ χειρώσωνται
τοῦτο ὃ ἂν θηρεύωνται, οὐ δύνανται τούτῳ χρῆσθαι, ἀλλ᾽ οἱ
10 μὲν κυνηγέται καὶ οἱ ἁλιῆς τοῖς ὀψοποιοῖς παραδιδόασιν, οἱ
c δ᾽ αὖ γεωμέτραι καὶ οἱ ἀστρονόμοι καὶ οἱ λογιστικοί—θηρευ-
τικοὶ γάρ εἰσι καὶ οὗτοι· οὐ γὰρ ποιοῦσι τὰ διαγράμματα
ἕκαστοι τούτων, ἀλλὰ τὰ ὄντα ἀνευρίσκουσιν—ἅτε οὖν χρῆσθαι αὐτοὶ αὐτοῖς οὐκ ἐπιστάμενοι, ἀλλὰ θηρεῦσαι μόνον,
5 παραδιδόασι δήπου τοῖς διαλεκτικοῖς καταχρῆσθαι αὐτῶν τοῖς
εὑρήμασιν, ὅσοι γε αὐτῶν μὴ παντάπασιν ἀνόητοί εἰσιν.
   Εἶεν, ἦν δ᾽ ἐγώ, ὦ κάλλιστε καὶ σοφώτατε Κλεινία·
τοῦτο οὕτως ἔχει;
   Πάνυ μὲν οὖν. καὶ οἵ γε στρατηγοί, ἔφη, οὕτω τὸν αὐτὸν
d τρόπον, ἐπειδὰν ἢ πόλιν τινὰ θηρεύσωνται ἢ στρατόπεδον,

ΕΥΘΥΔΗΜΟΣ 290 d

παραδιδόασι τοῖς πολιτικοῖς ἀνδράσιν—αὐτοὶ γὰρ οὐκ ἐπίστανται χρῆσθαι τούτοις ἃ ἐθήρευσαν—ὥσπερ οἶμαι οἱ
ὀρτυγοθῆραι τοῖς ὀρτυγοτρόφοις παραδιδόασιν. εἰ οὖν, ἦ δ'
ὅς, δεόμεθα ἐκείνης τῆς τέχνης, ἥτις ᾧ ἂν κτήσηται ἢ ποι- 5
ήσασα ἢ θηρευσαμένη αὐτὴ καὶ ἐπιστήσεται χρῆσθαι, καὶ ἡ
τοιαύτη ποιήσει ἡμᾶς μακαρίους, ἄλλην δή τινα, ἔφη,
ζητητέον ἀντὶ τῆς στρατηγικῆς.
ΚΡ. Τί λέγεις σύ, ὦ Σώκρατες; ἐκεῖνο τὸ μειράκιον e
τοιαῦτ' ἐφθέγξατο;
ΣΩ. Οὐκ οἴει, ὦ Κρίτων;
ΚΡ. Μὰ Δί' οὐ μέντοι. οἶμαι γὰρ αὐτὸν ἐγώ, εἰ ταῦτ'
εἶπεν, οὔτ' Εὐθυδήμου οὔτε ἄλλου οὐδενὸς ἔτ' ἀνθρώπου 5
δεῖσθαι εἰς παιδείαν.
ΣΩ. Ἀλλ' ἄρα, ὦ πρὸς Διός, μὴ ὁ Κτήσιππος ἦν ὁ ταῦτ'
εἰπών, ἐγὼ δὲ οὐ μέμνημαι;
ΚΡ. Ποῖος Κτήσιππος; 291
ΣΩ. Ἀλλὰ μὴν τόδε γε εὖ οἶδα, ὅτι οὔτε Εὐθύδημος οὔτε
Διονυσόδωρος ἦν ὁ εἰπὼν ταῦτα· ἀλλ', ὦ δαιμόνιε Κρίτων,
μή τις τῶν κρειττόνων παρὼν αὐτὰ ἐφθέγξατο; ὅτι γὰρ
ἤκουσά γε ταῦτα, εὖ οἶδα. 5
ΚΡ. Ναὶ μὰ Δία, ὦ Σώκρατες· τῶν κρειττόνων μέντοι
τις ἐμοὶ δοκεῖ, καὶ πολύ γε. ἀλλὰ μετὰ τοῦτο ἔτι τινὰ
ἐζητήσατε τέχνην; καὶ ηὕρετε ἐκείνην ἢ οὐχ ηὕρετε, ἧς
ἕνεκα ἐζητεῖτε;
ΣΩ. Πόθεν, ὦ μακάριε, ηὕρομεν; ἀλλ' ἦμεν πάνυ γελοῖοι· b
ὥσπερ τὰ παιδία τὰ τοὺς κορύδους διώκοντα, ἀεὶ ᾠόμεθα
ἑκάστην τῶν ἐπιστημῶν αὐτίκα λήψεσθαι, αἱ δ' ἀεὶ ὑπεξέφευγον. τὰ μὲν οὖν πολλὰ τί ἄν σοι λέγοιμι; ἐπὶ δὲ δὴ
τὴν βασιλικὴν ἐλθόντες τέχνην καὶ διασκοπούμενοι αὐτὴν 5
εἰ αὕτη εἴη ἡ τὴν εὐδαιμονίαν παρέχουσά τε καὶ ἀπεργαζομένη, ἐνταῦθα ὥσπερ εἰς λαβύρινθον ἐμπεσόντες, οἰόμενοι
ἤδη ἐπὶ τέλει εἶναι, περικάμψαντες πάλιν ὥσπερ ἐν ἀρχῇ τῆς
ζητήσεως ἀνεφάνημεν ὄντες καὶ τοῦ ἴσου δεόμενοι ὅσουπερ c
ὅτε τὸ πρῶτον ἐζητοῦμεν.

ΚΡ. Πῶς δὴ τοῦτο ὑμῖν συνέβη, ὦ Σώκρατες;

ΣΩ. Ἐγὼ φράσω. ἔδοξε γὰρ δὴ ἡμῖν ἡ πολιτικὴ καὶ
5 ἡ βασιλικὴ τέχνη ἡ αὐτὴ εἶναι.

ΚΡ. Τί οὖν δή;

ΣΩ. Ταύτῃ τῇ τέχνῃ ἥ τε στρατηγικὴ καὶ αἱ ἄλλαι
παραδιδόναι ἄρχειν τῶν ἔργων ὧν αὐταὶ δημιουργοί εἰσιν,
ὡς μόνῃ ἐπισταμένῃ χρῆσθαι. σαφῶς οὖν ἐδόκει ἡμῖν αὕτη
10 εἶναι ἣν ἐζητοῦμεν, καὶ ἡ αἰτία τοῦ ὀρθῶς πράττειν ἐν τῇ
d πόλει, καὶ ἀτεχνῶς κατὰ τὸ Αἰσχύλου ἰαμβεῖον μόνη ἐν
τῇ πρύμνῃ καθῆσθαι τῆς πόλεως, πάντα κυβερνῶσα καὶ
πάντων ἄρχουσα πάντα χρήσιμα ποιεῖν.

ΚΡ. Οὐκοῦν καλῶς ὑμῖν ἐδόκει, ὦ Σώκρατες;

5 ΣΩ. Σὺ κρινεῖς, ὦ Κρίτων, ἐὰν βούλῃ ἀκούειν καὶ τὰ μετὰ
ταῦτα συμβάντα ἡμῖν. αὖθις γὰρ δὴ πάλιν ἐσκοποῦμεν
ὧδέ πως· Φέρε, πάντων ἄρχουσα ἡ βασιλικὴ τέχνη τὶ ἡμῖν
e ἀπεργάζεται ἔργον ἢ οὐδέν; Πάντως δήπου, ἡμεῖς ἔφαμεν
πρὸς ἀλλήλους. Οὐ καὶ σὺ ἂν ταῦτα φαίης, ὦ Κρίτων;

ΚΡ. Ἔγωγε.

ΣΩ. Τί οὖν ἂν φαίης αὐτῆς ἔργον εἶναι; ὥσπερ εἰ σὲ
5 ἐγὼ ἐρωτῴην, πάντων ἄρχουσα ἡ ἰατρικὴ ὧν ἄρχει, τί ἔργον
παρέχεται; οὐ τὴν ὑγίειαν ⟨ἂν⟩ φαίης;

ΚΡ. Ἔγωγε.

ΣΩ. Τί δέ; ἡ ὑμετέρα τέχνη ἡ γεωργία, πάντων ἄρχουσα
292 ὧν ἄρχει, τί ἔργον ἀπεργάζεται; οὐ τὴν τροφὴν ἂν φαίης
τὴν ἐκ τῆς γῆς παρέχειν ἡμῖν;

ΚΡ. Ἔγωγε.

ΣΩ. Τί δέ; ἡ βασιλική, πάντων ἄρχουσα ὧν ἄρχει, τί
5 ἀπεργάζεται; ἴσως οὐ πάνυ γ᾽ εὐπορεῖς.

ΚΡ. Μὰ τὸν Δία, ὦ Σώκρατες.

ΣΩ. Οὐδὲ γὰρ ἡμεῖς, ὦ Κρίτων· ἀλλὰ τοσόνδε γε οἶσθα,
ὅτι εἴπερ ἐστὶν αὕτη ἣν ἡμεῖς ζητοῦμεν, ὠφέλιμον αὐτὴν δεῖ
εἶναι.

ΚΡ. Πάνυ γε.   10

ΣΩ. Οὐκοῦν ἀγαθόν γέ τι δεῖ ἡμῖν αὐτὴν παραδιδόναι;

ΚΡ. Ἀνάγκη, ὦ Σώκρατες.

ΣΩ. Ἀγαθὸν δέ γέ που ὡμολογήσαμεν ἀλλήλοις ἐγώ τε b
καὶ Κλεινίας οὐδὲν εἶναι ἄλλο ἢ ἐπιστήμην τινά.

ΚΡ. Ναί, οὕτως ἔλεγες.

ΣΩ. Οὐκοῦν τὰ μὲν ἄλλα ἔργα, ἃ φαίη ἄν τις πολιτικῆς
εἶναι—πολλὰ δέ που ταῦτ᾽ ἂν εἴη, οἷον πλουσίους τοὺς 5
πολίτας παρέχειν καὶ ἐλευθέρους καὶ ἀστασιάστους—πάντα
ταῦτα οὔτε κακὰ οὔτε ἀγαθὰ ἐφάνη, ἔδει δὲ σοφοὺς ποιεῖν
καὶ ἐπιστήμης μεταδιδόναι, εἴπερ ἔμελλεν αὕτη εἶναι ἡ
ὠφελοῦσά τε καὶ εὐδαίμονας ποιοῦσα.   c

ΚΡ. Ἔστι ταῦτα· τότε γοῦν οὕτως ὑμῖν ὡμολογήθη, ὡς
σὺ τοὺς λόγους ἀπήγγειλας.

ΣΩ. Ἆρ᾽ οὖν ἡ βασιλικὴ σοφοὺς ποιεῖ τοὺς ἀνθρώπους
καὶ ἀγαθούς;   5

ΚΡ. Τί γὰρ κωλύει, ὦ Σώκρατες;

ΣΩ. Ἀλλ᾽ ἆρα πάντας καὶ πάντα ἀγαθούς; καὶ πᾶσαν
ἐπιστήμην, σκυτοτομικήν τε καὶ τεκτονικὴν καὶ τὰς ἄλλας
ἁπάσας, αὕτη ἡ παραδιδοῦσά ἐστιν;

ΚΡ. Οὐκ οἶμαι ἔγωγε, ὦ Σώκρατες.   10

ΣΩ. Ἀλλὰ τίνα δὴ ἐπιστήμην; ἦ τί χρησόμεθα; τῶν d
μὲν γὰρ ἔργων οὐδενὸς δεῖ αὐτὴν δημιουργὸν εἶναι τῶν μήτε
κακῶν μήτε ἀγαθῶν, ἐπιστήμην δὲ παραδιδόναι μηδεμίαν
ἄλλην ἢ αὐτὴν ἑαυτήν. λέγωμεν δὴ οὖν τίς ποτέ ἐστιν
αὕτη, ἦ τί χρησόμεθα; βούλει φῶμεν, ὦ Κρίτων, ἦ ἄλλους 5
ἀγαθοὺς ποιήσομεν;

ΚΡ. Πάνυ γε.

ΣΩ. Οἳ τί ἔσονται ἡμῖν ἀγαθοὶ καὶ τί χρήσιμοι; ἢ ἔτι
λέγωμεν ὅτι ἄλλους ποιήσουσιν, οἱ δὲ ἄλλοι ἐκεῖνοι ἄλλους;
ὅ τι δέ ποτε ἀγαθοί εἰσιν, οὐδαμοῦ ἡμῖν φαίνονται, ἐπειδήπερ e
τὰ ἔργα τὰ λεγόμενα εἶναι τῆς πολιτικῆς ἠτιμάσαμεν, ἀλλ᾽
ἀτεχνῶς τὸ λεγόμενον ὁ Διὸς Κόρινθος γίγνεται, καὶ ὅπερ

ἔλεγον, τοῦ ἴσου ἡμῖν ἐνδεῖ ἢ ἔτι πλέονος πρὸς τὸ εἰδέναι τίς
5 ποτέ ἐστιν ἡ ἐπιστήμη ἐκείνη ἢ ἡμᾶς εὐδαίμονας ποιήσειε;
ΚΡ. Νὴ τὸν Δία, ὦ Σώκρατες, εἰς πολλήν γε ἀπορίαν,
ὡς ἔοικεν, ἀφίκεσθε.

ΣΩ. Ἔγωγε οὖν καὶ αὐτός, ὦ Κρίτων, ἐπειδὴ ἐν ταύτῃ
293 τῇ ἀπορίᾳ ἐνεπεπτώκη, πᾶσαν ἤδη φωνὴν ἠφίειν, δεόμενος
τοῖν ξένοιν, ὥσπερ Διοσκόρω ἐπικαλούμενος, σῶσαι ἡμᾶς,
ἐμέ τε καὶ τὸ μειράκιον, ἐκ τῆς τρικυμίας τοῦ λόγου, καὶ
παντὶ τρόπῳ σπουδάσαι, καὶ σπουδάσαντας ἐπιδεῖξαι τίς
5 ποτ' ἐστὶν ἡ ἐπιστήμη ἧς τυχόντες ἂν καλῶς τὸν ἐπίλοιπον
βίον διέλθοιμεν.
ΚΡ. Τί οὖν; ἠθέλησέν τι ὑμῖν ἐπιδεῖξαι ὁ Εὐθύδημος;
ΣΩ. Πῶς γὰρ οὔ; καὶ ἤρξατό γε, ὦ ἑταῖρε, πάνυ μεγαλο-
φρόνως τοῦ λόγου ὧδε—
b Πότερον δή σε, ἔφη, ὦ Σώκρατες, ταύτην τὴν ἐπιστήμην,
περὶ ἣν πάλαι ἀπορεῖτε, διδάξω, ἢ ἐπιδείξω ἔχοντα;
Ὦ μακάριε, ἦν δ' ἐγώ, ἔστι δὲ ἐπὶ σοὶ τοῦτο;
Πάνυ μὲν οὖν, ἔφη.
5 Ἐπίδειξον τοίνυν με νὴ Δί', ἔφην ἐγώ, ἔχοντα· πολὺ γὰρ
ῥᾷον ἢ μανθάνειν τηλικόνδε ἄνδρα.
Φέρε δή μοι ἀπόκριναι, ἔφη· ἔστιν ὅ τι ἐπίστασαι;—Πάνυ
γε, ἦν δ' ἐγώ, καὶ πολλά, σμικρά γε.—Ἀρκεῖ, ἔφη. ἆρ' οὖν
δοκεῖς οἷόν τέ τι τῶν ὄντων τοῦτο ὃ τυγχάνει ὄν, αὐτὸ τοῦτο
c μὴ εἶναι;—Ἀλλὰ μὰ Δί' οὐκ ἔγωγε.—Οὐκοῦν σὺ ἔφη,
ἐπίστασαί τι;—Ἔγωγε.—Οὐκοῦν ἐπιστήμων εἶ, εἴπερ ἐπίστασαι;—Πάνυ γε, τούτου γε αὐτοῦ.—Οὐδὲν διαφέρει· ἀλλ'
οὐκ ἀνάγκη σε ἔχει πάντα ἐπίστασθαι ἐπιστήμονά γε ὄντα;
5 —Μὰ Δί', ἔφην ἐγώ· ἐπεὶ πολλὰ ἄλλ' οὐκ ἐπίσταμαι.—
Οὐκοῦν εἴ τι μὴ ἐπίστασαι, οὐκ ἐπιστήμων εἶ.—Ἐκείνου γε,
ὦ φίλε, ἦν δ' ἐγώ.—Ἧττον οὖν τι, ἔφη, οὐκ ἐπιστήμων
εἶ; ἄρτι δὲ ἐπιστήμων ἔφησθα εἶναι· καὶ οὕτως τυγχάνεις ὢν
d αὐτὸς οὗτος ὃς εἶ, καὶ αὖ πάλιν οὐκ εἶ, κατὰ ταὐτὰ ἅμα.

Εἶεν, ἦν δ' ἐγώ, Εὐθύδημε· τὸ γὰρ λεγόμενον, καλὰ δὴ
πάντα λέγεις· πῶς οὖν ἐπίσταμαι ἐκείνην τὴν ἐπιστήμην
ἣν ἐζητοῦμεν; ὡς δὴ τοῦτο ἀδύνατόν ἐστιν τὸ αὐτὸ εἶναί τε
καὶ μή, εἴπερ ἓν ἐπίσταμαι, ἅπαντα ἐπίσταμαι—οὐ γὰρ 5
ἂν εἴην ἐπιστήμων τε καὶ ἀνεπιστήμων ἅμα—ἐπεὶ δὲ πάντα
ἐπίσταμαι, κἀκείνην δὴ τὴν ἐπιστήμην ἔχω· ἆρα οὕτως λέγεις,
καὶ τοῦτό ἐστιν τὸ σοφόν;
Αὐτὸς σαυτόν γε δὴ ἐξελέγχεις, ἔφη, ὦ Σώκρατες.   e
Τί δέ, ἦν δ' ἐγώ, ὦ Εὐθύδημε, σὺ οὐ πέπονθας τοῦτο τὸ
αὐτὸ πάθος; ἐγὼ γάρ τοι μετὰ σοῦ ὁτιοῦν ἂν πάσχων καὶ
μετὰ Διονυσοδώρου τοῦδε, φίλης κεφαλῆς, οὐκ ἂν πάνυ
ἀγανακτοίην. εἰπέ μοι, σφὼ οὐχὶ τὰ μὲν ἐπίστασθον τῶν 5
ὄντων, τὰ δὲ οὐκ ἐπίστασθον;
Ἥκιστά γε, ἔφη, ὦ Σώκρατες, ὁ Διονυσόδωρος.
Πῶς λέγετον; ἔφην ἐγώ· ἀλλ' οὐδὲν ἄρα ἐπίστασθον;
Καὶ μάλα, ἦ δ' ὅς.
Πάντ' ἄρα, ἔφην ἐγώ, ἐπίστασθον, ἐπειδήπερ καὶ ὁτιοῦν; 294
Πάντ', ἔφη· καὶ σύ γε πρός, εἴπερ καὶ ἓν ἐπίστασαι, πάντα
ἐπίστασαι.
Ὦ Ζεῦ, ἔφην ἐγώ, ὡς θαυμαστὸν λέγεις καὶ ἀγαθὸν μέγα
πεφάνθαι. μῶν καὶ οἱ ἄλλοι πάντες ἄνθρωποι πάντ' ἐπί- 5
στανται, ἢ οὐδέν;
Οὐ γὰρ δήπου, ἔφη, τὰ μὲν ἐπίστανται, τὰ δ' οὐκ ἐπί-
στανται, καὶ εἰσὶν ἅμα ἐπιστήμονές τε καὶ ἀνεπιστήμονες.
Ἀλλὰ τί; ἦν δ' ἐγώ.
Πάντες, ἦ δ' ὅς, πάντα ἐπίστανται, εἴπερ καὶ ἕν.   10
Ὦ πρὸς τῶν θεῶν, ἦν δ' ἐγώ, ὦ Διονυσόδωρε—δῆλοι γάρ b
μοί ἐστον ἤδη ὅτι σπουδάζετον, καὶ μόλις ὑμᾶς προυκαλε-
σάμην σπουδάζειν—αὐτὼ τῷ ὄντι πάντα ἐπίστασθον; οἷον
τεκτονικὴν καὶ σκυτικήν;
Πάνυ γ', ἔφη.   5
Ἦ καὶ νευρορραφεῖν δυνατώ ἐστον;
Καὶ ναὶ μὰ Δία καττύειν, ἔφη.

294 b ΠΛΑΤΩΝΟΣ

Ἦ καὶ τὰ τοιαῦτα, τοὺς ἀστέρας ὁπόσοι εἰσί, καὶ τὴν
ἄμμον;

10 Πάνυ γε, ἦ δ᾽ ὅς· εἶτ᾽ οὐκ ἂν οἴει ὁμολογῆσαι ἡμᾶς;
Καὶ ὁ Κτήσιππος ὑπολαβών· Πρὸς Διός, ἔφη, Διονυ-
c σόδωρε, τεκμήριόν τί μοι τούτων ἐπιδείξατον τοιόνδε, ᾧ
εἴσομαι ὅτι ἀληθῆ λέγετον.
Τί ἐπιδείξω; ἔφη.
Οἶσθα Εὐθύδημον ὁπόσους ὀδόντας ἔχει, καὶ ὁ Εὐθύδημος
5 ὁπόσους σύ;
Οὐκ ἐξαρκεῖ σοι, ἔφη, ἀκοῦσαι ὅτι πάντα ἐπιστάμεθα;
Μηδαμῶς, ἦ δ᾽ ὅς, ἀλλὰ τοῦτο ἔτι ἡμῖν μόνον εἴπατον καὶ
ἐπιδείξατον ὅτι ἀληθῆ λέγετον· καὶ ἐὰν εἴπητον ὁπόσους
ἑκάτερος ἔχει ὑμῶν, καὶ φαίνησθε γνόντες ἡμῶν ἀριθμη-
10 σάντων, ἤδη πεισόμεθα ὑμῖν καὶ τἆλλα.
d Ἡγουμένω οὖν σκώπτεσθαι οὐκ ἠθελέτην, ἀλλ᾽ ὡμο-
λογησάτην πάντα χρήματα ἐπίστασθαι, καθ᾽ ἓν ἕκαστον
ἐρωτώμενοι ὑπὸ Κτησίππου. ὁ γὰρ Κτήσιππος πάνυ ἀπαρακαλύπτως οὐδὲν ὅ τι οὐκ ἠρώτα τελευτῶν, καὶ τὰ αἴσχιστα, εἰ
5 ἐπισταίσθην· τὼ δὲ ἀνδρειότατα ὁμόσε ἤτην τοῖς ἐρωτήμασιν,
ὁμολογοῦντες εἰδέναι, ὥσπερ οἱ κάπροι οἱ πρὸς τὴν πληγὴν
ὁμόσε ὠθούμενοι, ὥστ᾽ ἔγωγε καὶ αὐτός, ὦ Κρίτων, ὑπ᾽
ἀπιστίας ἠναγκάσθην τελευτῶν ἐρέσθαι [τὸν Εὐθύδημον] εἰ
e καὶ ὀρχεῖσθαι ἐπίσταιτο ὁ Διονυσόδωρος· ὁ δέ, Πάνυ, ἔφη.
Οὐ δήπου, ἦν δ᾽ ἐγώ, καὶ ἐς μαχαίρας γε κυβιστᾶν καὶ
ἐπὶ τροχοῦ δινεῖσθαι τηλικοῦτος ὤν, οὕτω πόρρω σοφίας
ἥκεις;
5 Οὐδέν, ἔφη, ὅ τι οὔ.
Πότερον δέ, ἦν δ᾽ ἐγώ, πάντα νῦν μόνον ἐπίστασθον ἢ
καὶ ἀεί;
Καὶ ἀεί, ἔφη.
Καὶ ὅτε παιδία ἦστον καὶ εὐθὺς γενόμενοι ἠπίστασθε
10 πάντα;
Ἐφάτην ἅμα ἀμφοτέρω.

ΕΥΘΥΔΗΜΟΣ 295 a

Καὶ ἡμῖν μὲν ἄπιστον ἐδόκει τὸ πρᾶγμα εἶναι· ὁ δ' **295**
Εὐθύδημος, Ἀπιστεῖς, ἔφη, ὦ Σώκρατες;
Πλήν γ' ὅτι, ⟨ἦν δ'⟩ ἐγώ, εἰκὸς ὑμᾶς ἐστι σοφοὺς εἶναι.
Ἀλλ' ἤν, ἔφη, ἐθελήσῃς μοι ἀποκρίνεσθαι, ἐγὼ ἐπιδείξω
καὶ σὲ ταῦτα τὰ θαυμαστὰ ὁμολογοῦντα. 5
Ἀλλὰ μήν, ἦν δ' ἐγώ, ἥδιστα ταῦτα ἐξελέγχομαι. εἰ γάρ
τοι λέληθα ἐμαυτὸν σοφὸς ὤν, σὺ δὲ τοῦτο ἐπιδείξεις ὡς
πάντα ἐπίσταμαι καὶ ἀεί, τί μεῖζον ἔρμαιον αὐτοῦ ἂν εὕροιμι
ἐν παντὶ τῷ βίῳ;
Ἀποκρίνου δή, ἔφη. 10
Ὡς ἀποκρινουμένου ἐρώτα. b
Ἆρ' οὖν, ἔφη, ὦ Σώκρατες, ἐπιστήμων του εἶ ἢ οὔ;—
Ἔγωγε.—Πότερον οὖν ᾧ ἐπιστήμων εἶ, τούτῳ καὶ ἐπίστασαι,
ἢ ἄλλῳ τῳ;—Ὧι ἐπιστήμων. οἶμαι γάρ σε τὴν ψυχὴν
λέγειν· ἢ οὐ τοῦτο λέγεις; 5
Οὐκ αἰσχύνει, ἔφη, ὦ Σώκρατες; ἐρωτώμενος ἀντερωτᾷς;
Εἶεν, ἦν δ' ἐγώ· ἀλλὰ πῶς ποιῶ; οὕτω γὰρ ποιήσω
ὅπως ἂν σὺ κελεύῃς. ὅταν μὴ εἰδῶ ὅ τι ἐρωτᾷς, κελεύεις
με ὅμως ἀποκρίνεσθαι, ἀλλὰ μὴ ἐπανερέσθαι;
Ὑπολαμβάνεις γὰρ δήπου τι, ἔφη, ὃ λέγω; c
Ἔγωγε, ἦν δ' ἐγώ.
Πρὸς τοῦτο τοίνυν ἀποκρίνου ὃ ὑπολαμβάνεις.
Τί οὖν, ἔφην, ἂν σὺ μὲν ἄλλῃ ἐρωτᾷς διανοούμενος, ἐγὼ
δὲ ἄλλῃ ὑπολάβω, ἔπειτα πρὸς τοῦτο ἀποκρίνωμαι, ἐξαρκεῖ 5
σοι ἐὰν μηδὲν πρὸς ἔπος ἀποκρίνωμαι;
Ἔμοιγε, ἦ δ' ὅς· οὐ μέντοι σοί γε, ὡς ἐγῷμαι.
Οὐ τοίνυν μὰ Δία ἀποκρινοῦμαι, ἦν δ' ἐγώ, πρότερον
πρὶν ἂν πύθωμαι.
Οὐκ ἀποκρινεῖ, ἔφη, πρὸς ἃ ἂν ἀεὶ ὑπολαμβάνῃς, ὅτι ἔχων 10
φλυαρεῖς καὶ ἀρχαιότερος εἶ τοῦ δέοντος.
Κἀγὼ ἔγνων αὐτὸν ὅτι μοι χαλεπαίνοι διαστέλλοντι τὰ d
λεγόμενα, βουλόμενός με θηρεῦσαι τὰ ὀνόματα περιστήσας.
ἀνεμνήσθην οὖν τοῦ Κόννου, ὅτι μοι κἀκεῖνος χαλεπαίνει

ἑκάστοτε ὅταν αὐτῷ μὴ ὑπείκω, ἔπειτά μου ἧττον ἐπιμελεῖται
5 ὡς ἀμαθοῦς ὄντος· ἐπεὶ δὲ οὖν διενενοήμην καὶ παρὰ τοῦτον
φοιτᾶν, ᾠήθην δεῖν ὑπείκειν, μή με σκαιὸν ἡγησάμενος
φοιτητὴν μὴ προσδέχοιτο. εἶπον οὖν· 'Αλλ' εἰ δοκεῖ σοι,
e Εὐθύδημε, οὕτω ποιεῖν, ποιητέον· σὺ γὰρ πάντως που
κάλλιον ἐπίστασαι διαλέγεσθαι ἢ ἐγώ, τέχνην ἔχων ἰδιώτου
ἀνθρώπου. ἐρώτα οὖν πάλιν ἐξ ἀρχῆς.
'Αποκρίνου δή, ἔφη, πάλιν, πότερον ἐπίστασαί τῳ ἃ
5 ἐπίστασαι, ἢ οὔ;—Ἔγωγε, ἔφην, τῇ γε ψυχῇ.
296 Οὗτος αὖ, ἔφη, προσαποκρίνεται τοῖς ἐρωτωμένοις. οὐ
γὰρ ἔγωγε ἐρωτῶ ὅτῳ, ἀλλ' εἰ ἐπίστασαί τῳ.
Πλέον αὖ, ἔφην ἐγώ, τοῦ δέοντος ἀπεκρινάμην ὑπὸ ἀπαι-
δευσίας. ἀλλὰ συγγίγνωσκέ μοι· ἀποκρινοῦμαι γὰρ ἤδη
5 ἁπλῶς ὅτι ἐπίσταμαί τῳ ἃ ἐπίσταμαι.—Πότερον, ἦ δ' ὅς,
τῷ αὐτῷ τούτῳ γ' ἀεί, ἢ ἔστι μὲν ὅτε τούτῳ, ἔστιν δὲ
ὅτε ἑτέρῳ;—Ἀεί, ὅταν ἐπίστωμαι, ἦν δ' ἐγώ, τούτῳ.
Οὐκ αὖ, ἔφη, παύσει παραφθεγγόμενος;
'Αλλ' ὅπως μή τι ἡμᾶς σφήλῃ τὸ "ἀεὶ" τοῦτο.
b Οὔκουν ἡμᾶς γ', ἔφη, ἀλλ' εἴπερ, σέ. ἀλλ' ἀποκρίνου·
ἦ ἀεὶ τούτῳ ἐπίστασαι;—Ἀεί, ἦν δ' ἐγώ, ἐπειδὴ δεῖ ἀφελεῖν
τὸ "ὅταν."—Οὔκουν ἀεὶ μὲν τούτῳ ἐπίστασαι· ἀεὶ δ' ἐπιστάμενος πότερον τὰ μὲν τούτῳ ἐπίστασαι ᾧ ἐπίστασαι, τὰ δ'
5 ἄλλῳ, ἢ τούτῳ πάντα;—Τούτῳ, ἔφην ἐγώ, ἅπαντα, ἅ γ'
ἐπίσταμαι.
Τοῦτ' ἐκεῖνο, ἔφη· ἥκει τὸ αὐτὸ παράφθεγμα.
'Αλλ' ἀφαιρῶ, ἔφην ἐγώ, τὸ "ἅ γ' ἐπίσταμαι."
'Αλλὰ μηδὲ ἕν, ἔφη, ἀφέλῃς· οὐδὲν γάρ σου δέομαι.
c ἀλλά μοι ἀπόκριναι· δύναιο ἂν ἅπαντα ἐπίστασθαι, εἰ μὴ
πάντα ἐπίσταιο;
Τέρας γὰρ ἂν εἴη, ἦν δ' ἐγώ.
Καὶ ὃς εἶπε· Προστίθει τοίνυν ἤδη ὅτι βούλει· ἅπαντα
5 γὰρ ὁμολογεῖς ἐπίστασθαι.

Ἔοικα, ἔφην ἐγώ, ἐπειδήπερ γε οὐδεμίαν ἔχει δύναμιν τὸ
" ἃ ἐπίσταμαι," πάντα δὲ ἐπίσταμαι.

Οὐκοῦν καὶ ἀεὶ ὡμολόγηκας ἐπίστασθαι τούτῳ ᾧ ἐπίστασαι, εἴτε ὅταν ἐπίστῃ εἴτε ὅπως βούλει· ἀεὶ γὰρ ὡμολόγηκας
ἐπίστασθαι καὶ ἅμα πάντα. δῆλον οὖν ὅτι καὶ παῖς ὢν 10
ἠπίστω, καὶ ὅτ᾽ ἐγίγνου, καὶ ὅτ᾽ ἐφύου· καὶ πρὶν αὐτὸς d
γενέσθαι, καὶ πρὶν οὐρανὸν καὶ γῆν γενέσθαι, ἠπίστω
ἅπαντα, εἴπερ ἀεὶ ἐπίστασαι. καὶ ναὶ μὰ Δία, ἔφη, αὐτὸς
ἀεὶ ἐπιστήσει καὶ ἅπαντα, ἂν ἐγὼ βούλωμαι.

Ἀλλὰ βουληθείης, ἦν δ᾽ ἐγώ, ὦ πολυτίμητε Εὐθύδημε, 5
εἰ δὴ τῷ ὄντι ἀληθῆ λέγεις. ἀλλ᾽ οὔ σοι πάνυ πιστεύω
ἱκανῷ εἶναι, εἰ μή σοι συμβουληθείη ὁ ἀδελφός σου οὑτοσὶ
Διονυσόδωρος· οὕτω δὲ τάχα ἄν. εἴπετον δέ μοι, ἦν δ᾽ ἐγώ—
τὰ μὲν γὰρ ἄλλα οὐκ ἔχω ὑμῖν πῶς ἀμφισβητοίην, οὕτως e
εἰς σοφίαν τερατώδεσιν ἀνθρώποις, ὅπως ἐγὼ οὐ πάντα
ἐπίσταμαι, ἐπειδή γε ὑμεῖς φατε—τὰ δὲ τοιάδε πῶς φῶ
ἐπίστασθαι, Εὐθύδημε, ὡς οἱ ἀγαθοὶ ἄνδρες ἄδικοί εἰσιν;
φέρε εἰπέ, τοῦτο ἐπίσταμαι ἢ οὐκ ἐπίσταμαι; 5

Ἐπίστασαι μέντοι, ἔφη.

Τί; ἦν δ᾽ ἐγώ.

Ὅτι οὐκ ἄδικοί εἰσιν οἱ ἀγαθοί.

Πάνυ γε, ἦν δ᾽ ἐγώ, πάλαι. ἀλλ᾽ οὐ τοῦτο ἐρωτῶ· ἀλλ᾽ 297
ὡς ἄδικοί εἰσιν οἱ ἀγαθοί, ποῦ ἐγὼ τοῦτο ἔμαθον;

Οὐδαμοῦ, ἔφη ὁ Διονυσόδωρος.

Οὐκ ἄρα ἐπίσταμαι, ἔφην, τοῦτο ἐγώ.

Διαφθείρεις, ἔφη, τὸν λόγον, ὁ Εὐθύδημος πρὸς τὸν 5
Διονυσόδωρον, καὶ φανήσεται οὑτοσὶ οὐκ ἐπιστάμενος, καὶ
ἐπιστήμων ἅμα ὢν καὶ ἀνεπιστήμων. Καὶ ὁ Διονυσόδωρος
ἠρυθρίασεν.

Ἀλλὰ σύ, ἦν δ᾽ ἐγώ, πῶς λέγεις, ὦ Εὐθύδημε; οὐ δοκεῖ
σοι ὀρθῶς ἀδελφὸς λέγειν ὁ πάντ᾽ εἰδώς; b

Ἀδελφὸς γάρ, ἔφη, ἐγώ εἰμι Εὐθυδήμου, ταχὺ ὑπολαβὼν
ὁ Διονυσόδωρος;

Κἀγὼ εἶπον· Ἔασον, ὠγαθέ, ἕως ἂν Εὐθύδημός με διδάξῃ
5 ὡς ἐπίσταμαι τοὺς ἀγαθοὺς ἄνδρας ὅτι ἄδικοί εἰσι, καὶ μή
μοι φθονήσῃς τοῦ μαθήματος.
Φεύγεις, ἔφη, ὦ Σώκρατες, ὁ Διονυσόδωρος, καὶ οὐκ
ἐθέλεις ἀποκρίνεσθαι.
Εἰκότως γ', εἶπον ἐγώ· ἥττων γάρ εἰμι καὶ τοῦ ἑτέρου
10 ὑμῶν, ὥστε πολλοῦ δέω μὴ οὐ δύο γε φεύγειν. πολὺ γάρ
c πού εἰμι φαυλότερος τοῦ Ἡρακλέους, ὃς οὐχ οἷός τε ἦν τῇ
τε ὕδρᾳ διαμάχεσθαι, σοφιστρίᾳ οὔσῃ καὶ διὰ τὴν σοφίαν
ἀνιείσῃ, εἰ μίαν κεφαλὴν τοῦ λόγου τις ἀποτέμοι, πολλὰς
ἀντὶ τῆς μιᾶς, καὶ καρκίνῳ τινὶ ἑτέρῳ σοφιστῇ ἐκ θαλάττης
5 ἀφιγμένῳ, νεωστί μοι δοκεῖν καταπεπλευκότι· ὃς ἐπειδὴ
αὐτὸν ἐλύπει οὕτως ἐκ τοῦ ἐπ' ἀριστερὰ λέγων καὶ δάκνων,
τὸν Ἰόλεων τὸν ἀδελφιδοῦν βοηθὸν ἐπεκαλέσατο, ὁ δὲ αὐτῷ
d ἱκανῶς ἐβοήθησεν. ὁ δ' ἐμὸς Ἰόλεως [Πατροκλῆς] εἰ ἔλθοι,
πλέον ἂν θάτερον ποιήσειεν.
Ἀπόκριναι δή, ἔφη ὁ Διονυσόδωρος, ὁπότε σοι ταῦτα
ὕμνηται· πότερον ὁ Ἰόλεως τοῦ Ἡρακλέους μᾶλλον ἦν
5 ἀδελφιδοῦς ἢ σός;
Κράτιστον τοίνυν μοι, ὦ Διονυσόδωρε, ἦν δ' ἐγώ, ἀπο-
κρίνασθαί σοι. οὐ γὰρ μὴ ἀνῇς ἐρωτῶν, σχεδόν τι ἐγὼ
τοῦτ' εὖ οἶδα, φθονῶν καὶ διακωλύων, ἵνα μὴ διδάξῃ με
Εὐθύδημος ἐκεῖνο τὸ σοφόν.—Ἀποκρίνου δή, ἔφη.—Ἀπο-
10 κρίνομαι δή, εἶπον, ὅτι τοῦ Ἡρακλέους ἦν ὁ Ἰόλεως ἀδελ-
e φιδοῦς, ἐμὸς δ', ὡς ἐμοὶ δοκεῖ, οὐδ' ὁπωστιοῦν. οὐ γὰρ
Πατροκλῆς ἦν αὐτῷ πατήρ, ὁ ἐμὸς ἀδελφός, ἀλλὰ παραπλήσιον μὲν τοὔνομα Ἰφικλῆς, ὁ Ἡρακλέους ἀδελφός.—
Πατροκλῆς δέ, ἦ δ' ὅς, σός;—Πάνυ γ', ἔφην ἐγώ, ὁμομή-
5 τριός γε, οὐ μέντοι ὁμοπάτριος.—Ἀδελφὸς ἄρα ἐστί σοι
καὶ οὐκ ἀδελφός.—Οὐχ ὁμοπάτριός γε, ὦ βέλτιστε, ἔφην·
ἐκείνου μὲν γὰρ Χαιρέδημος ἦν πατήρ, ἐμὸς δὲ Σωφρονίσκος.
—Πατὴρ δὲ ἦν, ἔφη, Σωφρονίσκος καὶ Χαιρέδημος;—Πάνυ
298 γ', ἔφην· ὁ μέν γε ἐμός, ὁ δὲ ἐκείνου.—Οὐκοῦν, ἦ δ' ὅς, ἕτερος

ἦν Χαιρέδημος τοῦ πατρός;—Τοὐμοῦ γ᾽, ἔφην ἐγώ.—Ἀρ᾽
οὖν πατὴρ ἦν ἕτερος ὢν πατρός; ἢ σὺ εἶ ὁ αὐτὸς τῷ λίθῳ;
—Δέδοικα μὲν ἔγωγ᾽, ἔφην, μὴ φανῶ ὑπὸ σοῦ ὁ αὐτός· οὐ
μέντοι μοι δοκῶ.—Οὐκοῦν ἕτερος εἶ, ἔφη, τοῦ λίθου; — 5
Ἕτερος μέντοι.—Ἄλλο τι οὖν ἕτερος, ἢ δ᾽ ὅς, ὢν λίθου οὐ
λίθος εἶ; καὶ ἕτερος ὢν χρυσοῦ οὐ χρυσὸς εἶ;—Ἔστι ταῦτα.
—Οὐκοῦν καὶ ὁ Χαιρέδημος, ἔφη, ἕτερος ὢν πατρὸς οὐκ
ἂν πατὴρ εἴη.—Ἔοικεν, ἦν δ᾽ ἐγώ, οὐ πατὴρ εἶναι.

Εἰ γὰρ δήπου, ἔφη, πατήρ ἐστιν ὁ Χαιρέδημος, ὑπολαβὼν b
ὁ Εὐθύδημος, πάλιν αὖ ὁ Σωφρονίσκος ἕτερος ὢν πατρὸς
οὐ πατήρ ἐστιν, ὥστε σύ, ὦ Σώκρατες, ἀπάτωρ εἶ.

Καὶ ὁ Κτήσιππος ἐκδεξάμενος, Ὁ δὲ ὑμέτερος, ἔφη, αὖ
πατὴρ οὐ ταὐτὰ ταῦτα πέπονθεν; ἕτερός ἐστιν τοὐμοῦ πατρός; 5
—Πολλοῦ γ᾽, ἔφη, δεῖ, ὁ Εὐθύδημος.—Ἀλλά, ἦ δ᾽ ὅς, ὁ
αὐτός;—Ὁ αὐτὸς μέντοι.—Οὐκ ἂν συμβουλοίμην· ἀλλὰ
πότερον, ὦ Εὐθύδημε, ἐμὸς μόνον ἐστὶ πατὴρ ἢ καὶ τῶν c
ἄλλων ἀνθρώπων;—Καὶ τῶν ἄλλων, ἔφη· ἢ οἴει τὸν αὐτὸν
πατέρα ὄντα οὐ πατέρα εἶναι;—Ὤιμην δῆτα, ἔφη ὁ Κτήσιππος.—Τί δέ; ἢ δ᾽ ὅς· χρυσὸν ὄντα μὴ χρυσὸν εἶναι;
ἢ ἄνθρωπον ὄντα μὴ ἄνθρωπον;—Μὴ γάρ, ἔφη ὁ Κτήσιπ- 5
πος, ὦ Εὐθύδημε, τὸ λεγόμενον, οὐ λίνον λίνῳ συνάπτεις·
δεινὸν γὰρ λέγεις πρᾶγμα εἰ ὁ σὸς πατὴρ πάντων ἐστὶν
πατήρ.—Ἀλλ᾽ ἔστιν, ἔφη.—Πότερον ἀνθρώπων; ἢ δ᾽ ὃς
ὁ Κτήσιππος, ἢ καὶ ἵππων καὶ τῶν ἄλλων πάντων ζῴων;—
Πάντων, ἔφη.—Ἦ καὶ μήτηρ ἡ μήτηρ;—Καὶ ἡ μήτηρ γε. d
—Καὶ τῶν ἐχίνων ἄρα, ἔφη, ἡ σὴ μήτηρ μήτηρ ἐστὶ τῶν
θαλαττίων.—Καὶ ἡ σή γ᾽, ἔφη.—Καὶ σὺ ἄρα ἀδελφὸς
εἶ τῶν κωβιῶν καὶ κυναρίων καὶ χοιριδίων.—Καὶ γὰρ σύ,
ἔφη.—⟨Κάπρος⟩ ἄρα σοι πατήρ ἐστι καὶ κύων.—Καὶ γὰρ 5
σοί, ἔφη.

Αὐτίκα δέ γε, ἦ δ᾽ ὃς ὁ Διονυσόδωρος, ἄν μοι ἀποκρίνῃ,
ὦ Κτήσιππε, ὁμολογήσεις ταῦτα. εἰπὲ γάρ μοι, ἔστι σοι
κύων;—Καὶ μάλα πονηρός, ἔφη ὁ Κτήσιππος.—Ἔστιν οὖν

H 2

e αὐτῷ κυνίδια;—Καὶ μάλ', ἔφη, ἕτερα τοιαῦτα.—Οὐκοῦν
πατήρ ἐστιν αὐτῶν ὁ κύων;—Ἔγωγέ τοι εἶδον, ἔφη, αὐτὸν
ὀχεύοντα τὴν κύνα.—Τί οὖν; οὐ σός ἐστιν ὁ κύων;—Πάνυ
γ', ἔφη.—Οὐκοῦν πατὴρ ὢν σός ἐστιν, ὥστε σὸς πατὴρ
5 γίγνεται ὁ κύων καὶ σὺ κυναρίων ἀδελφός;
Καὶ αὖθις ταχὺ ὑπολαβὼν ὁ Διονυσόδωρος, ἵνα μὴ
πρότερόν τι εἴποι ὁ Κτήσιππος, Καὶ ἔτι γέ μοι μικρόν, ἔφη,
ἀπόκριναι· τύπτεις τὸν κύνα τοῦτον;—Καὶ ὁ Κτήσιππος
γελάσας, Νὴ τοὺς θεούς, ἔφη· οὐ γὰρ δύναμαι σέ.—Οὐκοῦν
10 τὸν σαυτοῦ πατέρα, ἔφη, τύπτεις;
299 Πολὺ μέντοι, ἔφη, δικαιότερον τὸν ὑμέτερον πατέρα
τύπτοιμι, ὅ τι μαθὼν σοφοὺς υἱεῖς οὕτως ἔφυσεν. ἀλλ' ἦ
που, ὦ Εὐθύδημε [ὁ Κτήσιππος], πόλλ' ἀγαθὰ ἀπὸ τῆς
ὑμετέρας σοφίας ταύτης ἀπολέλαυκεν ὁ πατὴρ ὁ ὑμέτερός
5 τε καὶ τῶν κυνιδίων.
Ἀλλ' οὐδὲν δεῖται πολλῶν ἀγαθῶν, ὦ Κτήσιππε, οὔτ'
ἐκεῖνος οὔτε σύ.
Οὐδὲ σύ, ἦ δ' ὅς, ὦ Εὐθύδημε, αὐτός;
Οὐδὲ ἄλλος γε οὐδεὶς ἀνθρώπων. εἰπὲ γάρ μοι, ὦ
b Κτήσιππε, εἰ ἀγαθὸν νομίζεις εἶναι ἀσθενοῦντι φάρμακον
πιεῖν ἢ οὐκ ἀγαθὸν εἶναι δοκεῖ σοι, ὅταν δέηται· ἢ εἰς
πόλεμον ὅταν ἴῃ, ὅπλα ἔχοντα μᾶλλον ἰέναι ἢ ἄνοπλον.—
Ἔμοιγε, ἔφη. καίτοι οἶμαί τί σε τῶν καλῶν ἐρεῖν.—Σὺ
5 ἄριστα εἴσει, ἔφη· ἀλλ' ἀποκρίνου. ἐπειδὴ γὰρ ὡμολόγεις
ἀγαθὸν εἶναι φάρμακον, ὅταν δέῃ, πίνειν ἀνθρώπῳ, ἄλλο τι
τοῦτο τὸ ἀγαθὸν ὡς πλεῖστον δεῖ πίνειν, καὶ καλῶς ἐκεῖ ἕξει,
ἐάν τις αὐτῷ τρίψας ἐγκεράσῃ ἐλλεβόρου ἄμαξαν;—Καὶ ὁ
Κτήσιππος εἶπεν· Πάνυ γε σφόδρα, ὦ Εὐθύδημε, ἐὰν ᾖ γε
c ὁ πίνων ὅσος ὁ ἀνδριὰς ὁ ἐν Δελφοῖς.—Οὐκοῦν, ἔφη, καὶ ἐν
τῷ πολέμῳ ἐπειδὴ ἀγαθόν ἐστιν ὅπλα ἔχειν, ὡς πλεῖστα δεῖ
ἔχειν δόρατά τε καὶ ἀσπίδας, ἐπειδήπερ ἀγαθόν ἐστιν;—
Μάλα δήπου, ἔφη ὁ Κτήσιππος· σὺ δ' οὐκ οἴει, ὦ Εὐθύδημε,
5 ἀλλὰ μίαν καὶ ἓν δόρυ;—Ἔγωγε.—Ἦ καὶ τὸν Γηρυόνην ἄν,

ἔφη, καὶ τὸν Βριάρεων οὕτως σὺ ὁπλίσαις; ἐγὼ δὲ ᾤμην σὲ δεινότερον εἶναι, ἅτε ὁπλομάχην ὄντα, καὶ τόνδε τὸν ἑταῖρον.

Καὶ ὁ μὲν Εὐθύδημος ἐσίγησεν· ὁ δὲ Διονυσόδωρος πρὸς τὰ πρότερον ἀποκεκριμένα τῷ Κτησίππῳ ἤρετο, Οὐκοῦν καὶ d χρυσίον, ἦ δ᾽ ὅς, ἀγαθὸν δοκεῖ σοι εἶναι ἔχειν;—Πάνυ, καὶ ταῦτά γε πολύ, ἔφη ὁ Κτήσιππος.—Τί οὖν; ἀγαθὰ οὐ δοκεῖ σοι χρῆναι ἀεί τ᾽ ἔχειν καὶ πανταχοῦ;—Σφόδρα γ᾽, ἔφη.—Οὐκοῦν καὶ τὸ χρυσίον ἀγαθὸν ὁμολογεῖς εἶναι;— 5 Ὡμολόγηκα μὲν οὖν, ἦ δ᾽ ὅς.—Οὐκοῦν ἀεὶ δεῖ αὐτὸ ἔχειν καὶ πανταχοῦ καὶ ὡς μάλιστα ἐν ἑαυτῷ; καὶ εἴη ἂν εὐδαιμονέστατος εἰ ἔχοι χρυσίου μὲν τρία τάλαντα ἐν τῇ γαστρί, e τάλαντον δ᾽ ἐν τῷ κρανίῳ, στατῆρα δὲ χρυσοῦ ἐν ἑκατέρῳ τὠφθαλμῷ;—Φασί γε οὖν, ὦ Εὐθύδημε, ἔφη ὁ Κτήσιππος, τούτους εὐδαιμονεστάτους εἶναι Σκυθῶν καὶ ἀρίστους ἄνδρας, οἳ χρυσίον τε ἐν τοῖς κρανίοις ἔχουσιν πολὺ τοῖς ἑαυτῶν, 5 ὥσπερ σὺ νυνδὴ ἔλεγες τὸν κύνα τὸν πατέρα, καὶ ὁ θαυμασιώτερόν γε ἔτι, ὅτι καὶ πίνουσιν ἐκ τῶν ἑαυτῶν κρανίων κεχρυσωμένων, καὶ ταῦτα ἐντὸς καθορῶσιν, τὴν ἑαυτῶν κορυφὴν ἐν ταῖς χερσὶν ἔχοντες.

Πότερον δὲ ὁρῶσιν, ἔφη ὁ Εὐθύδημος, καὶ Σκύθαι τε καὶ 300 οἱ ἄλλοι ἄνθρωποι τὰ δυνατὰ ὁρᾶν ἢ τὰ ἀδύνατα;—Τὰ δυνατὰ δήπου.—Οὐκοῦν καὶ σύ, ἔφη;—Κἀγώ.—Ὁρᾷς οὖν τὰ ἡμέτερα ἱμάτια;—Ναί.—Δυνατὰ οὖν ὁρᾶν ἐστιν ταῦτα.— Ὑπερφυῶς, ἔφη ὁ Κτήσιππος.—Τί δέ; ἦ δ᾽ ὅς.—Μηδέν. 5 σὺ δὲ ἴσως οὐκ οἴει αὐτὰ ὁρᾶν· οὕτως ἡδὺς εἶ. ἀλλά μοι δοκεῖς, Εὐθύδημε, οὐ καθεύδων ἐπικεκοιμῆσθαι καί, ⟨εἰ⟩ οἷόν τε λέγοντα μηδὲν λέγειν, καὶ σὺ τοῦτο ποιεῖν.

Ἦ γὰρ οὐχ οἷόν τ᾽, ἔφη ὁ Διονυσόδωρος, σιγῶντα b λέγειν;—Οὐδ᾽ ὁπωστιοῦν, ἦ δ᾽ ὃς ὁ Κτήσιππος.—Ἆρ᾽ οὐδὲ λέγοντα σιγᾶν;—Ἔτι ἧττον, ἔφη.—Ὅταν οὖν λίθους λέγῃς καὶ ξύλα καὶ σιδήρια, οὐ σιγῶντα λέγεις;—Οὔκουν εἴ γε ἐγώ, ἔφη, παρέρχομαι ἐν τοῖς χαλκείοις, ἀλλὰ φθεγγόμενα 5 καὶ βοῶντα μέγιστον τὰ σιδήρια λέγεται, ἐάν τις ἅψηται·

ὥστε τοῦτο μὲν ὑπὸ σοφίας ἔλαθες οὐδὲν εἰπών. ἀλλ' ἔτι
μοι τὸ ἕτερον ἐπιδείξατον, ὅπως αὖ ἔστιν λέγοντα σιγᾶν.

c   Καί μοι ἐδόκει ὑπεραγωνιᾶν ὁ Κτήσιππος διὰ τὰ παιδικά.
῞Οταν σιγᾷς, ἔφη ὁ Εὐθύδημος, οὐ πάντα σιγᾷς;—Ἔγωγε,
ἦ δ' ὅς.—Οὐκοῦν καὶ τὰ λέγοντα σιγᾷς, εἴπερ τῶν ἁπάντων
ἐστὶν τὰ λέγοντα.—Τί δέ; ἔφη ὁ Κτήσιππος, οὐ σιγᾷ
5 πάντα;—Οὐ δήπου, ἔφη ὁ Εὐθύδημος.—Ἀλλ' ἄρα, ὦ βέλτιστε, λέγει τὰ πάντα;—Τά γε δήπου λέγοντα.—Ἀλλά, ἦ
δ' ὅς, οὐ τοῦτο ἐρωτῶ, ἀλλὰ τὰ πάντα σιγᾷ ἢ λέγει;

d   Οὐδέτερα καὶ ἀμφότερα, ἔφη ὑφαρπάσας ὁ Διονυσόδωρος·
εὖ γὰρ οἶδα ὅτι τῇ ἀποκρίσει οὐχ ἕξεις ὅ τι χρῇ.
Καὶ ὁ Κτήσιππος, ὥσπερ εἰώθει, μέγα πάνυ ἀνακαγχάσας,
῏Ω Εὐθύδημε, ἔφη, ὁ ἀδελφός σου ἐξημφοτέρικεν τὸν λόγον,
5 καὶ ἀπόλωλέ τε καὶ ἥττηται.   Καὶ ὁ Κλεινίας πάνυ ἥσθη
καὶ ἐγέλασεν, ὥστε ὁ Κτήσιππος ἐγένετο πλεῖον ἢ δεκαπλάσιος.   ὁ δέ μοι ⟨δοκεῖ⟩ ἅτε πανοῦργος ὤν, ὁ Κτήσιππος,
παρ' αὐτῶν τούτων αὐτὰ ταῦτα παρηκηκόει· οὐ γάρ ἐστιν
ἄλλων τοιαύτη σοφία τῶν νῦν ἀνθρώπων.

e   Κἀγὼ εἶπον· Τί γελᾷς, ὦ Κλεινία, ἐπὶ σπουδαίοις οὕτω
πράγμασιν καὶ καλοῖς;
Σὺ γὰρ ἤδη τι πώποτ' εἶδες, ὦ Σώκρατες, καλὸν πρᾶγμα;
ἔφη ὁ Διονυσόδωρος.
5 ῎Εγωγε, ἔφην, καὶ πολλά γε, ὦ Διονυσόδωρε.

301 ῏Αρα ἕτερα ὄντα τοῦ καλοῦ, ἔφη, ἢ ταὐτὰ τῷ καλῷ;
Κἀγὼ ἐν παντὶ ἐγενόμην ὑπὸ ἀπορίας, καὶ ἡγούμην
δίκαια πεπονθέναι ὅτι ἔγρυξα, ὅμως δὲ ἕτερα ἔφην αὐτοῦ
γε τοῦ καλοῦ· πάρεστιν μέντοι ἑκάστῳ αὐτῶν κάλλος τι.
5 Ἐὰν οὖν, ἔφη, παραγένηταί σοι βοῦς, βοῦς εἶ, καὶ ὅτι
νῦν ἐγώ σοι πάρειμι, Διονυσόδωρος εἶ;
Εὐφήμει τοῦτό γε, ἦν δ' ἐγώ.
Ἀλλὰ τίνα τρόπον, ἔφη, ἑτέρου ἑτέρῳ παραγενομένου
τὸ ἕτερον ἕτερον ἂν εἴη;

ᾎρα τοῦτο, ἔφην ἐγώ, ἀπορεῖς; Ἤδη δὲ τοῖν ἀνδροῖν b
τὴν σοφίαν ἐπεχείρουν μιμεῖσθαι, ἅτε ἐπιθυμῶν αὐτῆς.

Πῶς γὰρ οὐκ ἀπορῶ, ἔφη, καὶ ἐγὼ καὶ οἱ ἄλλοι ἅπαντες
ἄνθρωποι ὃ μὴ ἔστι;

Τί λέγεις, ἦν δ' ἐγώ, ὦ Διονυσόδωρε; οὐ τὸ καλὸν καλόν 5
ἐστιν καὶ τὸ αἰσχρὸν αἰσχρόν;—Ἐὰν ἔμοιγε, ἔφη, δοκῇ.—
Οὐκοῦν δοκεῖ;—Πάνυ γ', ἔφη.—Οὐκοῦν καὶ τὸ ταὐτὸν ταὐτὸν
καὶ τὸ ἕτερον ἕτερον; οὐ γὰρ δήπου τό γε ἕτερον ταὐτόν, ἀλλ'
ἔγωγε οὐδ' ἂν παῖδα ᾤμην τοῦτο ἀπορῆσαι, ὡς οὐ τὸ ἕτερον c
ἕτερόν ἐστιν. ἀλλ', ὦ Διονυσόδωρε, τοῦτο μὲν ἑκὼν παρῆκας,
ἐπεὶ τὰ ἄλλα μοι δοκεῖτε ὥσπερ οἱ δημιουργοὶ οἷς ἕκαστα
προ ηκει ἀπεργάζεσθαι, καὶ ὑμεῖς τὸ διαλέγεσθαι παγκάλως
ἀπεργάζεσθαι. 5

Οἶσθα οὖν, ἔφη, ὅ τι προσήκει ἑκάστοις τῶν δημιουργῶν;
πρῶτον τίνα χαλκεύειν προσήκει, οἶσθα;—Ἔγωγε· ὅτι χαλκέα.—Τί δέ, κεραμεύειν;—Κεραμέα.—Τί δέ, σφάττειν τε
καὶ ἐκδέρειν καὶ τὰ μικρὰ κρέα κατακόψαντα ἕψειν καὶ ὀπτᾶν;
—Μάγειρον, ἦν δ' ἐγώ.—Οὐκοῦν ἐάν τις, ἔφη, τὰ προσή- d
κοντα πράττῃ, ὀρθῶς πράξει;—Μάλιστα.—Προσήκει δέ γε,
ὡς φῄς, τὸν μάγειρον κατακόπτειν καὶ ἐκδέρειν; ὡμολόγησας
ταῦτα ἢ οὔ;—Ὡμολόγησα, ἔφην, ἀλλὰ συγγνώμην μοι ἔχε.
—Δῆλον τοίνυν, ἦ δ' ὅς, ὅτι ἄν τις σφάξας τὸν μάγειρον καὶ 5
κατακόψας ἑψήσῃ καὶ ὀπτήσῃ, τὰ προσήκοντα ποιήσει· καὶ
ἐὰν τὸν χαλκέα τις αὐτὸν χαλκεύῃ καὶ τὸν κεραμέα κεραμεύῃ,
καὶ οὗτος τὰ προσήκοντα πράξει.

Ὦ Πόσειδον, ἦν δ' ἐγώ, ἤδη κολοφῶνα ἐπιτιθεὶς τῇ e
σοφίᾳ. ἆρά μοί ποτε αὕτη παραγενήσεται ὥστε μοι οἰκεία
γενέσθαι;

Ἐπιγνοίης ἂν αὐτήν, ὦ Σώκρατες, ἔφη, οἰκείαν γενο-
μένην; 5

Ἐὰν σύ γε βούλῃ, ἔφην ἐγώ, δῆλον ὅτι.

Τί δέ, ἦ δ' ὅς, τὰ σαυτοῦ οἴει γιγνώσκειν;

Εἰ μή τι σὺ ἄλλο λέγεις· ἀπὸ σοῦ γὰρ δεῖ ἄρχεσθαι,
τελευτᾶν δ' εἰς Εὐθύδημον τόνδε.

10 Ἆρ' οὖν, ἔφη, ταῦτα ἡγῇ σὰ εἶναι, ὧν ἂν ἄρξῃς καὶ ἐξῇ
302 σοι αὐτοῖς χρῆσθαι ὅ τι ἂν βούλῃ; οἷον βοῦς καὶ πρόβατον,
ἆρ' ἂν ἡγοῖο ταῦτα σὰ εἶναι, ἅ σοι ἐξείη καὶ ἀποδόσθαι
καὶ δοῦναι καὶ θῦσαι ὅτῳ βούλοιο θεῶν; ἃ δ' ἂν μὴ οὕτως
ἔχῃ, οὐ σά;
5 Κἀγώ (ἤδη γὰρ ὅτι ἐξ αὐτῶν καλόν τι ἀνακύψοιτο τῶν
ἐρωτημάτων, καὶ ἅμα βουλόμενος ὅτι τάχιστ' ἀκοῦσαι)
Πάνυ μὲν οὖν, ἔφην, οὕτως ἔχει· τὰ τοιαῦτά ἐστιν μόνα
ἐμά.—Τί δέ; ζῷα, ἔφη, οὐ ταῦτα καλεῖς ἃ ἂν ψυχὴν ἔχῃ;
b —Ναί, ἔφην.—Ὁμολογεῖς οὖν τῶν ζῴων ταῦτα μόνα εἶναι
σά, περὶ ἃ ἄν σοι ἐξουσία ᾖ πάντα ταῦτα ποιεῖν ἃ νυνδὴ
ἐγὼ ἔλεγον;—Ὁμολογῶ.—Καὶ ὅς, εἰρωνικῶς πάνυ ἐπισχὼν
ὥς τι μέγα σκοπούμενος, Εἰπέ μοι, ἔφη, ὦ Σώκρατες, ἔστιν
5 σοι Ζεὺς πατρῷος;—Καὶ ἐγὼ ὑποπτεύσας ἥξειν τὸν λόγον
οἷπερ ἐτελεύτησεν, ἄπορόν τινα στροφὴν ἔφευγόν τε καὶ
ἐστρεφόμην ἤδη ὥσπερ ἐν δικτύῳ εἰλημμένος· Οὐκ ἔστιν, ἦν
δ' ἐγώ, ὦ Διονυσόδωρε.—Ταλαίπωρος ἄρα τις σύ γε ἄνθρω-
c πος εἶ καὶ οὐδὲ Ἀθηναῖος, ᾧ μήτε θεοί πατρῷοί εἰσιν μήτε
ἱερὰ μήτε ἄλλο μηδὲν καλὸν καὶ ἀγαθόν.—Ἔα, ἦν δ' ἐγώ,
ὦ Διονυσόδωρε, εὐφήμει τε καὶ μὴ χαλεπῶς με προδίδασκε.
ἔστι γὰρ ἔμοιγε καὶ βωμοὶ καὶ ἱερὰ οἰκεῖα καὶ πατρῷα καὶ
5 τὰ ἄλλα ὅσαπερ τοῖς ἄλλοις Ἀθηναίοις τῶν τοιούτων.—
Εἶτα τοῖς ἄλλοις, ἔφη, Ἀθηναίοις οὐκ ἔστιν Ζεὺς ὁ πατρῷος;
—Οὐκ ἔστιν, ἦν δ' ἐγώ, αὕτη ἡ ἐπωνυμία Ἰώνων οὐδενί,
οὔθ' ὅσοι ἐκ τῆσδε τῆς πόλεως ἀπῳκισμένοι εἰσὶν οὔθ' ἡμῖν,
d ἀλλὰ Ἀπόλλων πατρῷος διὰ τὴν τοῦ Ἴωνος γένεσιν· Ζεὺς
δ' ἡμῖν πατρῷος μὲν οὐ καλεῖται, ἕρκειος δὲ καὶ φράτριος,
καὶ Ἀθηναία φρατρία.—Ἀλλ' ἀρκεῖ γ', ἔφη ὁ Διονυσόδωρος·
ἔστιν γάρ σοι, ὡς ἔοικεν, Ἀπόλλων τε καὶ Ζεὺς καὶ Ἀθηνᾶ.
5 —Πάνυ, ἦν δ' ἐγώ.—Οὐκοῦν καὶ οὗτοι σοὶ θεοὶ ἂν εἶεν;
ἔφη.—Πρόγονοι, ἦν δ' ἐγώ, καὶ δεσπόται.—Ἀλλ' οὖν σοί
γε, ἔφη· ἢ οὐ σοὺς ὡμολόγηκας αὐτοὺς εἶναι;—Ὡμολόγηκα,
ἔφην· τί γὰρ πάθω;—Οὐκοῦν, ἔφη, καὶ ζῷά εἰσιν οὗτοι οἱ

θεοί; ὡμολόγηκας γὰρ ὅσα ψυχὴν ἔχει ζῷα εἶναι. ἢ οὗτοι e
οἱ θεοὶ οὐκ ἔχουσιν ψυχήν;—Ἔχουσιν, ἦν δ᾽ ἐγώ.—Οὐκοῦν
καὶ ζῷά εἰσιν;—Ζῷα, ἔφην.—Τῶν δέ γε ζῴων, ἔφη, ὡμολόγηκας ταῦτ᾽ εἶναι σά, ὅσα ἄν σοι ἐξῇ καὶ δοῦναι καὶ
ἀποδόσθαι καὶ θῦσαι δὴ θεῷ ὅτῳ ἂν βούλῃ.—Ὡμολόγηκα, 5
ἔφην· οὐκ ἔστιν γάρ μοι ἀνάδυσις, ὦ Εὐθύδημε.—Ἴθι δή μοι
εὐθύς, ἦ δ᾽ ὅς, εἰπέ· ἐπειδὴ σὸν ὁμολογεῖς εἶναι τὸν Δία
καὶ τοὺς ἄλλους θεούς, ἆρα ἔξεστί σοι αὐτοὺς ἀποδόσθαι 303
ἢ δοῦναι ἢ ἄλλ᾽ ὅ τι ἂν βούλῃ χρῆσθαι ὥσπερ τοῖς ἄλλοις
ζῴοις;

Ἐγὼ μὲν οὖν, ὦ Κρίτων, ὥσπερ πληγεὶς ὑπὸ τοῦ λόγου,
ἐκείμην ἄφωνος· ὁ δὲ Κτήσιππός μοι ἰὼν ὡς βοηθήσων, 5
Πυππὰξ ὦ Ἡράκλεις, ἔφη, καλοῦ λόγου.—Καὶ ὁ Διονυσόδωρος, Πότερον οὖν, ἔφη, ὁ Ἡρακλῆς πυππάξ ἐστιν ἢ ὁ
Πυππὰξ Ἡρακλῆς;—Καὶ ὁ Κτήσιππος, Ὦ Πόσειδον, ἔφη,
δεινῶν λόγων. ἀφίσταμαι· ἀμάχω τὼ ἄνδρε.

Ἐνταῦθα μέντοι, ὦ φίλε Κρίτων, οὐδεὶς ὅστις οὐ τῶν b
παρόντων ὑπερεπῄνεσε τὸν λόγον καὶ τὼ ἄνδρε, καὶ γελῶντες
καὶ κροτοῦντες καὶ χαίροντες ὀλίγου παρετάθησαν. ἐπὶ μὲν
γὰρ τοῖς ἔμπροσθεν ἐφ᾽ ἑκάστοις πᾶσι παγκάλως ἐθορύβουν
μόνοι οἱ τοῦ Εὐθυδήμου ἐρασταί, ἐνταῦθα δὲ ὀλίγου καὶ οἱ 5
κίονες οἱ ἐν τῷ Λυκείῳ ἐθορύβησάν τ᾽ ἐπὶ τοῖν ἀνδροῖν καὶ
ἥσθησαν. ἐγὼ μὲν οὖν καὶ αὐτὸς οὕτω διετέθην, ὥστε
ὁμολογεῖν μηδένας πώποτε ἀνθρώπους ἰδεῖν οὕτω σοφούς, c
καὶ παντάπασι καταδουλωθεὶς ὑπὸ τῆς σοφίας αὐτοῖν ἐπὶ
τὸ ἐπαινεῖν τε καὶ ἐγκωμιάζειν αὐτὼ ἐτραπόμην, καὶ εἶπον·
Ὦ μακάριοι σφὼ τῆς θαυμαστῆς φύσεως, οἳ τοσοῦτον πρᾶγμα
οὕτω ταχὺ καὶ ἐν ὀλίγῳ χρόνῳ ἐξείργασθον. πολλὰ μὲν 5
οὖν καὶ ἄλλα οἱ λόγοι ὑμῶν καλὰ ἔχουσιν, ὦ Εὐθύδημέ τε
καὶ Διονυσόδωρε· ἐν δὲ τοῖς καὶ τοῦτο μεγαλοπρεπέστατον,
ὅτι τῶν πολλῶν ἀνθρώπων καὶ τῶν σεμνῶν δὴ καὶ δοκούντων
τὶ εἶναι οὐδὲν ὑμῖν μέλει, ἀλλὰ τῶν ὁμοίων ὑμῖν μόνον. d
ἐγὼ γὰρ εὖ οἶδα ὅτι τούτους τοὺς λόγους πάνυ μὲν ἂν ὀλίγοι

ἀγαπῷεν ἄνθρωποι ὅμοιοι ὑμῖν, οἱ δ' ἄλλοι οὕτω νοοῦσιν
αὑτούς, ὥστ' εὖ οἶδα ὅτι αἰσχυνθεῖεν ἂν μᾶλλον ἐξελέγχοντες
5 τοιούτοις λόγοις τοὺς ἄλλους ἢ αὐτοὶ ἐξελεγχόμενοι. καὶ
τόδε αὖ ἕτερον δημοτικόν τι ͵αὶ πρᾷον ἐν τοῖς λόγοις·
ὁπόταν φῆτε μήτε καλὸν εἶναι μηδὲν μήτε ἀγαθὸν πρᾶγμα
μήτε λευκὸν μηδ' ἄλλο τῶν τοιούτων μηδέν, μηδὲ τὸ παράπαν
e ἑτέρων ἕτερον, ἀτεχνῶς μὲν τῷ ὄντι συρράπτετε τὰ στόματα
τῶν ἀνθρώπων, ὥσπερ καὶ φατέ· ὅτι δ' οὐ μόνον τὰ τῶν
ἄλλων, ἀλλὰ δόξαιτε ἂν καὶ τὰ ὑμέτερα αὐτῶν, τοῦτο πάνυ
χαρίεν τέ ἐστιν καὶ τὸ ἐπαχθὲς τῶν λόγων ἀφαιρεῖται. τὸ
5 δὲ δὴ μέγιστον, ὅτι ταῦτα οὕτως ἔχει ὑμῖν καὶ τεχνικῶς
ἐξηύρηται, ὥστ' ἐ⟨ν⟩ πάνυ ὀλίγῳ χρόνῳ ὁντινοῦν ἂν μαθεῖν
ἀνθρώπων· ἔγνων ἔγωγε καὶ τῷ Κτησίππῳ τὸν νοῦν προσέ-
χων ὡς ταχὺ ὑμᾶς ἐκ τοῦ παραχρῆμα μιμεῖσθαι οἷός τε ἦν.
304 τοῦτο μὲν οὖν τοῦ πράγματος σφῶν τὸ σοφὸν πρὸς μὲν τὸ
ταχὺ παραδιδόναι καλόν, ἐναντίον δ' ἀνθρώπων διαλέγεσθαι
οὐκ ἐπιτήδειον, ἀλλ' ἄν γέ μοι πείθησθε, εὐλαβήσεσθε μὴ
πολλῶν ἐναντίον λέγειν, ἵνα μὴ ταχὺ ἐκμαθόντες ὑμῖν μὴ
5 εἰδῶσιν χάριν. ἀλλὰ μάλιστα μὲν αὐτὼ πρὸς ἀλλήλω μόνω
διαλέγεσθον· εἰ δὲ μή, εἴπερ ἄλλου του ἐναντίον, ἐκείνου
μόνου ὃς ἂν ὑμῖν διδῷ ἀργύριον. τὰ αὐτὰ δὲ ταῦτα, ἐὰν
b σωφρονῆτε, καὶ τοῖς μαθηταῖς συμβουλεύσετε, μηδέποτε
μηδενὶ ἀνθρώπων διαλέγεσθαι ἀλλ' ἢ ὑμῖν τε καὶ αὑτοῖς·
τὸ γὰρ σπάνιον, ὦ Εὐθύδημε, τίμιον, τὸ δὲ ὕδωρ εὐωνό-
τατον, ἄριστον ὄν, ὡς ἔφη Πίνδαρος. ἀλλ' ἄγετε, ἦν δ'
5 ἐγώ, ὅπως κἀμὲ καὶ Κλεινίαν τόνδε παραδέξεσθον.
Ταῦτα, ὦ Κρίτων, καὶ ἄλλα ἄττα ἔτι βραχέα διαλε-
χθέντες ἀπῇμεν. σκόπει οὖν ὅπως συμφοιτήσεις παρὰ τὼ
c ἄνδρε, ὡς ἐκείνω φατὸν οἵω τε εἶναι διδάξαι τὸν ἐθέλοντ'
ἀργύριον διδόναι, καὶ οὔτε φύσιν οὔθ' ἡλικίαν ἐξείργειν
οὐδεμίαν—ὃ δὲ καὶ σοὶ μάλιστα προσήκει ἀκοῦσαι, ὅτι οὐδὲ
τοῦ χρηματίζεσθαί φατον διακωλύειν οὐδέν—μὴ οὐ παρα-
5 λαβεῖν ὁντινοῦν εὐπετῶς τὴν σφετέραν σοφίαν.

ΚΡ. Καὶ μήν, ὦ Σώκρατες, φιλήκοος μὲν ἔγωγε καὶ ἡδέως ἄν τι μανθάνοιμι, κινδυνεύω μέντοι κἀγὼ εἷς εἶναι τῶν οὐχ ὁμοίων Εὐθυδήμῳ, ἀλλ᾽ ἐκείνων ὧν δὴ καὶ σὺ ἔλεγες, τῶν ἥδιον ἂν ἐξελεγχομένων ὑπὸ τῶν τοιούτων d λόγων ἢ ἐξελεγχόντων. ἀτὰρ γελοῖον μέν μοι δοκεῖ εἶναι τὸ νουθετεῖν σε, ὅμως δέ, ἅ γ᾽ ἤκουον, ἐθέλω σοι ἀπαγγεῖλαι. τῶν ἀφ᾽ ὑμῶν ἀπιόντων ἴσθ᾽ ὅτι προσελθών τίς μοι περιπατοῦντι, ἀνὴρ οἰόμενος πάνυ εἶναι σοφός, τούτων 5 τις τῶν περὶ τοὺς λόγους τοὺς εἰς τὰ δικαστήρια δεινῶν, Ὦ Κρίτων, ἔφη, οὐδὲν ἀκροᾷ τῶνδε τῶν σοφῶν;—Οὐ μὰ τὸν Δία, ἦν δ᾽ ἐγώ· οὐ γὰρ οἷός τ᾽ ἦ προσστὰς κατακούειν ὑπὸ τοῦ ὄχλου.—Καὶ μήν, ἔφη, ἄξιόν γ᾽ ἦν ἀκοῦσαι.—Τί δέ; ἦν δ᾽ ἐγώ.—Ἵνα ἤκουσας ἀνδρῶν διαλεγομένων οἳ νῦν e σοφώτατοί εἰσι τῶν περὶ τοὺς τοιούτους λόγους.—Κἀγὼ εἶπον· Τί οὖν ἐφαίνοντό σοι;—Τί δὲ ἄλλο, ἦ δ᾽ ὅς, ἢ οἷάπερ ἀεὶ ἄν τις τῶν τοιούτων ἀκοῦσαι ληρούντων καὶ περὶ οὐδενὸς ἀξίων ἀναξίαν σπουδὴν ποιουμένων; (οὑτωσὶ γάρ πως καὶ 5 εἶπεν τοῖς ὀνόμασιν).—Καὶ ἐγώ, Ἀλλὰ μέντοι, ἔφην, χαρίεν γέ τι πρᾶγμά ἐστιν ἡ φιλοσοφία.—Ποῖον, ἔφη, χαρίεν, ὦ μακάριε; οὐδενὸς μὲν οὖν ἄξιον. ἀλλὰ καὶ εἰ νῦν παρεγένου, 305 πάνυ ἄν σε οἶμαι αἰσχυνθῆναι ὑπὲρ τοῦ σεαυτοῦ ἑταίρου· οὕτως ἦν ἄτοπος, ἐθέλων ἑαυτὸν παρέχειν ἀνθρώποις οἷς οὐδὲν μέλει ὅτι ἂν λέγωσιν, παντὸς δὲ ῥήματος ἀντέχονται. καὶ οὗτοι, ὅπερ ἄρτι ἔλεγον, ἐν τοῖς κράτιστοί εἰσι τῶν 5 νῦν. ἀλλὰ γάρ, ὦ Κρίτων, ἔφη, τὸ πρᾶγμα αὐτὸ καὶ οἱ ἄνθρωποι οἱ ἐπὶ τῷ πράγματι διατρίβοντες φαῦλοί εἰσιν καὶ καταγέλαστοι. Ἐμοὶ δέ, ὦ Σώκρατες, τὸ πρᾶγμα ἐδόκει οὐκ ὀρθῶς ψέγειν οὔθ᾽ οὗτος οὔτ᾽ εἴ τις ἄλλος ψέγει· τὸ b μέντοι ἐθέλειν διαλέγεσθαι τοιούτοις ἐναντίον πολλῶν ἀνθρώπων ὀρθῶς μοι ἐδόκει μέμφεσθαι.

ΣΩ. Ὦ Κρίτων, θαυμάσιοί εἰσιν οἱ τοιοῦτοι ἄνδρες. ἀτὰρ οὔπω οἶδα ὅ τι μέλλω ἐρεῖν. ποτέρων ἦν ὁ προσελθών 5 σοι καὶ μεμφόμενος τὴν φιλοσοφίαν; πότερον τῶν ἀγωνί-

305 b ΠΛΑΤΩΝΟΣ

σασθαι δεινῶν ἐν τοῖς δικαστηρίοις, ῥήτωρ τις, ἢ τῶν τοὺς
τοιούτους εἰσπεμπόντων, ποιητὴς τῶν λόγων οἷς οἱ ῥήτορες
ἀγωνίζονται;

c ΚΡ. Ἥκιστα νὴ τὸν Δία ῥήτωρ, οὐδὲ οἶμαι πώποτ᾽ αὐτὸν
ἐπὶ δικαστήριον ἀναβεβηκέναι· ἀλλ᾽ ἐπαΐειν αὐτόν φασι
περὶ τοῦ πράγματος νὴ τὸν Δία καὶ δεινὸν εἶναι καὶ δεινοὺς
λόγους συντιθέναι.

5 ΣΩ. Ἤδη μανθάνω· περὶ τούτων καὶ αὐτὸς νυνδὴ ἔμελ-
λον λέγειν. οὗτοι γάρ εἰσιν μέν, ὦ Κρίτων, οὓς ἔφη Πρόδικος μεθόρια φιλοσόφου τε ἀνδρὸς καὶ πολιτικοῦ, οἴονται
δ᾽ εἶναι πάντων σοφώτατοι ἀνθρώπων, πρὸς δὲ τῷ εἶναι
καὶ δοκεῖν πάνυ παρὰ πολλοῖς, ὥστε παρὰ πᾶσιν εὐδοκιμεῖν
d ἐμποδὼν σφίσιν εἶναι οὐδένας ἄλλους ἢ τοὺς περὶ φιλοσοφίαν ἀνθρώπους. ἡγοῦνται οὖν, ἐὰν τούτους εἰς δόξαν
καταστήσωσιν μηδενὸς δοκεῖν ἀξίους εἶναι, ἀναμφισβητήτως
ἤδη παρὰ πᾶσιν τὰ νικητήρια εἰς δόξαν οἴσεσθαι σοφίας
5 πέρι. εἶναι μὲν γὰρ τῇ ἀληθείᾳ σφᾶς σοφωτάτους, ἐν δὲ
τοῖς ἰδίοις λόγοις ὅταν ἀποληφθῶσιν, ὑπὸ τῶν ἀμφὶ Εὐθύδημον κολούεσθαι. σοφοὶ δὲ ἡγοῦνται εἶναι πάνυ εἰκότως·
μετρίως μὲν γὰρ φιλοσοφίας ἔχειν, μετρίως δὲ πολιτικῶν,
e πάνυ ἐξ εἰκότος λόγου—μετέχειν γὰρ ἀμφοτέρων ὅσον ἔδει,
ἐκτὸς δὲ ὄντες κινδύνων καὶ ἀγώνων καρποῦσθαι τὴν σοφίαν.

ΚΡ. Τί οὖν; δοκοῦσί σοί τι, ὦ Σώκρατες, λέγειν; οὐ
γάρ τοι ἀλλὰ ὅ γε λόγος ἔχει τινὰ εὐπρέπειαν τῶν ἀνδρῶν.

5 ΣΩ. Καὶ γὰρ ἔχει ὄντως, ὦ Κρίτων, εὐπρέπειαν μᾶλλον
306 ἢ ἀλήθειαν. οὐ γὰρ ῥᾴδιον αὐτοὺς πεῖσαι ὅτι καὶ ἄνθρωποι
καὶ τἆλλα πάντα ὅσα μεταξύ τινοιν δυοῖν ἐστιν καὶ ἀμφο-
τέροιν τυγχάνει μετέχοντα, ὅσα μὲν ἐκ κακοῦ καὶ ἀγαθοῦ,
τοῦ μὲν βελτίω, τοῦ δὲ χείρω γίγνεται· ὅσα δὲ ἐκ δυοῖν
5 ἀγαθοῖν μὴ πρὸς ταὐτόν, ἀμφοῖν χείρω πρὸς ὃ ἂν ἑκάτερον
ᾖ χρηστὸν ἐκείνων ἐξ ὧν συνετέθη· ὅσα δ᾽ ἐκ δυοῖν κακοῖν
συντεθέντα μὴ πρὸς τὸ αὐτὸ ὄντοιν ἐν τῷ μέσῳ ἐστίν, ταῦτα
b μόνα βελτίω ἑκατέρου ἐκείνων ἐστίν, ὧν ἀμφοτέρων μέρος

μετέχουσιν. εἰ μὲν οὖν ἡ φιλοσοφία ἀγαθόν ἐστιν καὶ ἡ πολιτικὴ πρᾶξις, πρὸς ἄλλο δὲ ἑκατέρα, οὗτοι δ᾽ ἀμφοτέρων μετέχοντες τούτων ἐν μέσῳ εἰσίν, οὐδὲν λέγουσιν—ἀμφοτέρων γάρ εἰσι φαυλότεροι—εἰ δὲ ἀγαθὸν καὶ κακόν, τῶν 5 μὲν βελτίους, τῶν δὲ χείρους· εἰ δὲ κακὰ ἀμφότερα, οὕτως ἄν τι λέγοιεν ἀληθές, ἄλλως δ᾽ οὐδαμῶς. οὐκ ἂν οὖν οἶμαι αὐτοὺς ὁμολογῆσαι οὔτε κακὼ αὐτὼ ἀμφοτέρω εἶναι οὔτε c τὸ μὲν κακόν, τὸ δὲ ἀγαθόν· ἀλλὰ τῷ ὄντι οὗτοι ἀμφοτέρων μετέχοντες ἀμφοτέρων ἥττους εἰσὶν πρὸς ἑκάτερον πρὸς ὃ ἥ τε πολιτικὴ καὶ ἡ φιλοσοφία ἀξίω λόγου ἐστόν, καὶ τρίτοι ὄντες τῇ ἀληθείᾳ ζητοῦσι πρῶτοι δοκεῖν εἶναι. 5 συγγιγνώσκειν μὲν οὖν αὐτοῖς χρὴ τῆς ἐπιθυμίας καὶ μὴ χαλεπαίνειν, ἡγεῖσθαι μέντοι τοιούτους εἶναι οἷοί εἰσιν· πάντα γὰρ ἄνδρα χρὴ ἀγαπᾶν ὅστις καὶ ὁτιοῦν λέγει ἐχόμενον φρονήσεως πρᾶγμα καὶ ἀνδρείως ἐπεξιὼν διαπονεῖται. d

ΚΡ. Καὶ μήν, ὦ Σώκρατες, καὶ αὐτὸς περὶ τῶν υἱέων, ὥσπερ ἀεὶ πρός σε λέγω, ἐν ἀπορίᾳ εἰμὶ τί δεῖ αὐτοῖς χρήσασθαι. ὁ μὲν οὖν νεώτερος ἔτι καὶ σμικρός ἐστιν, Κριτόβουλος δ᾽ ἤδη ἡλικίαν ἔχει καὶ δεῖταί τινος ὅστις 5 αὐτὸν ὀνήσει. ἐγὼ μὲν οὖν ὅταν σοὶ συγγένωμαι, οὕτω διατίθεμαι ὥστ᾽ ἐμοὶ δοκεῖ μανίαν εἶναι τὸ ἕνεκα τῶν παίδων ἄλλων μὲν πολλῶν σπουδὴν τοιαύτην ἐσχηκέναι, καὶ περὶ τοῦ γάμου ὅπως ἐκ γενναιοτάτης ἔσονται μητρός, καὶ e περὶ τῶν χρημάτων ὅπως ὡς πλουσιώτατοι, αὐτῶν δὲ περὶ παιδείας ἀμελῆσαι· ὅταν δὲ εἴς τινα ἀποβλέψω τῶν φασκόντων ἂν παιδεῦσαι ἀνθρώπους, ἐκπέπληγμαι καί μοι δοκεῖ εἷς ἕκαστος αὐτῶν σκοποῦντι πάνυ ἀλλόκοτος εἶναι, 5 ὥς γε πρὸς σὲ τἀληθῆ εἰρῆσθαι· ὥστε οὐκ ἔχω ὅπως 307 προτρέπω τὸ μειράκιον ἐπὶ φιλοσοφίαν.

ΣΩ. Ὦ φίλε Κρίτων, οὐκ οἶσθα ὅτι ἐν παντὶ ἐπιτηδεύματι οἱ μὲν φαῦλοι πολλοὶ καὶ οὐδενὸς ἄξιοι, οἱ δὲ σπουδαῖοι ὀλίγοι καὶ παντὸς ἄξιοι; ἐπεὶ γυμναστικὴ οὐ καλὸν δοκεῖ 5 σοι εἶναι, καὶ χρηματιστικὴ καὶ ῥητορικὴ καὶ στρατηγία;

ΚΡ. Ἔμοιγε πάντως δήπου.

ΣΩ. Τί οὖν; ἐν ἑκάστῃ τούτων τοὺς πολλοὺς πρὸς
b ἕκαστον τὸ ἔργον οὐ καταγελάστους ὁρᾷς;

ΚΡ. Ναὶ μὰ τὸν Δία, καὶ μάλα ἀληθῆ λέγεις.

ΣΩ. Ἦ οὖν τούτου ἕνεκα αὐτός τε φεύξῃ πάντα τὰ
ἐπιτηδεύματα καὶ τῷ υἱεῖ οὐκ ἐπιτρέψεις;

5 ΚΡ. Οὔκουν δίκαιόν γε, ὦ Σώκρατες.

ΣΩ. Μὴ τοίνυν ὅ γε οὐ χρὴ ποίει, ὦ Κρίτων, ἀλλ᾽ ἐάσας
χαίρειν τοὺς ἐπιτηδεύοντας φιλοσοφίαν, εἴτε χρηστοί εἰσιν
εἴτε πονηροί, αὐτὸ τὸ πρᾶγμα βασανίσας καλῶς τε καὶ εὖ,
c ἐὰν μέν σοι φαίνηται φαῦλον ὄν, πάντ᾽ ἄνδρα ἀπότρεπε,
μὴ μόνον τοὺς υἱεῖς· ἐὰν δὲ φαίνηται οἷον οἶμαι αὐτὸ ἐγὼ
εἶναι, θαρρῶν δίωκε καὶ ἄσκει, τὸ λεγόμενον δὴ τοῦτο, αὐτός
τε καὶ τὰ παιδία.

NOTES ON THE TEXT OF
EUTHYDEMUS

NOTES

ἐν Λυκείῳ. Cf. Pausanias i. 44 : 'The Lyceum is named from **271** Lycus the son of Pandion, but was from the first considered, as it **a** ɪ is now, a temple of Apollo, who was here first called Lyceus.' After Aristotle had made the περίπατος, or covered walk, of the Lyceum the place for teaching his pupils, a scene very similar to that which is described in the *Euthydemus* occurred there. In the *Panathenaicus* 236 D Isocrates says that he had heard how 'some three or four of the vulgar Sophists who pretend to know everything had been sitting in the Lyceum' and railing against him.

ἢ πολύς. The affirmative ἢ in Plato usually begins an answer to **2** a previous speaker, as in *Pol.* 453 E, 530 C, 567 E, *Euthyphr.* 14 B : but Heindorf's proposal to omit it here is rightly rejected by Bekker as too arbitrary.

περιειστήκει. The common reading is περιεστήκει : but Schanz, *Praef.* xiii, refers to Choeroboscus, *Dict.* 596, 27 ἐγένετο εἰστήκειν διὰ τῆς εἰ διφθόγγου.

ὑπερκύψας, 'having leant over.' Cf. Hom. *Epigr.* xiv. 22 ὃς δέ χ' **3** ὑπερκύψῃ, πυρὶ τούτου πᾶν τὸ πρόσωπον φλεχθείη.

Ὁπότερον BT. Cf. *Lys.* 212 C ὁπότερος οὖν αὐτῶν ποτέρου φίλος **6** ἐστίν; *Pol.* 348 B 'Οποτέρως οὖν σοι, ἦν δ' ἐγώ, ἀρέσκει, 'Gentler and less direct than ποτέρως, Would you tell me which of the two ways you prefer? Cf. *Euthyd.* 271 B' (Jowett and L. Campbell). On *Pol.* 348 B, cf. Adam : 'Hermann writes ποτέρως, but the text ought not to be changed either here or in *Euthyd.* 271 A.' In *Lys.* 212 C there is apparently no various reading, and it would be difficult to accommodate Hermann's remarkable conjecture ὁ πότερος, adopted by Adam, to ὁποτέρως, *Pol.* 348 B. Cf. Jann. 2038 : 'The use of the relatives in indirect questions brought them into association with the ordinary or direct interrogatives, and thus rendered them admissible in questions also, *especially in A dialogue,*' i.e. in the dialogue of Classical Antiquity, 500–300 B.C.

8 τρίτος ἀπὸ σοῦ, 'next but one to you,' Socrates himself being counted in.

b 1 'Αξιόχου. Cf. Ps.-Plat. *Ax och.* 364 A Κλεινίαν ὁρῶ τὸν 'Αξιόχου. The sons of the elder Alcibiades were Cleinias (Hdt. viii. 17) and Axiochus, and their sons were the famous Alcibiades and this younger Cleinias, who were therefore first cousins.

3 ἡλικίαν. The first meaning of the word is 'size,' 'stature,' as in Lucian, *Vera Hist.* i. 40 ἄνδρας μεγάλους ὅσον ἡμισταδιαίους τὰς ἡλικίας. But 'stature' being in early years an indication of 'age,' ἡλικία is commonly used in the latter sense, as here.

ἐκεῖνος μὲν ... οὗτος δέ. These words are wrongly referred by Routh and Winckelmann to the two Sophists. In correcting this error Stallbaum seems to fall into another by referring ἐκεῖνος to Cleinias, and οὗτος to Critobulus. In reality ἐκεῖνος indicates the one who is thought of as more remote (ἐκεῖ, *yonder*), being only incidentally mentioned, namely Critobulus, οὗτος the nearer in thought, namely Cleinias, of whom Crito has been chiefly speaking. Cf. Xen. *Mem.* i. 3, 13 τοῦτο τὸ θηρίον, ὃ καλοῦσι καλὸν καὶ ὡραῖον, τοσούτῳ δεινότερόν ἐστι τῶν φαλαγγίων, ὅσῳ ἐκεῖνα μὲν ἁψάμενα, τοῦτο δὲ οὐδ' ἁπτόμενον, ἐὰν δέ τις αὐτὸ θεᾶται, ἐνίησί τι. Demosth. *De Cherson.* 108 τὸ βέλτιστον ἀεί, μὴ τὸ ῥᾷστον ἅπαντας λέγειν· ἐπ' ἐκεῖνο μὲν γὰρ ἡ φύσις αὐτὴ βαδιεῖται, ἐπὶ τοῦτο δὲ τῷ λόγῳ δεῖ προάγεσθαι διδάσκοντα τὸν ἀγαθὸν πολίτην. Cf. Kühner-Blass, *Gr. Gr.* § 467.

Schanz, *N. C. P.* p. 69, understands ἡλικίαν as referring to 'stature,' and ἐκεῖνος to Cleinias, and quotes Xen. *Conv.* iv. 11–12 as proving the superior beauty of Critobulus, though the passage evidently means the very reverse. For after speaking of his own desire to be thought handsome Critobulus says : 'I take more delight in looking upon Cleinias than in all other beautiful things in the world : and I would choose rather to be blind to all other beautiful things than to him alone. And I am vexed by the night and by sleep, because I do not see him, but most thankful to the day and the sun, because they show me Cleinias again.'

4 σκληφρός T, σκλῆφρος B, 'thin,' 'slender,' 'puny': cf. Hesych. σκληφροί· οἱ ἰσχνοὶ καὶ λεπτοὶ τοῖς σώμασιν. Schol. in *Euthyd.* σκληφρὸς ὁ τῷ μὲν χρόνῳ πρεσβύτερος, τῇ δὲ ὄψει νεώτερος δοκῶν.

2

Προφερὴς δὲ ὁ τῷ μὲν χρόνῳ νεώτερος, τῇ δὲ ὄψει πρεσβύτερος. In B there is a marginal note on σκλῆφρος· Οὕτω λέγεται καὶ παρὰ 'Αριστοτέλει ὁ ἰσχνὸς καὶ λεπτὸς τὸ σῶμα. Cf. Aristot. *Somn.* iii. 17, *Probl.* i. 30, 14, where σκληφροί is a better reading than Bekker's σκληροί.

καλὸς καὶ ἀγαθὸς τὴν ὄψιν, 'of a noble presence ' : so Plato describes Parmenides, *Parmen.* 127 B. In Xen. *Conviv.* iii. 7, iv. 10, v. 1 Cleinias is represented as especially proud of his acknowledged beauty.

μετέχει ΒΤ. Heindorf's conjecture μετεῖχε, adopted by Stallbaum 8 and Badham, is quite unnecessary. Socrates is referring to the custom of the two brothers, not merely to yesterday's exhibition.

καινοί τινες αὖ οὗτοι, ὡς ἔοικε, σοφισταί. This sentence formerly 9 assigned by Ficinus, Routh, and others to Socrates, is rightly transferred by recent editors to Crito. The conjecture, ὡς ἔοικε, is much more appropriate to Crito than to Socrates, who knew all about the two Sophists. Stallbaum after σοφισταί interpolates Σω. Ναί. unnecessarily.

αὖ, 'again,' implies that in Crito's opinion they had already had Sophists enough in Athens.

ἐντεῦθέν ποθεν, i.e. from some part of Greece including the islands. C 2

Θουρίους. Thurii or Thurium was a town of Magna Graecia on 3 the Gulf of Tarentum, deriving its name from a neighbouring fountain Thuria. After the destruction of Sybaris by the people of Crotona an Athenian colony was sent out by Pericles (*circ.* 443 B.C.) to found a new city near the ruins. The history of Sybaris and Thurii is given by Strabo, 263, and more fully by Diodorus Siculus, xii. 9–11.

φεύγοντες. Heindorf's conjecture φυγόντες is unnecessary, as φεύγειν means not only ' to go into exile,' but also 'to be in exile.' Both these meanings are well illustrated by Hdt. vi. 103 Κίμωνα τὸν Στησαγόρεω κατέλαβε φυγεῖν ἐξ 'Αθηνέων Πεισίστρατον τὸν 'Ιππαράτεος· καὶ αὐτῷ φεύγοντι ὀλυμπιάδα ἀνελέσθαι τεθρίππῳ συνέβη.

ἐκεῖθεν, i.e. from Thurii. Heindorf points out the error in the 4 statement of Athenaeus xi. 506 ὀνειδίζειν αὐτοῖς (τὸν Πλάτωνα) καὶ τὴν ἐκ Χίου τῆς πατρίδος φυγήν, ἀφ' ἧς ἐν Θουρίοις κατῳκίσθησαν.

περὶ τούσδε τοὺς τόπους, i.e. Greece, in distinction from Italy or Magna Graecia.

3   I 2

271 C   NOTES

5   ὃ δὲ σὺ ἐρωτᾷς τὴν σοφίαν αὐτοῖν, 'but as to what you ask about
their wisdom.' Cf. Xen. *Anab.* v. 5, 20 °Ο δὲ λέγεις βίᾳ παρελθόντας
σκηνοῦν, vi. 1, 29 °Ο δὲ ὑμεῖς ἐννοεῖτε, ὅτι ἧττον ἂν στάσις εἴη, *Oecon.*
c. 15, 6 ὃ δὲ εἶπας ὡς δεῖ μαθεῖν . . . καὶ ἃ δεῖ ποιεῖν, καὶ ὡς δεῖ καὶ
ὁπότε ἕκαστα, *Hier.* c. 6, 12 ὃ δὲ ἐζήλωσας ἡμᾶς, ὡς τοὺς μὲν φίλους
μάλιστα εὖ ποιεῖν δυνάμεθα, *Hellen.* ii. 3, 45 ἃ δ' αὖ εἶπας, ὡς ἐγώ εἰμι
οἷος ἀεί ποτε μεταβάλλεσθαι.
In such passages 'the neuter ὅ, referring to what follows, stands
at the beginning of a proposition, in order to carry back the
thoughts to a preceding assertion' (Matth. *Gk. Gr.* 478). Very
similar to this is the use of *quod* in Latin: cf. Madvig, *Lat. Gr.*
398, Obs. 2.
    τὴν σοφίαν. For the accusative after ἐρωτᾷς cf. *Protag.* 351 E
τὴν ἡδονὴν αὐτὴν ἐρωτῶν εἰ οὐκ ἀγαθόν ἐστιν. *Phileb.* 19 B.
    θαυμασία, ὦ Κρίτων B, Stallbaum, Schanz. This reading is better
than any of the variations proposed. The sense is quite clear:
'What is their wisdom? A marvellous wisdom, Crito, they are
absolutely all-wise.'
6   πάσσοφοι ἀτεχνῶς τώ γε B, Vind. Cf. Kühner-Blass, *Gr. Gr.*
459. i., who refers to 291 A 1 Ἀλλὰ μὴν τό γε εὖ οἶδα, and *Polit.* 305 C
τό γε δὴ κατανοητέον, and adds 'mit durchaus epischer Färbung.'
For τώ γε Bekker and Stallbaum adopt ὡς ἔγωγε T, Ficinus 'equi-
dem,' and regard τώ γε as an error of transcription arising from
the accidental omission of ὡς in ἀτεχνῶς ὡς ἔγωγε, and the subsequent change of ΕΓ into Τ.
    If the latter reading were adopted, ὡς would have its consecutive
sense, 'so that I did not even know before what pancratiasts were.'
Cf. Hdt. i. 163, ii. 135; Xen. *Cyr.* v. 4, 11.
    But the reading of BV is not to be set aside without absolute
necessity. 'Apud Platonem saepius quam apud alios scriptores
articulus demonstrativi pronominis munere fungitur' (Schanz,
N. C. P. p. 79).
    ὅ τι εἶεν. On the recent fashion of printing both the pronoun
and the conjunction as one word, ὅτι, see Introduction, p. 48.
7   παγκρατιασταί. Cf. Schol. in Plat. *Pol.* 338 C παγκρατιαστὴς ὁ
παγκράτιον ἀγωνιζόμενος· ἔστι δὲ τοῦτο ἀγών τις ἐξ ἀτελοῦς πάλης καὶ
ἀτελοῦς πυγμῆς συγκείμενος.
    οὐ ⟨καθ' ἃ⟩ τὼ Ἀκαρνᾶνε ἐγενέσθην. κατὰ B, Vind. ἐγενέσθην is

4

NOTES   271 C

omitted in T, and by Schanz and C. F. Hermann (Teubner), and placed by Badham after μάχεσθαι.

But the tense of ἐγενέσθην shows that its subject is τὼ 'Ακαρνᾶνε, not the Sophists, and instead of removing ἐγενέσθην we need only for κατά read καθ' ἅ. A careful inspection of Codex Clarkianus shows that there has been an erasion after the first a in κα τα (*sic*). Cf. Xen. *Mem.* iv. 6, 5 ὁ εἰδὼς ἅ ἐστι νόμιμα, καθ' ἃ δεῖ πως ἀλλήλοις χρῆσθαι, νόμιμος ἂν εἴη. *Hellen.* i. 7, 29 αὐτὰ τὰ πράγματα, καθ' ἃ καὶ αἱ ἁμιρτίαι δοκοῦσι γεγενῆσθαι.

καὶ μάχῃ, ᾗ πάντων ἔστι κρατεῖν TV, ἔστι om. B : Schanz omits ᾗ d 2 and ἔστι, Madvig conjectures μάχῃ ἡ πάντων κρατεῖ, Badham and Burnet omit the whole clause. Ficinus follows the text of TV : 'hi vero corpore primum pugnare maxime possunt, et eo genere pugnae quo omnia (omnes?) superantur.' Heindorf, rightly retaining the text of TV, explains it as follows : 'Pugnae genere, quod verum est παγκράτιον. Spectant haec liquido ad superiora illa ὅ τι εἶεν οἱ παγκρατιάσται.' But the real meaning of the clause is most clearly shown by what immediately follows, ἐν ὅπλοις γὰρ ... μάχεσθαι. The art of fighting in armour with the real weapons of war was the perfection of military training, as described by Nicias, *Lach.* 181 E, 'he who understands this art could certainly not be hurt at all by any single assailant, perhaps not even by many, but in every way would thus have an advantage.' In *Gorg.* 456 D ἔμαθέ τις πυκτεύειν τε καὶ παγκρατιάζειν καὶ ἐν ὅπλοις μάχεσθαι, ὥστε κρείττων εἶναι καὶ φίλων καὶ ἐχθρῶν, the most important art is named last. Cf. *Legg.* 813 E, 833 E.

καὶ ἀγωνίσασθαι. Schanz omits καί without sufficient reason : in 272 ἀγωνίσασθαι there is an allusion to speaking in person, which is here a 2 contrasted with teaching others.

συγγράφεσθαι λόγους, 'to get speeches composed.' Cf. Quintil. 3 *Inst. Orat.* ii. 15 'Socrates inhonestam sibi credidit orationem quam ei Lysias reo composuerat ; et tum maxime scribere litigatoribus quae illi pro se ipso dicerent erat moris, atque ita iuri quo non licebat pro altero agere fraus adhibebatur.'

παγκρατιαστικῇ τέχνῃ. 'Vellem, interiecto articulo, τῇ παγκρα- 5 τιαστικῇ τέχνῃ' (Heindorf). The article would be out of place, or at least, unnecessary, as 'pancratiastic art' is not here limited to the well-known bodily exercise.

5

272 a   NOTES

6 **ἀργός.** Cf. Eur. *Phoen.* 766 ἐν δ' ἐστὶν ἡμῖν ἀργόν. Schol. ἀργόν·
ἄ-ρακτον καὶ παραλελειμμένον, ὀφεῖλον γενέσθαι καὶ μὴ γενόμενον
(Heindorf).

7 **μηδ' ἀντᾶραι.** Cf. Demosth. 24 Λακεδαιμονίοις μέν ποτε, ὦ ἄνδρες
᾿Αθηναῖοι, ὑπὲρ τῶν δικαίων ἀντήρατε. Thuc. iii. 32 ; Xen. *Cyr.* v. 4, 25.

8 **ἐν τοῖς λόγοις μάχεσθαι,** an allusion to ἐν ὅπλοις μάχεσθαι, 'to fight
in their armour of words.'

b 2 **παραδοῦναι ἐμαυτόν,** 'to give myself over as a pupil.' Cf. 285 c
παραδίδωμι ἐμαυτὸν Διονυσοδώρῳ τούτῳ. *Legg.* vii. 811 E τοὺς νέους
αὐτοῖς παραδιδόναι διδάσκειν τε καὶ παιδεύειν.

7 **ἔχων** Τ, **ἔχω** Β ; cf. 285 E ἀκούω Β (Schanz).

8 **παραμύθιον τοῦ μὴ φοβεῖσθαι.** The article with the infinitive
expresses the purpose or effect of the παραμύθιον. Cf. Aesch. *Prom.*
V. 243 ἐξελυσάμην βροτοὺς τοῦ μὴ διαρραισθέντας εἰς ῞Αιδου μολεῖν.
See Hermann on Viger, *De Idiot. Gr.* not. 271. Paley's suggestion
that in τοῦ μή two constructions are mixed, τὸ μή for ὥστε μή, and
τοῦ μολεῖν is unnecessary.

9 **τῆς σοφίας ἧς ἔγωγε ἐπιθυμῶ, τῆς ἐριστικῆς.** Diogenes Laertius in
his life of Protagoras (ix. 55) names first in a list of the works of
Protagoras then extant Τέχνη ἐριστικῶν. In Plato the word ἐριστικός
first appears in *Lys.* 211 B ἀλλὰ ὅρα ὅπως ἐπικουρήσεις μοι, ἐάν με
ἐλέγχειν ἐπιχειρῇ ὁ Μενέξενος· ἢ οὐκ οἶσθα ὅτι ἐριστικός ἐστιν ; In the
Meno, 80 E, the argument that a man cannot inquire about that
which he knows, or about that which he does not know, is termed
an ἐριστικὸς λόγος, and contrasted with the doctrine that the soul
is immortal and knows all things by reminiscence : 'and therefore
we must not believe this ἐριστικῷ λόγῳ for it would make us idle,
and is sweet to the ear of the feeble.' Cf. *Meno* 75 C, *Soph.*
225 D.

In Aristot. *Soph. El.* xi we find the following definition : 'Eristice
is illegitimate fighting in disputation. The competitor who is bent
on victory at all hazards sticks at no artifice ; no more does the
eristic reasoner. If victory is his final motive, he is called contentious and eristic (ἐριστικοὶ καὶ φιλέριδες) ; if professional reputation
and lucre, sophistic. For Sophistic is, as I said before, a money-
making art ' (Poste).

c 1 **αὖ** Β, **αὐτός** Τ. αὖ has its usual sense 'again,' for Socrates adds
that he had already brought disgrace upon one of his teachers.

6

NOTES 272 C

περιάψω, 'hoc proprie adhibetur de infamia vel labe, qua quem 2
aspergimus' (Heindorf). Cf. Lysias 164, 1 εἰ σωθεὶς αἰσχρῶς ὀνείδη
καὶ ἐμαυτῷ καὶ ἐκείνοις περιάψω.
Κόννῳ τῷ Μητροβίου. Cf. 295 D, *Menex*. 235 E. On the supposed
identity of Κόννος with Κοννᾶς, who gave the name to a comedy of
Ameipsias, see the long dissertation of Winckelmann, *Prolegomena*,
cap. viii.
τῷ κιθαριστῇ... κιθαρίζειν. Badham proposed to omit the former,
and Schanz the latter, but without authority or necessity. On the
affinity of music to philosophy cf. *Lach*. 188 D καὶ κομιδῇ μοι δοκεῖ
μουσικὸς ὁ τοιοῦτος εἶναι ἁρμονίαν καλλίστην ἡρμοσμένος οὐ λύραν οὐδὲ
παιδιᾶς ὄργανα, ἀλλὰ τῷ ὄντι ζῆν ἡρμοσμένος. Athen. 632 C Κἀμοὶ δὲ
διὰ τοῦτο φαίνεται φιλοσοφητέον εἶναι περὶ μουσικῆς. Καὶ γὰρ Πυθαγόρας
ὁ Σάμιος, τηλικαύτην δόξαν ἔχων ἐπὶ φιλοσοφίᾳ καταφανής ἐστιν ἐκ
πολλῶν οὐ παρέργως ἁψάμενος μουσικῆς... τὸ δὲ ὅλον ἔοικεν ἡ παλαιὰ
τῶν Ἑλλήνων σοφία τῇ μουσικῇ μάλιστα εἶναι δεδομένη... καὶ πάντας
τοὺς χρωμένους τῇ τέχνῃ ταύτῃ σοφιστὰς ἀπεκάλουν, ὥσπερ καὶ Αἰσχυλος
ἐποίησεν 'Εἴτ' οὖν σοφιστὴς καλὰ παραπαίων χέλυν.'
οἱ συμφοιτηταί μου ἐμοῦ τε... ΒΤ. Badham omits μου, for 4
which Stallbaum and Schanz adopt μοι from Vindob. But it is
not likely that μοι, if original, would be changed into μου immediately before ἐμοῦ. There is not the same reason for μοι here as in
συμμαθητάς μοι φοιτᾶν below. In B there is a light stroke, seemingly meant for a comma, between μου, and ἐμοῦ.
ἴσως φοβούμενοι τάχα. 'Obvius hic apud Atticos pleonasmus in 6
Platone quidem frequentissimus est. ἴσως τάχ' ἄν *Tim*. 38 E, *Legg*.
iii. 676 C, 686 D, *Apol*. 31 A' (Heind.).
καὶ σὺ τί οὐ συμφοιτᾷς; ὡς Winckelmann. The objection to the d 1
reading of the best MSS. καὶ σύ τί που συμφοῖτα· ἴσως ΒΤ is that
πού seems never to be joined with an imperative.
ἄξομεν T et ἔξομεν Vind., ἔξομεν B. 'And as a bait for them we 2
will take with us your sons.'
υἱεῖς. 'The late accusative singular υἱέα, reprehended by Phrynichus, with its consort υἱέας, has not found its way into any
Attic text' (Rutherford, *N. Phryn*. 143). Cf. Kühner-Blass,
i. § 138 Anmerk. 3: Schanz, Plat. *Legg*. Praef. p. viii. § 5
'P. Foucart hanc observationem ex inscriptionibus Atticis elicuit
(*Revue de Philologie*, i. 35): une série d'exemples, depuis le
7

cinquième siècle jusqu'au deuxième avant notre ère, montre que, au moins en prose, les Athéniens employaient toujours la forme *ὑός.*' Schanz adds : 'In Clarkiano huius scripturae, quod sciam, nullum est vestigium ; in Parisino omnibus fere locis *ὑός* reperitur.' The Codex Clarkianus being our best authority in the *Euthydemus,* which is not contained in the Parisinus, I have not taken upon myself to rewrite our chief MS. in respect of this word.

6   ὅ τι καὶ μαθησόμεθα, 'what it is we are going to learn.' On the force of καί see Riddell, Plat. *Apol.* 176.

7   οὐκ ἂν φθάνοις ἀκούων, 'iamiam audies.' The ordinary explanation, 'you cannot hear it too soon,' is far better than Hermann's elaborate and confusing note on Viger, *De Idiotismis Gr.* 320. Cf. Kühner-Jelf, § 694, Obs. 2.

e 1   κατὰ θεὸν γάρ τινα. Cf. Plat. *Legg.* iii. 682 A κατὰ θεόν πως εἰρημένα καὶ κατὰ φύσιν. The phrase is generally used in a favourable sense, 'by some good providence,' but sometimes in a bad sense, as in Eur. *Iph. in Aul.* 411 Ἑλλὰς δὲ σὺν σοὶ κατὰ θεὸν νοσεῖ τινα, 'according to the will of some god.'

3   ἀναστῆναι, 'to rise up and go away.' Cf. Plat. *Protag.* 311 A ἀναστάντες εἰς τὴν αὐλὴν περιῇμεν. *Phaed.* 116 A ἀνίστατο εἰς οἴκημά τι ὡς λουσόμενος.

τὸ εἰωθὸς σημεῖον τὸ δαιμόνιον. Cf. *Phaedr.* 242 B. In the *Apologia* 31 D Socrates describes this as a divine intimation which had come to him ever since he was a child (θεῖόν τι καὶ δαιμόνιον ... ἐκ παιδὸς ἀρξάμενον): he calls it a voice which only came to forbid something that he was about to do, but never commanded him to do anything. It was no kind of personal being, no 'genius familiaris,' nor any 'strange god,' as Meletus had misrepresented it in his indictment, but a sudden and spontaneous impression and conviction, which Socrates regarded as a divine intimation. This was usually prohibitive according to Plato, as here, forbidding him to move : but according to Xenophon, *Mem.* i. 1, 4, it was positive as well as negative, bidding as well as forbidding. For fuller accounts see Zeller, *Socrates* 82 ; Riddell, *Plato's Apology of Socrates,* Appendix A; Xen. *Mem.* Kühner, *Proleg.* 22 ; Plutarch. *Mor.* 575, *De Genio Socratis* ; W. Pater, *Plato* 78; Montaigne, *Of Prognostications* : 'The Daemon of Socrates, &c.'

8

NOTES 273 a

μαθηταί. By placing this immediately before ἐμοὶ δοκεῖν Badham 273
makes the connexion more evident.   a 2
καὶ ἄλλοι μαθηταὶ ἅμα αὖ πολλοὶ ἐμοὶ δοκεῖν. αὖ is found in B,
but omitted in T Vind., and altered by Schanz to αὐτοῖν.
If retained it may be rendered 'besides' or 'also,' as in *Protag.*
323 A τόδε αὖ λαβὲ τεκμήριον, 326 A οἵ τ' αὖ κιθαρισταί. Badham places
μαθηταί immediately before ἐμοὶ δοκεῖν, in order to make the connexion clearer, 'disciples as it seemed to me.' Without this
transposition Ficinus gives the same sense: 'et alii multi cum illis,
qui illorum mihi discipuli videbantur.' Schanz supposes that ξένοι
or some such word has dropped out before ἐμοὶ δοκεῖν. There is
probably some error in the text of B, for αὖ seems to be superfluous after καὶ ἄλλοι μαθηταὶ ἅμα, 'and disciples besides with them.'
On αὖ and other 'expletives' see Jannaris 1700 (1).

εἰσελθόντες δὲ περιεπατείτην BT, εἰσελθόντε π. Vind. 'probavit 3
Cobet' (Schanz). The dual and plural are so frequently inter-
changed in the context that it is hardly necessary to alter the
reading of BT.

δρόμῳ. Cf. Ruhnk. *Tim. Lex.* Δρόμοι sunt loca cursibus destinata,
sive ambulacra publica. *Theaet.* 15 B ἄρτι γὰρ ἐν τῷ ἔξω δρόμῳ
ἠλείφοντο. Ubi Scholiastes: τόποι τινὲς ἦσαν, ὁ μὲν ἐκτὸς ἄστεος, ὁ δὲ
ἐντός, ἀπὸ τῶν ἐν αὐτοῖς τελουμένων ὑπὸ τῶν νέων Δρόμοι καλούμενοι.
Cf. *Phaedr.* 227 A κατὰ τὰς ὁδοὺς ποιοῦμαι τοὺς περιπάτους· φησὶ γὰρ
ἀκοπωτέρους εἶναι τῶν ἐν τοῖς δρόμοις.

οὔπω... περιεληλυθότε ἥστην, καὶ εἰσέρχεται. On this use of καί 4
after a definition of time, so frequent in the New Testament, cf.
277 B οὔπω... ταῦτα εἴρητο... καὶ ὁ Διονυσόδωρος... Thuc. i. 50
Ἤδη δὲ ἦν ὀψὲ καὶ οἱ Κορίνθιοι ἐξαπίνης πρύμναν ἐκρούοντο. Xen. *Cyr.*
ii. 1, 10 σχεδόν τε ἕτοιμα ἦν καὶ τῶν Περσῶν οἱ ὁμότιμοι παρῆσαν. *Anab.*
i. 2, 18.

πολλοί τε [καὶ] ἄλλοι καὶ Κτήσιππος. Cf. Schanz, *Nov. Com. Plat.* 6
p. 56 'quod coniectando invenimus, optimo libro Clarkiano con-
firmatum vidimus, qui καί omisit.'

Παιανιεύς. Paeania was a borough (δῆμος) of the tribe Pandionis. 7
Demosthenes belonged to Paeania.

ὅσον μὴ ὑβριστὴς [δὲ] διὰ τὸ νέος εἶναι BT. Winckelmann omits 8
δέ as an error caused by διά following, and compares 301 B *Ἤδη δὲ
τοῖν ἀνδροῖν τὴν σοφίαν ἐπεχείρουν μιμεῖσθαι*, where for δέ cod. B has

9

διά. ὅσον μὴ ὑβριστής quite literally means 'as far as he was not boisterous,' i.e. 'except that he was boisterous.' The construction is the same as in *Phaed.* 64 D καθ' ὅσον μὴ πολλὴ ἀνάγκη μετέχειν αὐτῶν, 'except so far as it is absolutely necessary to have to do with them': ibid. 83 A πείθουσα δὲ ἐκ τούτων μὲν ἀναχωρεῖν ὅσον μὴ ἀνάγκη αὐτοῖς χρῆσθαι. Plut. *Timol.* iii. πρᾷος διαφερόντως ὅσα μὴ σφόδρα μισοτύραννος εἶναι.

b 1 ἀπὸ τῆς εἰσόδου, 'having from the entrance caught sight of me sitting alone.'

4 ἐπιστάντε διελεγέσθην, 'stopped short and began to talk to each other.' Cf. 172 A κἀγὼ ἐπιστὰς περιέμεινα. *Symp.* 212 D ἐπιστῆναι ἐπὶ τὰς θύρας.

ἄλλην καὶ ἄλλην ἀποβλέποντε, sc. ὄψιν, 'glancing now and then.' 'Usitatius fuisset ἄλλῃ καὶ ἄλλῃ'(Heind.); but that would have meant 'this way and that,' which is not the meaning here.

6 ἰόντε, 'they came and sat down, one of them, Euthydemus, beside the youth, and the other beside myself on the left.'

7 Εὐθύδημος B, ὁ Εὐθύδημος T. Schanz adopts the article in his edition, 1880, though he had shown in the *Novae Commentationes Platonicae*, p. 64, that it is often omitted even in a renewed mention of the name as in 289 E, 294 C, 297 B, D, and elsewhere frequently.

παρ' αὐτὸν ἐμέ. Winckelmann reads παρ' αὖ τὸν ἐμέ, and for the position of αὖ between a preposition and its case refers to *Pol.* 371 D τοῖς δὲ ἀντὶ αὖ ἀργυρίου διαλλάττειν: *Politic.* 302 D ἐκ δ' αὖ τῶν μὴ πολλῶν ἐκ δ' αὖ τῶν πολλῶν: *Phaed.* 71 A ἀπὸ δ' αὖ τοῦ ἑτέρου. For τὸν ἐμέ cf. *Theaet.* 166 A γέλωτα δὴ τὸν ἐμὲ ἐν τοῖς λόγοις ἀπέδειξε. The conjecture though simple and ingenious is unnecessary.

c 2 μέντοι seems to have an explanatory as well as an assertive force; giving a reason why he welcomed them: 'These two gentlemen, you know, Cleinias, are skilled not in trifling things, but in those of great importance.'

6 καὶ ὅσα ἐν ὅπλοις μάχεσθαι διδακτέον. Schanz brackets μάχεσθαι, following Badham, but suggests as a better reading καὶ ἐν ὅπλοις μάχεσθαι, omitting both ὅσα and διδακτέον. There seems to be no need for any alteration in the text of the MSS., 'and all necessary teaching to fight in arms.'

d 1 κατεφρονήθην is the inference which Socrates drew from their looks and laughter: 'I saw that they despised me.'

βλέψαντες εἰς ἀλλήλους B, βλέψαντες εἰς ἀλλήλους T. Cf. Plat. 2
Phaedr. 278 B νὼ καταβάντε ἐς τὸ Νυμφῶν, where καταβάντες (Steph.)
may be due to the ἐς following. Here, however, βλέψαντες
was probably the original reading, corresponding to ἀλλήλους,
for ἀλλήλω T² is a very doubtful correction. On the combination of
a dual subject with a plural participle see Kühner-Blass, § 368;
Jannaris, *Gk. Gr.* 1172; Xen. *Mem.* i. 2, 33 καλέσαντες ὅ τε Κριτίας
καὶ ὁ Χαρικλῆς τὸν Σωκράτην τόν τε νόμον ἐδεικνύτην αὐτῷ.

τὸ ἔργον . . . πάρεργα, 'your work must be something grand, if 5
matters so great as these are your amusements.'

Ὠ Ζεῦ, ἦν δ' ἐγώ. The reading of BT, ἔφην ἦν δ' ἐγώ, may e 1
probably have arisen from a marginal quotation or reminiscence
of 294 A Ὠ Ζεῦ, ἔφην ἐγώ, since ἔφην in our present passage is an
evident gloss or interpretation.

λέγετον πρᾶγμα. Cobet would omit λέγετον without any sufficient
reason.

ἑρμαῖον. Any great good fortune or unexpected gain was 2
attributed to the influence of Hermes. Cf. 295 A, *Symp.* 217 A
ἑρμαῖον ἡγησάμην εἶναι καὶ εὐτύχημα ἐμὸν θαυμαστόν. Ruhnk. *Tim.*
Lex. Ἑρμαῖον· εὕρεμα. Stallb. Plat. *Phaed.* 107 C 'ἑρμαῖον interprete
Scholiasta est τὸ ἀπροσδόκητον κέρδος· ἀπὸ τῶν ἐν ταῖς ὁδοῖς τιθεμένων
ἀπαρχῶν, ἃς οἱ ὁδοιπόροι κατεσθίουσι· ταίτας δὲ τῷ Ἑρμῇ ἀφιεροῦσιν ὡς
ὄντι καὶ τούτῳ ἐνὶ τῶν ἐνοδίων θεῶν.' Preller, *Gr. Myth.* 403.

τοῦτο is not to be joined with τὸ πολύ, but is explained by ἐν 3
ὅπλοις μάχεσθαι, 'clever for the most part in this, I mean in fighting
in armour.'

ἐπεδημησάτην BV, γρ. T; ἐπεδημείτην T. The imperfect would 5
imply that they were at home in Athens, the aorist that they came
to it as visitors. Cf. *Protag.* 310 E ἔτι γὰρ παῖς ἦν ὅτε τὸ πρῶτον
ἐπεδήμησεν.

τοῦτο μέμνημαι σφὼ ἐπαγγελλομένω. 'Non satis notum est Graecos
verbis recordandi participia temporis praesentis adiungere . . . .
Charm. 156 A μέμνημαι Κριτία τῷδε συνόντα σε, *Prot.* 359 C μέμνησαι,
ὦ Πρωταγόρα, ταῦτα ἀποκρινόμενος;' (Schanz, *Nov. Com. Plat.*
p. 70).

ἵλεω εἴητον, 'be merciful.' Cf. Plat. *Phaedr.* 257 A ἀλλὰ τῶν 6
προτέρων τε συγγνώμην καὶ τῶνδε χάριν ἔχων, εὐμενὴς καὶ ἵλεως τὴν

ἐρωτικήν μοι τέχνην, ἣν ἔδωκας, μήτε ἀφέλῃ μήτε πηρώσῃς δι' ὀργήν : ibid.
'εὐμενὴς καὶ ἴλεως solennis est dictio de diis *volentibus propitiisque*' (Heind.).

274 ἐλέγετον BT, 'sed ἐ *in ras. additum videtur* in B' (Schanz).
a 2 'Videte utrum vera loquamini' (Ficinus). Stallbaum sees no reason to alter the reading of the MSS.
7 μέγαν βασιλέα. As every one knew who the 'Great King' was the article was unnecessary, as in the case of a proper name. Cf. Xen. *Mem.* iii. 5, 26 ἐν τῇ βασιλέως χώρᾳ : ibid. *Conv.* iii. 13 τὰ βασιλέως χρήματα.
b 2 ὅτι μέν B, ἀλλ' ὅτι μέν T. That ἀλλά is an unnecessary addition is shown by Schanz, *N. C. P.* p. 63, quoting *Pol.* 412 B, *Phaed.* 87 A. οἱ μὴ ἔχοντες. 'Intell. αὐτήν' (Stallbaum): i. e. 'the unwise will wish to learn of you'; a rather sarcastic compliment.
3 ἐγγυῶμαι. The active voice means 'to give a pledge,' the middle 'I pledge myself,' that is 'I make myself an ἐγγυητής or bail.' Cf. *Protag.* 336 D ἐπεὶ Σωκράτη γε ἐγὼ ἐγγυῶμαι μὴ ἐπιλήσεσθαι.
7 κἀμοὶ δοκεῖν ὡς. Badham rightly argues that ἐμοὶ δοκεῖν BT refers to ἐπεσκόπει, not to ἔτυχε καθεζόμενος, which was not a matter of opinion but of evident fact. He therefore reads κἀμοὶ δοκεῖν ὡς, or ἐμοὶ δὲ δοκεῖν ὡς, either of which is preferable to the awkward conjecture of Schanz πόρρω καθεζόμενος τοῦ Κλεινίου ἐμοὶ δοκεῖν· ὥσθ' ὡς.
c 1 ἐπεσκόπει. The verb seems to be used by Plato only here, but is not uncommon in the Orators and Polybius, and occurs also in Aristot. *Rhet.* i. 1, 7 ἐπισκοπεῖν τῇ κρίσει τὸ ἴδιον ἡδὺ ἢ λυπηρόν.
d 2 αὐτώ Bt, αὐτῷ T. Here T has been corrected, probably from B.
6 ἐπιδείξατον BV, ἐπιδείξασθον T. The reading of B is retained by Winckelmann, Stallbaum, Badham, and Schanz, and justified by 274 A ὡς ἐπιδείξοντε καὶ διδάξοντε, and the many passages of Plato quoted by Winckelmann. As the exhibition is to be made at the request of others, not for their own sake, the active is the right voice, not the middle as in 278 C 4.
τὰ μὲν οὖν πλεῖστα, 'the main part.'
e 2 τὸ πρᾶγμα τὴν ἀρετήν. Hirschig and Badham would omit τὸ πρᾶγμα, and Cobet τὴν ἀρετήν, changing αὐτῆς into αὐτοῦ. Possibly τὸ πρᾶγμα is a marginal gloss intended to explain the use of μαθητόν as a predicate of τὴν ἀρετήν. Cf. Plutarch, *Mor.* 439 Ὅτι διδακτὸν

12

NOTES   274 e

ἡ ἀρετή. Schanz however(*N. C. P.* p. 70) defends τὸ πρᾶγμα, referring
to *Prot.* 327 A τούτου τοῦ πράγματος τῆς ἀρετῆς. See also Jann.
Gk. Gr. 1178 ᵇ.

φέρε, like *age* in Latin, is often found before a question, as if 3
pressing for an immediate answer: ' Come, tell me.' Cf. Plat.
Gorg. 514 D φέρε πρὸς θεῶν, αὐτὸς δὲ ὁ Σωκράτης πῶς ἔχει τὸ σῶμα
πρὸς ὑγίειαν; *Legg.* i. 633 C τὴν ἀνδρείαν δὲ φέρε τί θῶμεν; Aristoph.
Thesmoph. 788 φέρε δή νυν, | εἰ κακόν ἐσμεν, τί γαμεῖθ' ὑμεῖς;
    ἄλλης B², ἄλλως BT : the correction in B was probably made by 5
Arethas.

ἂν προτρέψαιτε. Winckelmann retains the reading of BT, προ- 275
τρέψετε, but the future indicative with ἄν is, to say the least, so a 1
unusual that προτρέψαιτε is certainly to be preferred. Schanz refers
to 278 C 4, where there is a similar variation between ἐνδείξεσθον B,
ἐνδείξαισθον T, and ἐνδείξασθον Vind. i.

υἱός. Schanz and Burnett read ὑός, without any remark. Cf. 10
Zonaras, 1763, ap. Lobeck. *Phryn.* 40 Ὑός, ἄνευ τοῦ ῑ, Ἀττικοί.
Rutherford, *New Phryn.* 143 : ' It is probable that throughout the
Attic period the iota was never written. At all events Herwerden
(*Lapid. de Dial. Att. Test.* pp. 11, 12) distinctly states that in no
Attic inscription of a good age does any form but ὑός appear except
in verse, and even in that case ὑός, ὑεῖς, &c. are sometimes found. ...
The reason for the prevalence of υἱός, υἱέος, &c. in the manuscripts
of Attic writers is not far to seek. Those forms gradually took the
place of ὑός, ὑέος, &c., in stone records after the time of Alexander.'
In Homer, *Il.* vi. 130, xvii. 575, 590, iv. 473, v. 612, vii. 47, where
the word is printed with a diphthong, a *short syllable is required*.
See 272 D 2, note.

αὐτανέψιος, ' own cousin ' : see 271 B 1, note. Cf. Eur. *Heracleid.*
987 ἤδη γε σοὶ μὲν αὐτανέψιος γεγώς. Aesch. *Suppl.* 933, 984.

περὶ αὐτῷ B, περὶ αὐτοῦ T. Both constructions occur frequently, b 2
the dative chiefly in cases of *fearing for* or the contrary. Cf. Thuc.
i. 60 δεδιότες περὶ τῷ χωρίῳ. *Phaed.* 114 D θαρρεῖν χρὴ περὶ τῇ ἑαυτοῦ
ψυχῇ.

εἰ μή τι διαφέρει ὑμῖν. The same phrase occurs in Plat. *Lach.* 187 D 5
εἰ οὖν ὑμῖν μή τι διαφέρει.

ἅμα ἀνδρείως τε καὶ θαρραλέως. Badham objects to ἅμα : ' Absurde 8
praeponitur ἅμα duabus rebus tam similibus quam sunt ἀνδρεία et

13

θάρρος.' Schanz, *N. C. P.* p. 71 replies: 'At ἅμα non pertinet ad ἀνδρείως καὶ θαρραλέως, sed ad ἔφη,' i. e. 'No sooner had I spoken than Euthydemus said,' &c. But in fact 'bravely' and 'confidently' are not synonymous, and ἔφη is too far from ἅμα to be referred to it by 'hyperbaton.'

c 1   ἀποκρίνεσθαι B, ἀποκρίνασθαι T: cf. c 3 τὸ ἀποκρίνασθαι B, τὸ ἀποκρίνεσθαι T. In both passages B gives the better reading: in dependence on the present ἐὰν ἐθέλῃ, indicating a *general* willingness to answer, ἀποκρίνεσθαι alone is right. In c 3 the aorist ἀποκρίνασθαι is rightly used of the answer to be given to a *particular* question: cf. 275 E 1 ἀπόκριναι ἀνδρείως.

2   Ἀλλὰ μὲν δή, 'Why, in truth.' Cf. *Gorg.* 466 B, 471 A, 492 E, 506 B, D.

6   τὸ ἔργον δύνασθαι. Schanz, ibid. p. 71, quotes Xen. *Cyr.* ii. 2, 11 τὰς ψυχὰς αὐτῶν θήγειν ὑμέτερον τὸ ἔργον.

ἀναλαβεῖν διεξιόντα, literally 'to recollect in narrating.' Cf. Plat. *Apol.* 18 D σκιαμαχεῖν ἀπολογούμενον, 'to fight with shadows in defending myself.'

7   διεξιόντα, 'going through in detail': cf. Plat. *Phaed.* 84 c πολλὰς γὰρ δὴ ἔτι ἔχει ὑποψίας καὶ ἀντιλαβάς, εἴ γε δή τις αὐτὰ μέλλει ἱκανῶς διεξιέναι. σοφίαν ἀμήχανον ὅσην. ἀμήχανον as well as ὅσην agrees with σοφίαν. Cf. *Pol.* ix. 588 A ἀμηχάνῳ δὴ ὅσῳ πλείονι νικήσει, vii. 527 E ἀμηχάνως ὡς εὖ δόξεις λέγειν.

d 1   Μούσας τε καὶ Μνήμην. Cf. *Phaedr.* 237 A Ἄγετε δή, ὦ Μοῦσαι, ξύμ μοι λάβεσθε τοῦ μύθου. It is evident that Μνήμη is here not one of the Muses, but their mother, who is more commonly called Μνημοσύνη. Plat. *Theaetet.* 191 D τῆς τῶν Μουσῶν μητρὸς Μνημοσύνης. Aesch. *Prom. V.* 461 μνήμην θ' ἁπάντων μουσομήτορ' ἐργάτιν. Cf. Paus. 795 'The sons of Aloeus thought the Muses were three in number, and named them Μελέτη, Μνήμη, and Ἀοιδή.' Hom. *Hymn in Herm.* 429 Μνημοσύνην μὲν πρῶτα θεῶν ἐγέραιρεν ἀοιδῇ | μητέρα Μουσάων. *Il.* ii. 491 Ὀλυμπιάδες Μοῦσαι, Διὸς αἰγιόχοιο | θυγατέρες. *Od.* xxiv. 60 Μοῦσαι δ' ἐννέα πᾶσαι. Hes. *Theog.* 53:

Μοῦσαι Ὀλυμπιάδες, κοῦραι Διὸς αἰγιόχοιο,
τὰς ἐν Πιερίῃ Κρονίδῃ τέκε πατρὶ μιγεῖσα
Μνημοσύνη.

On the various families of Muses see Plut. *Mor.* 703; Diod. Sic. iv. 7; Cic. *De Nat. Deor.* iii. 21.

NOTES 275 d

μεγάλου. 'H. l. idem est quod χαλεποῦ, prorsus ut Latine 5
magna quaestio dicitur pro difficili. *Hipp. Mai.* 287 Β οὐ μέγα
ἐστὶ τὸ ἐρώτημα, ἀλλὰ καὶ πολὺ τούτου χαλεπώτερα ἂν ἀποκρίνασθαι
ἐγώ σε διδάξαιμι ' (Heindorf). Cic. *Tusc.* i. 4, 23 ' magna quaestio est.'

ἔβλεπεν B, ' began to look,' or ' kept looking ': ἐνέβλεψεν T, ' cast 6
a look.'

πάνυ μειδιάσας, ' with a broad smile.' e 4
ἐξεγένετο. Cf. *Parmen.* 128 E οὐδὲ βουλεύσασθαι ἐξεγένετο. Isocr. 8
De Antidos. 312 οὕτως ἂν ἐκγενέσθαι μοι μάλιστα διαλεχθῆναι περὶ
ἁπάντων ὧν τυγχάνω βουλόμενος.

κιθαριστής. The ' cithara,' ' cittern,' or ' guitar ' was very similar 276
to the lyre, on which see the article *Lyra* in Smith's *Dict. of Gk.* a 5
and R. Antiquities.

γραμματιστής in Herodotus means the scribe or registrar who
kept the accounts of a treasury (ii. 28, iii. 123), or numbered the
army of Xerxes (vii. 100) : but here it evidently means the ' writing-
master,' as in 277 A, and *Charm.* 159 c ἐν γραμματιστοῦ τὰ ὅμοια
γράμματα γράφειν ταχὺ ἢ ἡσυχῇ ;

εἰ μὴ σοφοί, ἀμαθεῖς. The Sophist's trick depends wholly upon b 2
the unfair use of σοφοί and ἀμαθεῖς in two different senses, as
referring (1) to the wish and ability to learn, (2) to the fact of being
at present learned or unlearned. The remedy for this fallacy is to
define the sense in which the terms are used in the present
question.

Οἱ ἀμαθεῖς ἄρα [σοφοὶ] μανθάνουσιν B : σοφοί is omitted in T 4
Vind. If retained, as by Winckelmann and Stallbaum, it must
be taken proleptically, ' learn to be wise.' But a superfluous idea
is thus brought into the argument, and σοφοί is better omitted, as
by most editors.

ὥσπερ ὑπὸ διδασκάλου χορὸς ἀποσημήναντος. Cf. Ps.-Aristot. *De* 6
Mundo vi. 20 καθάπερ δὲ ἐν χορῷ κορυφαίου κατάρξαντος συνεπηχεῖ
πᾶς ὁ χορὸς ἀνδρῶν κτλ.

ἀνεθορύβησαν, ' cheered.' ' Vox ἀναθορυβεῖν propria est de *secunda* 7
admurmuratione. Isocrat. *Panath.* 291 οὐκ ἐθορύβησαν, ὃ ποιεῖν
εἰώθασιν ἐπὶ τοῖς χαριέντως διειλεγμένοις, ἀλλ' ἀνεβόησαν.'

ἐκδεξάμενος, ' took up the discourse,' a metaphor from catching c 2
a ball or anything passed from hand to hand : cf. 277 B ὥσπερ

15

276 c   NOTES

σφαῖραν ἐκδεξάμενος τὸν λόγον. 298 A. *Sympos.* 189 A ἐκδεξάμενον
οὖν ἔφη εἰπεῖν τὸν Ἀριστοφάνη.

3 ἀποστοματίζοι. Cf. Ruhnk. *Tim. Lex.* Ἀποστοματίζειν· ἀπὸ μνήμης
λέγειν. ‘Timaeus et ex eo Suidas h. l. (277 A) exponunt *memoriter
recitare, ore, non scripto, proferre.* At Pollux ii. 102 Ἀποστοματί-
ζεσθαι δὲ τοὺς παῖδας Πλάτων που λέγει, ἤγουν ὑπὸ τῶν διδασκάλων
ἐρωτᾶσθαι τὰ μαθήματα, ὡς ἀπὸ στόματος λέγειν. Polluci consentit
vetus Grammaticus apud Suidam : Ἀποστοματίζειν φασὶ τὸν διδάσκαλον, ὅταν κελεύῃ τὸν παῖδα λέγειν ἅττα ἀπὸ στόματος.’ In our
present passage the former interpretation is to be preferred, for in
ἀποστοματίζοι ὑμῖν the dative shows that it is the master who speaks
ἀπὸ μνήμης and ἀπὸ στόματος.   In St. Luke xi. 53, ἀποστοματίζειν
αὐτὸν περὶ πλειόνων, the other sense is to be preferred, ‘to make Him
speak off-hand of many things,’ as is evident from the accusative
αὐτόν, and from what follows, θηρεῦσαί τι ἐκ τοῦ στόματος αὐτοῦ.

4 ἐμάνθανον ... τὰ ἀποστοματιζόμενα. Cf. Aristot. *De Soph. Elench.*
iv. 526 εἰσὶ δὲ παρὰ μὲν τὴν ὁμωνυμίαν οἱ τοιοῦτοι τῶν λόγων, οἷον ὅτι
μανθάνουσιν οἱ ἐπιστάμενοι· τὰ γὰρ ἀποστοματιζόμενα μανθάνουσιν οἱ
γραμματικοί· τὸ γὰρ μανθάνειν ὁμώνυμον, τό τε ξυνιέναι χρώμενον τῇ
ἐπιστήμῃ καὶ τὸ λαμβάνειν ἐπιστήμην.   See Introduction § vi.   In this
passage οἱ γραμματικοί are of course the pupils, ‘those who know
their letters,’ as in Xen. *Mem.* iv. 2, 20.

7 οὐκ εὖ σύ Burnet : ‘οὐκ εὐθύς BT : οὐκ εὖ scripsit Schanz.’
This good correction by Schanz is still further improved by Burnet’s
addition of σύ.

d 1 καὶ πάνυ μέγα T Vind. It is of course possible that μέγα, which is
omitted in B, may be an interpolation, as Schanz seems to suppose,
from 300 D μέγα πάνυ ἀνακαγχάσας : on the other hand πάνυ ἐγέλασαν
is a very questionable phrase, while the constant use of neuter
adjectives with γελᾶν, and of μέγα with similar verbs such as λέγειν,
βοᾶν, φωνεῖν, ᾄδειν, makes the omission of it here very doubtful.

5 ἠρώτα καί, ‘T Vind. ἠρώτα B : seclusit Schanz’ (Burnet). It is
more likely that καί should have been dropped out in B than ἠρώτα
interpolated in T. Vind., and Schanz therefore was not justified in
omitting the clause.

ὥσπερ οἱ ἀγαθοὶ ὀρχησταί. The dancers in a chorus reversed
their course in the strophe and antistrophe, but something more
complicated than this is indicated in the next words.

16

NOTES 276 d

διπλᾶ ἔστρεφε, 'began to give a double twist to his questions on 6
the same point.' Stallbaum refers to Aristoph. *Thesmoph*. 982
ἔξαιρε δὴ προθύμως διπλῆν χάριν χορείας. Cf. Hesych. διπλῆ· ὀρχήσεως
εἶδος.

μανθάνουσιν ἃ ἐπίστανται ἢ ἃ μὴ ἐπίστανται; The same para- 7
doxical question is brought forward in *Meno* 80 E: 'Do you see
what an eristic argument this is that you are importing, that it is
forsooth impossible for a man to inquire about either what he
knows or what he does not know.' The solution depends on the
double meaning of μανθάνω as explained in Arist. *Soph. El.* iv. 526
and 529 μανθάνει νῦν γράμματα, εἴπερ ἐμάνθανεν ἃ ἐπίσταται.

ὑμῖν BT Vind. The reading of all the MSS. seems to have e 3
been too hastily rejected in favour of ἡμῖν the conjecture of
Stephanus, which is followed by Ficinus. But in the answer of
Socrates there is a fine irony involved in καλὸν ὑμῖν ἐφάνη, 'the
former question was a fine revelation for you.' For this sense of
ἐφάνη, indicating a wonderful or unexpected appearance, cf. 294 A
ὦ Ζεῦ, ἔφην ἐγώ, ὡς θαυμαστὸν λέγεις καὶ ἀγαθὸν μέγα πεφάνθαι.
Pol. 368 D ἕρμαιον ἂν ἐφάνη.

ἐρωτῶμεν ἄφυκτα, 'in all our questions of this kind we leave no 5
escape.'

ἃ οὐκ ἐπίσταιντο. In 276 D, ἃ μὴ ἐπίστανται, there is merely a 9
supposition that the learners are ignorant. In the answer there
is a definite assertion, which in direct oration would be μανθάνουσιν
ἃ οὐκ ἐπίστανται.

οὐκ ἐπίστασαι σὺ γράμματα; The ambiguity of the question is 277
noticed by Aristotle, *Rhet.* ii. 24, 3 τὸν τὰ στοιχεῖα ἐπιστάμενον ὅτι τὸ a 1
ἔπος οἶδεν· τὸ γὰρ ἔπος τὸ αὐτό ἐστιν.

ἆρα σὺ⟨οὐ⟩ μανθάνεις Γ (Coislinianus) Routh, Heindorf: BT omit 6
οὐ. From the antithetical clause ὁ δὲ μὴ ἐπιστάμενος ... μανθάνει
it is evident that both σύ and οὐ are necessary.

There is a similar confusion in *Phaedr.* 230 C, D, where σύ (CY) is
twice corrupted into οὐ (OY) both in B and T, also in 286 E σὺ δ'
ἐκέλευες;

ἢ δ' ὅς. ἔφη B Vind., εἰδώς T. The origin of the corrupt εἰδώς 8
is shown in Routh's ingenious conjecture ἢ δ' ὅς.

ὥσπερ σφαῖραν ἐκδεξάμενος. Cf. Plut. *De Genio Socratis*, ii. 582 F b 4
ὁ δὲ μὴ δεξάμενος ὥσπερ σφαῖραν εὖ φερομένην κατῄσχυνεν ἀτελῆ

EUTHYDEMUS   17   K

πεσοῦσαν. The game of passing the ball to and fro was called in Latin 'ludere datatim,' Plaut. *Curculio*, ii. 3, 17.

6   τὸ μανθάνειν οὐκ ἐπιστήμην ἐστὶ λαμβάνειν; Cf. 276 C 4 note.

c 2   ἢ οἵ ἂν μὴ ἔχωσιν; Burnet, 'ἔχωσιν huc transp. Badham : post μή B.T : *secl*. Schanz.' ἔχωσιν is certainly wanted in the question rather than in the answer.

d 1   ἐπὶ τὸ τρίτον ... ὥσπερ πάλαισμα. The victory in wrestling was not gained till the third fall. Cf. Aesch. *Eumen*. 586 ᾿Εν μὲν τόδ᾽ ἤδη τῶν τριῶν παλαισμάτων. Plat. *Pol*. 583 B, *Phaedr*. 256 B τῶν τριῶν παλαισμάτων τῶν ὡς ἀληθῶς ᾿Ολυμπιακῶν.

καταβαλών Heindorf, καταβαλών BT, om. Badham, Schanz. καταβαλών cannot be omitted unless τὸν νεανίσκον is omitted also (Cobet). If καταβαλών is retained it can only mean 'after throwing the youth was once more setting out for the third bout.' But the future is better.

2   βαπτιζόμενον. Cf. Plut. *Mor*. 9 B ψυχὴ τοῖς μὲν συμμέτροις αὔξεται πόνοις, τοῖσδ᾽ ὑπερβάλλουσι βαπτίζεται.

5   ἀήθεις T, is much better than ἀληθεῖς B Vind. which Winckelmann tries to defend.

7   τῇ τελετῇ τῶν Κορυβάντων. Cf. Lucian, *De Saltat*. 272 Πρῶτον δέ φασι ῾Ρέαν ἡσθεῖσαν τῇ τέχνῃ ἐν Φρυγίᾳ μὲν τοὺς Κορύβαντας ἐν Κρήτῃ δὲ τοὺς Κουρῆτας ὀρχεῖσθαι κελεῦσαι. Ibid. 277 ᾿Εῶ λέγειν ὅτι τελετὴν οὐδὲ μίαν ἀρχαίαν ἔστιν εὑρεῖν ἄνευ ὀρχήσεως. Ibid. σὺν ῥυθμῷ καὶ ὀρχήσει μνεῖσθαι. Hence the phrase ἐξορχεῖσθαι τὰ μυστήρια. Cf. Eur. *Bacch*. 123 ; Hor. *Od*. i. 16, 7 ; Preller, *Gr. Myth*. 656 ; Lobeck, *Aglaoph*. 640, 1153 ; Verg. *Aen*. iii. 111 ; Ov. *Met*. iv. 282 ; Lucian, *Tragoedo-Podagra* 36 :

παραπλῆγες δ᾽ ἀμφὶ ῥόπτροις
κελαδοῦσι Κρητὶ ῥυθμῷ
νόμον Κορύβαντες εὐάν.

On the dance of the Corybantes see Smith's *Dict. Class. Antiq*. SALTATIO, 1005 a.

9   χορηγία BTV : χορεία t, V marg. As it was the office of the Choregus (χορηγία) to supply a chorus for the dramatist, the use of the word here implies that the Sophists were providing a similar entertainment, and at the same time indicates the dramatic character of the dialogue.

εἰ ἄρα καὶ τετέλεσαι. In this use of εἰ ἄρα there is an

18

NOTES 277 d

ellipsis of the apodosis : ' *as you know*, if, that is, you have been initiated.'

τὰ πρῶτα τῶν ἱερῶν, 'the first part of the Sophistic mysteries.' e 2 There is a similar allusion to the greater and lesser mysteries in *Sympos.* 210 A ταῦτα μὲν οὖν τὰ ἐρωτικὰ ἴσως, ὦ Σώκρατες, κἂν σὺ μυηθείης· τὰ δὲ τέλεα καὶ ἐποπτικά, ὧν ἕνεκα καὶ ταῦτ' ἔστιν, ἐάν τις ὀρθῶς μετίῃ, οὐκ οἶδ' εἰ οἷός τ' ἂν εἴης. ὥς φησι Πρόδικος. Cf. *Charm.* 163 D καὶ γὰρ Προδίκου μυρία τινὰ 4 ἀκήκοα περὶ ὀνομάτων διαιροῦντος. *Crat.* 384 B εἰ μὲν οὖν ἐγὼ ἤδη ἠκηκόη παρὰ Προδίκου τὴν πεντηκοντάδραχμον ἐπίδειξιν ... εἰδέναι τὴν ἀλήθειαν περὶ ὀνομάτων ὀρθότητος· νῦν δὲ οὐκ ἀκήκοα, ἀλλὰ τὴν δραχμιαίαν. Cf. Aristot. *Rhet.* xiv. 9 Τοῦτο δ' ἐστίν, ὥσπερ ἔφη Πρόδικος, ὅτε νυστάζοιεν οἱ ἀκροαταί, παρεμβάλλειν τῆς πεντηκονταδράχμου αὐτοῖς. Aristophanes, before he had learned to appreciate Socrates, contrasts him unfavourably with Prodicus (*Nub.* 361). On the philological works ascribed to Prodicus see Jann. *Gk. Gr.* App. ii. 12, note 1.

ταύτῃ τῇ ἐπιστήμῃ. Cf. Aristot. *Soph. El.* iv, quoted in the note 278 on 276 C 4. a 2

ταὐτὸν ὄνομα ἐπ' ἀνθρώποις ἐναντίως ἔχουσιν κείμενον. The fallacy 6 depending on the equivocal use of words is described by Aristot. *Categ.* i. 1 Ὁμώνυμα λέγεται ὧν ὄνομα μόνον κοινόν, ὁ δὲ κατὰ τοὔνομα λόγος τῆς οὐσίας ἕτερος, οἷον ζῷον ὅ τε ἄνθρωπος καὶ τὸ γεγραμμένον, i.e. ζῷον may mean either a living man, or a picture.

σκολύθρια, 'stools': a word occurring only here in Plato. Cf. b 8 Ruhnk. *Tim. Lex.* Σκολύθρια· ταπεινὰ διφρία παρὰ τοῖς Θεσσάλοις, ἅ τινες θρανία καλοῦσιν.

αὑτοῖν ἵνα μοι BT. Winckelmann regarding the repetition of the c syllable ιν as a corruption conjectures αὑτοῖν ἅ μοι, and the alteration is adopted by Schanz in opposition to the best MSS. The only change required is to correct the itacism ἀποδώσειν in BT into ἀποδῶσιν, as Burnet does with many MSS.

ἐπιδείξασθαι BT, ἐπιδείξεσθαι Steph. Schanz. The change to the 5 future is quite unnecessary ; cf. Hdt. i. 53 προλέγουσαι Κροίσῳ ... μεγάλην ἀρχήν μιν καταλῦσαι. Plat. *Sympos.* 193 D ἐλπίδας παρέχεται ... ἡμᾶς ... εὐδαίμονας ποιῆσαι. *Phaed.* 97 B πολλὴ ἐλπὶς κτήσασθαι. Thuc. v. 22 οὐκ ἔφασαν δέξασθαι. Cf. Routh 'ἐπιδείξεσθαι *Steph. Edit.* veteri relicta lectione sine idonea causa opinor.'

παῖσαι T, παίξαι B, παῖξαι Vt. Cf. Rutherford, *N. Phryn.* p. 91: 6

19 K 2

'The Attic form was doubtless παίσομαι, as all forms with ξ, like παίξας and πέπαιγμαι, were unquestionably un-Attic, and should be removed, with manuscript authority, from such passages as Plato, *Euthyd.* 278 C.'

νῦν δέ μοι δοκεῖ BT, νῦν δ', ἐμοὶ δοκεῖ Heindorf, Bekker, Schanz, νῦν δέ, μοι δοκεῖ, Stallbaum, Badham, Burnet. Heindorf's dictum, ' Immo ἐμοὶ δοκεῖ, ut semper scribitur in hac formula (v. Reitz ad Lucian. *de Astrolog.* 9),' seems to have misled subsequent editors. In Lucian ἐμοὶ δὲ δοκέει is at the beginning of a sentence, where of course the enclitic μοι is impossible, and the pronoun in antithesis to τῶν ἄλλων is necessarily emphatic. Stallbaum writes ' etiam μοί ita in parenthesi collocari nuper a multis est observatum.' It is better to leave the reading of BT unaltered, instead of inserting commas to make μοι δοκεῖ into a formal parenthesis : cf. *Menex.* 236 B where all editors agree in writing ὅτε μοι δοκεῖ συνετίθει. See the note on 297 C νεωστί μοι δοκεῖν.

d 1   πεπαίσθω T, 'let there be an end of this sport,' a less discourteous phrase than πεπαύσθω B, 'let this be stopped.'

7   ἀπαυτοσχεδιάσαι V, ἀπ' αὐτὸ σχεδιάσαι B, αὐτοσχεδιάσαι T. The verb αὐτοσχεδιάζω is found both in earlier dialogues, *Euthyphro* 5 A, 16 A, *Apol.* 20, and in later *Crat.* 413 D, *Phaedr.* 236 D, as well as in Thucydides, Xenophon, and Aristotle. The compound with ἀπό seems to occur only in this passage, and, for the intensive force of ἀπό, may be compared with ἀπαυθαδιζόμενος *Apol.* 37 A, ἀπαναισχυντῆσαι ibid. 31 B, ἀποτολμάω *Pol.* 503 B.

e 1   ἀνάσχεσθον T : ἀνάσχετον B does not give the meaning required.

3   Ἀρά γε πάντες . . . 289 B is used in an abridged form by Iamblichus, *Protrept.* C 5.

εὖ πράττειν, 'to do well.' 'An ambiguous phrase. In its usual acceptation it would rather mean "faring well" than "acting well." It occurs in the *Gorgias* of Plato, p. 507 C, in a way which seems to contain the transition between these two ideas—πολλὴ ἀνάγκη, ὦ Καλλίκλεις, τὸν σώφρονα, ὥσπερ διήλθομεν, δίκαιον ὄντα καὶ ἀνδρεῖον καὶ ὅσιον ἀγαθὸν ἄνδρα εἶναι τελέως, τὸν δὲ ἀγαθὸν εὖ τε καὶ καλῶς πράττειν ἃ ἂν πράττῃ, τὸν δ' εὖ πράττοντα μακάριόν τε καὶ εὐδαίμονα εἶναι, τὸν δὲ πονηρὸν καὶ κακῶς πράττοντα ἄθλιον. Aristotle was at no pains to solve the ambiguity. Cf. *Eth.* vi. 2, 5.' (GRANT, *Aristot. Eth.* i. 4, 2.)

NOTES 279 a

Εἶεν is frequently used, as here, in passing on from one point to 279
another. 'Well then, as to the next point.' Cf. Reisig ad Soph. a 1
Oed. Col. 1308 'εἶεν] Hac voce utuntur Graeci in omni genere
sermonis, ubi ad alia progrediuntur ; atque est plane, ut Grammatici definiunt, συγκατάθεσις μὲν τῶν εἰρημένων, συναφὴ δὲ πρὸς τὰ
μέλλοντα.'

σεμνοῦ ἀνδρός, 'the task of a great man.' ' σεμνὸς ἀνήρ est quem 6
alias dicit οὐ φαῦλον' (Heind.). Cf. 303 C τῶν σεμνῶν δὴ καὶ
δοκούντων τι εἶναι.

εὐπορεῖν, 'to be well provided.' Cf. Plat. *Ion* 533 A εὐπορεῖ ὅ τι 7
εἴπῃ, a passage which shows that εὑρεῖν (Τ) is an unnecessary
change.

τὸ ὑγιαίνειν. Health is rightly put before beauty and riches in 8
Plat. *Legg.* 661 A λέγεται γὰρ ὡς ἄριστον μὲν ὑγιαίνειν, δεύτερον δὲ
κάλλος, τρίτον δὲ πλοῦτος. Cf. *Meno* 87 E ὑγίεια, φαμέν, καὶ ἰσχὺς
καὶ κάλλος καὶ πλοῦτος δή.

τἆλλα κατὰ τὸ σῶμα ἱκανῶς παρεσκευάσθαι. Cf. Iambl. *Protrept.* b 1
ὥστε ἱκανῶς αὐτὸ παρεσκευάσθαι πρὸς τὴν κατὰ φύσιν συμμετρίαν καὶ
κρᾶσιν καὶ ῥώμην.

ἐν τῇ ἑαυτοῦ. Iamblichus completes the phrase by adding πατρίδι. 3
τοῦ χοροῦ. The choir or band of the cardinal virtues, or rather c 1
of goods in general, is incomplete without σοφία. Routh compares
Aristeid. *Or. pro Miltiad.* ii. 161 Μιλτιάδην δὲ τὸν ἐν Μαραθῶνι ποῦ
χοροῦ τάξομεν.

παραλείπωμεν ΒΤ : Cobet, followed by Schanz, alters this to παρε- 3
λίπομεν. But the subjunctive is rightly retained by Burnet, being
defended by Heindorf on the ground that ἐνθυμοῦ expresses anxious
care, as in *Hipp. Mai.* 300 D ἐνθυμοῦμαι, ὦ ἑταῖρε, μὴ παίζῃς πρός με.

'Ολίγου ... ἐγενόμεθα, 'we were near to becoming.' Cf. Plat. *Apol.* 9
22 A ἔδοξάν μοι ὀλίγου δεῖν τοῦ πλείστου ἐνδεεῖς εἶναι : ibid. 17 A ὀλίγου
ἐμαυτοῦ ἐπελαθόμην.

ἐν τοῖς ἔμπροσθεν, 'in our former list.' d 2
'Η σοφία δήπου ... εὐτυχία ἐστίν. The pretence of having for- 6
gotten to include εὐτυχία, and then remembering that it was included
in σοφία, is intended to draw especial attention to the contrast between the Socratic doctrine, that virtue consists in wisdom or true
knowledge, and the view of the Sophists that it is the result of
good fortune, a kind of divine gift, as in the *Meno* 99 C. Cf. *Euthyd.*

21

280 B σοφίας παρούσης, ᾧ ἂν παρῇ μηδὲν προσδεῖσθαι εὐτυχίας. Bonitz, *Platon. Stud.* 251 note, observes that it is difficult to find (in German, as it is in English) a single word expressing the two meanings of εὐτυχία, an accidental concurrence of favourable circumstances, and success resulting from the agent's judicious choice of means.

7 κἂν παῖς γνοίη. Cf. 301 C 1 οὐδ' ἂν παῖδα ᾤμην τοῦτο ἀπορῆσαι. *Lys.* 205 C 1, *Symp.* 204 B.

καὶ ὅς. Here, as in ἦ δ' ὅς, we see that ὅς was in its original sense demonstrative.

e 1 περὶ αὐλημάτων εὐπραγίαν, 'success in flute-tunes.' 'εὐπραγίαν delendum videtur' (Schanz). On the contrary εὐπραγίαν is most appropriate as carrying on the idea that εὐτυχία is an element in εὖ πράττειν.

280 Ἆρ' οὐκ . . . ὅτι, 'Is it not because . . . ?' 'Vulgo ἆρ' οὖν.' 'Nus-
a 4 quam vidi οὖν infeliciter positum, Ἆρ' οὐκ ex Platonico more reposui: sic enim loqui solet qui alterius responsum ante capit' (Badham). Οὖν has probably been introduced here, because ἆρ' οὖν occurs so frequently in the context immediately following, 280 B (*bis*), D, 281 A, B.

b 1 ἐν κεφαλαίῳ, 'in general,' i.e. as a summary induction from the particular cases mentioned.

2 ᾧ ἂν παρῇ, a good emendation supplied from Casaubon's unpublished notes by Routh: it indicates the subject to be understood before προσδεῖσθαι, which is left without any subject by the reading ὅταν παρῇ BT Vind. 1.

4 πῶς ἂν ἡμῖν ἔχοι, 'how our former agreements would stand,' i.e. how they would be affected by this conclusion about σοφία. Badham's conjecture ἆρ' for ἂν is therefore no improvement.

c 1 ὠφελοῖ, εἰ εἴη Iamblichus: ὠφελοίη η B: ὠφέλοιη εἰ ἦι T. The scribes of B and T both seem to have been misled by glancing back at ὠφελοῖ ἢ εἰ ὠφελοῖ. Iamblichus is, of course, a much earlier witness to the true reading.

2 ποτόν. After σίτια the plural would be more usual, as in *Protag.* 314 A, 334 A, *Phaedr.* 259 C, *Pol.* 332. But Stallbaum retains ποτόν as the reading of all MSS., and Winckelmann quotes in support of it a similar combination in Max. Tyr. *Or.* xxxi. 108 ἐμπιπλάμενοι ποτοῦ καὶ σιτίων.

4 οἱ δημιουργοὶ πάντες. The term δημιουργός, 'one who works for

the people,' includes all who practise any profession, trade, or craft for pay, from physicians to artisans.

δεῖν BT Vind.; δεῖ Iamblichus. I have allowed the reading of d 4 the MSS. to stand, but not without hesitation. It is more likely that δεῖν should have been altered to δεῖ, in order to make the construction regular, than the reverse. Cf. Aesch. *Persae* 188 τούτω στάσιν τιν', ὡς ἐγὼ 'δοκοῦν ὁρᾶν, τεύχειν ἐν ἀλλήλαισι: and Soph. *Trach.* 1238 ἀνὴρ ὅδ', ὡς ἔοικεν, οὐ νεμεῖν ἐμοὶ φθίνοντι μοῖραν. But in these passages the infinitive follows ὡς ἔοικεν, and the passages quoted by Winckelmann, to prove that it may precede, are not altogether convincing. More satisfactory, so far as poetry is concerned, is the passage Aesch. *Pers.* 564 τυτθὰ δ' ἐκφυγεῖν ἄνακτ' αὐτὸν ὡς ἀκούομεν.

ὡς οὐδὲν ὄφελος τῆς κτήσεως γίγνεται, BT. For ὡς Iamblichus 6 has ἥ, *Protrept.* c.v., which has been adopted by Routh, Schanz, and Burnet. Schanz, however, had previously written (*N. C. P.* p. 74): 'Amplecterer ergo Routhii coniecturam (?), ni artis palaeographicae rationem spretam viderem; nam permutationis verborum ἥ et ὡς nullum novi exemplum.' Stallbaum retains ὡς, laying an emphasis on τῆς κτήσεως, as does Ficinus: 'nihil enim *sola* possessio iuvat.' This is justified by the consideration that τῆς κτήσεως here, like τὴν τούτων κτῆσιν in D 4, still connotes the negative idea expressed in χρῷτο δὲ αὐτοῖς μή and μόνον κεκτῆσθαι.

Ἆρ' οὖν ... οὔτε ἀγαθόν, D 7–281 A 1, quoted by Stobaeus, *Florileg.* 7 103, 29.

ἤδη τοῦτο ἱκανόν T, Stob. This is strangely corrupted in B into e 1 the senseless ὃ δὴ τούτωι καλλίωι. ἤδη means 'at once,' i. e. 'without anything more,' 'of itself.' Cf. *Gorg.* 486 E εὖ οἶδ' ὅτι ... ταῦτ' ἤδη ἐστὶν αὐτὰ τἀληθῆ. On the various uses of ἤδη in Plato cf. Lutoslawski, 106, 118.

ἢ καὶ ἐὰν μή; BT. καί, omitted by Stobaeus, is necessary to the 4 exact sense, '*an etiam si non recte?*' (Ficinus).

καλῶς γε, Stob., a necessary emendation of καλῶς δέ, BTV.

θάτερον, 'harm,' is often used as equivalent to τὸ κακόν, in order 5 to avoid a word of ill omen. Cf. 297 D πλέον ἂν θάτερον ποιήσειεν, 'would do more harm than good.'

ἄλλο τί ... ἢ ἐπιστήμη; 'is that which effects the right use 281 anything else than knowledge of carpentering?' a 3

23

3 τὸ ἀπεργαζόμενον ὀρθῶς χρῆσθαι. A second τό seems to be required before ὀρθῶς, as in A 5 and A 8; ἀπεργάζομαι is apparently not one of the verbs which are followed by the anarthrous infinitive; cf. Jannaris 2085.

4 ἀλλὰ μήν που καί, 'but surely also in the work pertaining to household furniture.' The whole sentence ἀλλὰ μήν που . . . Συνέφη is bracketed by Hirschig and Badham, but without apparent reason.

6 τὴν χρείαν, 'the use' in the sense of 'usefulness.' Cf. Gorg. 480 A τίς ἡ μεγάλη χρεία ἐστὶ τῆς ῥητορικῆς;

8 τὸ ὀρθῶς πᾶσι τοῖς τοιούτοις χρῆσθαι. Bracketed by Schanz without good reason: for τό Badham would prefer τοῦ, but the accusative rightly represents the area or extent of the verb's action: 'in regard to the right use of all these was it knowledge that leads the way?' Cf. Soph. Philoct. 99 τὴν γλῶσσαν, οὐχὶ τἄργα, πάνθ' ἡγουμένην, 'the tongue in all things takes the lead.'

b 1 ἦν ⟨ἡ⟩ ἡγουμένη. The article ἡ seems to have been dropped out. Badham supplied it, but omitted ἦν, which is supported by BT.

2 οὐ μόνον ἄρα εὐτυχίαν ἀλλὰ καὶ εὐπραγίαν. Cf. Aristot. Eth. Eud. vii. 14, 1 Ἐπεὶ δ' οὐ μόνον ἡ φρόνησις ποιεῖ τὴν εὐπραγίαν καὶ ἀρετήν, ἀλλά φαμεν καὶ τοὺς εὐτυχεῖς εὖ πράττειν ὡς καὶ τῆς εὐτυχίας εὖ ποιούσης εὐπραγίαν καὶ τὰ αὐτὰ τῆς ἐπιστήμης, σκεπτέον ἆρ' ἐστὶ φύσει ὁ μὲν εὐτυχὴς ὁ δ' ἀτυχής, ἢ οὔ; On this passage Zeller, Plato 51, n. 13 writes: 'Eudemus, Eth. Eud. vii. 14 (1247 b 15) must refer to the Euthydemus (279 D sq., 281 B), inasmuch as what is here quoted as Socratic is to be found there and there only.' Eth. Eud. vii. 13, 10 καὶ ὀρθῶς τὸ Σωκρατικόν, ὅτι οὐδὲν ἰσχυρότερον φρονήσεως. 'Ἀλλ' ὅτι ἐπιστήμην ἔφη οὐκ ὀρθόν· ἀρετὴ γάρ ἐστι καὶ οὐκ ἐπιστήμη. Cf. Plut. Moral. 440 B οὐκοῦν ἔτι γελοιότερος ὁ μόνην τὴν φρόνησιν μὴ διδακτὴν ἀποφαίνων, ἧς ἄνευ τῶν ἄλλων τεχνῶν ὄφελος οὐδὲν οὔτε ὄνησίς ἐστιν;

7 ἢ μᾶλλον ὀλίγα; The words νοῦν ἔχων, which follow in BT, are omitted by Iamblichus, and rightly rejected by Badham and Schanz. For in the following argument there is no place for an antithesis between νοῦν ἔχων and νοῦν μὴ ἔχων, but only between πολλά and ὀλίγα· 'Would a man devoid of understanding be benefited by possessing and by doing many things, or rather (by possessing and by doing) few things?'

c 2 ἧττον δὲ κακῶς πράττων, 'and doing less ill.' The phrase κακῶς πράττειν may mean either 'to do evil' or 'to do (fare) badly.'

Socrates here falls into the same fallacy as the Sophists by using
πράττων in two different senses, but the purpose and effect of his
argument are totally different. Cf. *Charmid.* 172 A ἐν πάσῃ πράξει
καλῶς καὶ εὖ πράττειν ἀναγκαῖον ... τοὺς δὲ εὖ πράττοντας εὐδαίμονας
εἶναι. See Heindorf's note on that passage.

Πότερον οὖν ἂν μᾶλλον ἐλάττω κτλ., 'In which case then would a 3
man be more likely to do fewer things, if he were poor or rich?' 'Cave
μᾶλλον cum ἐλάττω coniungas, quod fecit Heindorfius' (Stallbaum).

ἔντιμος ἢ ἄτιμος; Cobet would substitute ἐπίτιμος, but Schanz, 5
N. C. P. p. 75, rightly argues that ἔντιμος and ἄτιμος are both
referred to social as well as legal honour, while ἐπίτιμος is limited
to the latter.

ἀνδρεῖος ὤν. The addition [καὶ σώφρων] seems to be inappropriate, 6
and is rejected by Badham and Schanz.

ἐν κεφαλαίῳ κτλ. 'To sum up then, Cleinias,' said I, 'as to all d 2
things which we at first said were good, the argument probably
does not turn upon this question, how they are by nature good of
themselves alone.' In the beginning of the sentence σύμπαντα is
the subject of κινδυνεύει and of an infinitive dependent upon it, such
as ταύτῃ σκοπεῖσθαι δεῖν (Stallbaum); but Plato afterwards passes
by an anacoluthon to περὶ τούτου ὁ λόγος αὐτοῖς εἶναι, 'a change of
construction in consequence of the more convenient form of the
continuation' (Engelhardt ap. Lutosl. 76).

πέφυκεν ἀγαθὰ [εἶναι]. There is no objection to the construction 5
πέφυκεν εἶναι, which occurs in *Legg.* 723 D, 870 B, but εἶναι is
omitted in B Vind., and apparently added in T from Iamblichus.

μείζω κακὰ εἶναι. The infinitive depends on ὧδ᾽ ἔχει. Cf. *Phaed.* 6
70 C εἰ τοῦθ᾽ οὕτως ἔχει, πάλιν γίγνεσθαι ἐκ τῶν ἀποθανόντων τοὺς
ζῶντας (Winckelmann).

ὄν. The participle is dependent on συμβαίνει, the effect of which e 3
extends to the whole passage. The same construction is found in
Pol. 490 C ξυνέβη προσῆκον τούτοις ἀνδρία, and in *Crat.* 422 A, *Menex.*
237 C. The infinitive is, however, more usual, as in *Phaed.* 74 A,
92 B, *Parmen.* 134 A.

τὸ λοιπόν, i.e. the conclusion that remains to be drawn. 282

ἐπειδή T: ἐπειδὴ δέ B: ἐπειδὴ δή Stallbaum's conjecture, which a 1
illustrates the origin of the error in B as a repetition of the last
syllable in ἐπειδή.

25

2 ἐφάνημεν . . . γιγνόμενοι, 'it was shown that we become.'

4 ἐπιστήμη ἡ παρέχουσα. Supply ἐφάνη from ἐφάνημεν. Iamblichus has ἐστίν : Heindorf, Bekker, and Badham without authority add ἦν, 'is, as we said.'

5 ἐκ παντὸς τρόπου. The same phrase is found in *Pol.* 499 A, *Legg.* 938 C. The dative is much more usual.

6 τοῦτο, used here in its 'prospective' sense, is explained by ὅπως κτλ.

7 καὶ παρὰ πατρός γε δήπου τοῦτο οἰόμενον . . . ὑπηρετεῖν. 'And when a man thinks that this is what he ought certainly to receive much rather than money from his father, and from guardians and friends, especially those who profess to love him, whether strangers or citizens, and entreats and beseeches them to impart wisdom,— for this purpose, Cleinias, there is no cause for shame or blame in serving or slaving either for a lover or for any man, and being willing to perform any honourable service from the desire to become wise.'

With this passage Routh compares *Sympos.* 184 C νενόμισται κτλ., where the same subject is treated at length in the speech of Pausanias.

b 6 ἢ οὐ δοκεῖ σοι; . . . Πάνυ μὲν οὖν εὖ κτλ. 'Or do you not think so? Nay, I think you speak quite rightly.'

c 1 Εἰ ἔστι γε. 'Yes, Cleinias,' said I, 'if at least wisdom can be taught.'

4 Ἀλλ' ἔμοιγε . . . 'But in my opinion, Socrates, it can be taught.'

6 ἀπαλλάξας. 'Pro ἀπαλλάττων' (Heind.). Stallbaum corrects Heindorf's error, showing that the aorist is required to express a single and as it were momentary action, and comparing *Phaed.* 60 C εὖ γ' ἐποίησας ἀναμνήσας με : Xen. *Cyr.* i. 14, 3, and many other passages.

8 διδακτὸν δοκεῖ καὶ . . . ποιεῖν. Badham adds εἶναι after δοκεῖ on account of ποιεῖν following. The construction δοκεῖ διδακτόν may be compared with 289 B οὐδὲ ταύτης ἔοικεν ὄφελος οὐδέν, and *Gorg.* 475 E ὁ ἔλεγχος . . . οὐδὲν ἔοικεν. *Tim.* 37 D καθάπερ οὖν αὐτὸ τυγχάνει ζῷον ἀίδιον.

The question, εἰ διδακτὸν ἡ ἀρετή, in other words the relation of knowledge to virtue, has been already discussed in several of the early dialogues and especially in the *Protagoras*, where Socrates

26

begins by denying but ends by affirming that virtue can certainly be taught. Cf. *Protag.* 361 B.

οἴων ἐπιθυμῶ τῶν προτρεπτικῶν λόγων εἶναι. In the reading of BT, d 5 οἶον ... τῶν προτρεπτικῶν λόγον, τῶν προτρεπτικῶν cannot well stand without a substantive: Routh proposed to read οἴων and λόγων, and this emendation is accepted by Stallbaum, οἴων being regarded as a rather unusual form of attraction, 'my example of what I desire protreptic arguments to be': Schanz prefers the emendation found in Cod. Angelic. C. I. 4, a copy of B, οἷον ἐπιθυμῶ τὸν προτρεπτικὸν λόγον εἶναι. Cobet cuts the knot by omitting the whole clause.

ἰδιωτικὸν ἴσως κτλ., 'unskilful perhaps and long and ill-ex- 6 pressed.'

ταὐτὸν τοῦτο τέχνῃ πράττων ἐπιδειξάτω, 'give us a specimen of 8 treating this same subject according to rules of art.'

τὸ ἑξῆς κτλ., 'show the youth what follows in order from the e 1 point at which I left off.'

ἣν δεῖ λαβόντα εὐδαιμονεῖν, 'which he must acquire in order to be 3 happy.' Cf. 289 C ἣν ἔδει κεκτημένους ἡμᾶς εὐδαίμονας εἶναι. *Pol.* 427 B. In this construction δεῖ properly applies to the notion of λαβόντα, κεκτημένους, &c.

ὥσπερ γὰρ ἔλεγον. Coislin.[2]: γάρ om. BTV. 4

τυγχάνει ὂν κτλ. For a full discussion of this use of τυγχάνω 5 with a participle see Rutherford, *N. Phryn.* p. 342, and cf. 290 A 4, *Tim.* 19 A, *Theaet.* 165 C, *Protag.* 313 C ὁ σοφιστὴς τυγχάνει ὢν ἔμπορός τις, 2 Macc. iii. 9.

ἄψοιντο Heindorf: ἄψαιντο BTV. Schanz regards ἄψαιντο as an 283 error in the original archetype. Cf. Xen. *Conv.* iii. 2 ἐξηγοῦ ποίων a 3 λόγων ἁπτόμενοι μάλιστ' ἂν ταῦτα ποιοῖμεν.

θαυμασίους ... θαυμαστόν. Plato seems to use either form in- 7 differently both of things and persons: cf. Riddell, *Digest*, § 314.

κατῆρχεν λόγον. The accusative after the active voice of this b 2 verb is unusual in prose: but see Pind. *Nem.* iii. 10 ἄρχε δ' οὐρανοῦ πολυνεφέλα κρέοντι, θύγατερ, δόκιμον ὕμνον. Cf. Kühner-Blass, *Gr. Gr.* § 416, Anmerk 7. After the middle voice the accusative is not uncommon in poetry: Hom. *Od.* iii. 445 χέρνιβά τ' οὐλοχύτας τε κατήρχετο. Eur. *Hec.* 685 κατάρχομαι νόμον βακχεῖον. *Or.* 949 κατάρχομαι στεναγμόν. A poetical construction is not out of place in such a writer as Plato, after a formal invocation of the Muses, 276 D.

4 Εἰπέ μοι, with a plural vocative, is found also in *Protag.* 311
D εἰπέ μοι, ὦ Σώκρατές τε καὶ Ἱππόκρατες.

8 ᾠηθήτην ἄρα, 'they supposed, as I thought:' ἄρα refers to 278 D
ταῦτα μὲν οὖν ... πεπαίσθω τε ὑμῖν καὶ ἴσως ἱκανῶς ἔχει.

C 4 ἔξαρνος ἴσει ἃ νῦν λέγεις. Cf. *Charm.* 158 C ἐξάρνῳ εἶναι τὰ ἐρω-
τώμενα.

5 Τί οὖν; ἔφη. Schanz's conjecture ἦ οὖν is quite arbitrary and
unnecessary.

7 οὔκουν φησί γέ πω. Stallbaum quotes many instances of the
separation of πω from the negative, *Men.* 72 D, 83 E, *Pol.* 434 D
&c.

8 ἀλαζών, 'untruthful,' one who wanders (ἀλᾶται) from the truth;
'mendax' (Heindorf). Stallbaum, with Ficinus ('iactabundus')
and Winckelmann, retains the more usual meaning as explaining
why Cleinias does not claim to be σοφός, 'he says at least that he
is not yet wise, for he is no braggart.'

d 2 ὃς μὲν οὐκ ἔστιν. As ὅς is sometimes used in the sense of οἷος, the
Sophist prepares to play upon the double meaning. Cf. Soph.
Ajax 1259 μαθὼν ὃς εἶ φύσιν. Eur. *Suppl.* 737 δρῶμέν τε τοιαῦθ'
ἂν σὺ τυγχάνῃς θέλων. Plat. *Phaedr.* 243 E ἕωσπερ ἂν ᾖς ὃς εἶ.

4 ὑπολαβών ... ἔφη, 'took me up and said.'

ἀπολωλέναι, 'to be dead,' or 'destroyed.'

καίτοι πολλοῦ ἂν ἄξιοι κτλ. 'Very precious forsooth must such
friends and lovers be!'

e 2 εἰ μὴ ἀγροικότερον, ἔφη, ἦν εἰπεῖν, 'if it were not rather a rude
thing to say.' The same phrase is used in *Apol.* 32 D.

3 Σοὶ εἰς κεφαλήν, 'In caput tuum istuc recidat,' sc. τὸ ἀπολωλέναι:
'On your head be it.' Cf. Aristoph. *Plut.* 525, 669, *Pax* 1063
H. ὦ μέλεοι θνητοὶ καὶ νήπιοι, Τρ. ἐς κεφαλὴν σοί.

ὅ τι μαθών. Cf. 299 A, *Apol.* 36 B τί ἄξιός εἰμι παθεῖν ἢ ἀπο-
τῖσαι, ὅ τι μαθὼν ἐν τῷ βίῳ οὐχ ἡσυχίαν ἦγον, 'for having taken it
into my head not to lead a quiet life.' As the indirect form of
τί μαθών the phrase must be written with the pronoun ὅ τι, not
with the conjunction ὅτι: cf. Hermann ad Viger, *De Idiot. Gr.*
758. The latter could only be justified if μαθών were ever used
alone in this sense. Schanz, following Hermann on Viger, *De
Idiotism.* 759 sq., wrongly changes μαθών into παθών. The two
phrases are rightly distinguished by L. and Sc., *Lex.* μανθάνω. 'Τί

μαθών; on what *belief* or *persuasion* ...? implying voluntary
action :—τί παθών; on what *compulsion*?' or, 'What ailed you to
do this or that?'

καταψεύδει ... ἐξολωλέναι, 'falsely charge me and the rest of us 4
with a thing of which I think it wicked even to speak,—as that
I should wish my friend here to be dead.'
Badham omits the latter part of the sentence, ὡς ... ἐξολωλέναι,
but without reason.

οἷόν τε εἶναι ψεύδεσθαι. Cf. *Sophist.* 236 E ' How it is possible to 7
speak anything false or to suppose that it really exists, and to say
this without being involved in a contradiction, is difficult in the
extreme. Why so? Because the statement has the boldness to
assume that Not-being exists. But when we were boys the great
Parmenides testified to us from first to last both in prose and in
metre in these words—"For this you ne'er can learn that non-
existent things exist."' The fallacy depends on the ambiguity of
the phrase λέγειν τι, meaning properly 'to speak about a thing,'
and only improperly 'to speak a thing.' The *words* spoken do
exist as words, but are not true unless the *thing* exists, and exists
as it is spoken of (Routh). Examples of the fallacy παρ' ἀμφιβολίαν
are given in the *Soph. El.* iv. 4 (527), among them δυνατὰ ὁρᾶν
and σιγῶντα λέγειν 300 B.

Πότερον λέγοντα, 'by speaking or by not speaking the thing that
may be in question?'

οὐκ ἄλλο λέγει τῶν ὄντων, 'he speaks no other existing thing than 284
that very thing which he speaks.' τῶν ὄντων is bracketed by a 2
Badham and Schanz, but rightly retained by Burnet. See the
next note.

Ἐν μὴν κἀκεῖνό γ' ἐστὶν τῶν ὄντων. This καί proves that there has 3
been a previous mention of τῶν ὄντων. 'Moreover that which he
speaks is one existing thing, independently of the rest.'

τἀληθῆ rejected by Badham, so as to leave the statement, 'he 6
that speaks τὸ ὄν speaks also τὰ ὄντα.' But the alteration is
unnecessary. The extension of τὸ ὄν into καὶ τὰ ὄντα is justified
by the comprehensive phrase περὶ οὗ ἂν ᾖ ὁ λόγος. Ficinus renders
rightly: 'Enim vero quicunque quod est quaeve sunt dicit, vera
loquitur.'

Ναί, ἔφη· ἀλλ' ὁ ταῦτα λέγων. Ctesippus admits that Diodorus b 1

29

speaks truth, *if* he speaks that which is; but then immediately adds that this condition is not fulfilled in the present case. Stallbaum argues that ὁ ταῦτα λέγων means Euthydemus, 'the present speaker'; but it is the falsehood of Dionysodorus that is under discussion throughout the argument, as is evident from C 5 ἀλλ' εἴπερ λέγει Διονυσόδωρος, τἀληθῆ τε καὶ τὰ ὄντα λέγει.

Plato is referring throughout the passage 283 E 7—284 C 6 to the doctrine of Parmenides, 'Only that which can be can be thought,' as stated in his *Proëm.* 33-40, and more briefly in 43 Χρὴ τὸ λέγειν τε νοεῖν τ' ἐὸν ἔμμεναι, ἔστι γὰρ εἶναι, μηδὲν δ' οὐκ εἶναι· τά σ' ἐγὼ φράζεσθαι ἄνωγα. Cf. Mullach, *Fragmenta Philos. Gr.* i. 118, and Zeller, *Pre-Socr. Philos.* i. 584.

3 Τὰ δὲ μὴ ὄντα κτλ. 'But is it not the fact that non-existing things are not?'

4 Ἄλλο τι κτλ. 'Then non-existing things are nowhere existing?' The whole question and answer, Ἄλλο τι... Οὐδαμοῦ, are omitted by Badham, but only the second ὄντα by Schanz: this ὄντα, however, is supported by the following τὰ μηδαμοῦ ὄντα.

6 ⟨ὥστε καὶ εἶναι⟩. This is Hermann's excellent emendation of various corruptions in the MSS., ὥς γε Κλεινίᾳ BV, ὥσγ' ἐκλεινίᾳ T, with the marginal conjecture ὥστ' ἐκεῖνα in T Vind. Κλεινίᾳ is certainly wrong, for Cleinias is not included among those of whom Ctesippus says in E 3 μου καὶ τῶν ἄλλων καταψεύδει. Also ἐκεῖνα is very questionable as a repetition of ταῦτα τὰ μὴ ὄντα, and at all events superfluous, whereas καὶ εἶναι adds much to the force of the passage: 'Is it possible that any one, whosoever he may be, could do anything about these non-existing things so as to make the things that exist nowhere actually to exist?' Badham and Schanz bracket τὰ μὴ ὄντα, as not absolutely necessary. The fallacy employed is that of the equivocal use of words, and, in this instance, of the word λέγειν. He who speaks speaks *about* something cannot properly be said *to speak the thing* ('rem loqui'). The *words* which he utters in speaking have a real existence, but unless the *things* really exist in the mode indicated by the words, these are not true. *Cratyl.* 385 B ὃς ἂν τὰ ὄντα λέγῃ ὡς ἔστιν, ἀληθής· ὃς δ' ἂν ὡς οὐκ ἔστιν, ψευδής; Ναί. 'Quod innuit quoque Ctesippus infra' (Routh). Cf. 283 E 7, note.

C 1 εἴπερ πράττουσι, καὶ ποιοῦσι, 'if they do, they also make.' Cf.

Charmid. 163 B οὐ ταὐτὸν καλεῖς τὸ ποιεῖν καὶ τὸ πράττειν; Οὐ μέντοι, ἔφη. Ibid. ποίησιν πράξεως καὶ ἐργασίας ἄλλο ἐνόμιζεν.

Οὐκ ἄρα τά γε μὴ ὄντ', ἔφη, λέγει οὐδείς. 'No one then, said he, 2 speaks what is not; for (in speaking) he would at once make something ; and you have admitted that it is impossible for any one to make what is not.' In ποιοῖ γὰρ ἂν ἤδη τί Heindorf would either omit τί or substitute αὐτά, meaning τὰ μὴ ὄντα. Cf. *Sophist.* 238 C οὔτε φθέγξασθαι δυνατὸν ὀρθῶς οὔτ' εἰπεῖν οὔτε διανοηθῆναι τὸ μὴ ὂν αὐτὸ καθ' αὑτό, ἀλλ' ἔστιν ἀδιανόητόν τε καὶ ἄρρητον καὶ ἄφθεγκτον καὶ ἄλογον.

κατὰ τὸν σὸν λόγον TV: λόγον om. B. 'Huius ellipsis alterum 5 exemplum novimus nullum' (Stallb.).

Εἰσὶν μέντοι ... 'Surely there are. Gentlemen, and those who d 1 speak the truth.'

τοὺς γοῦν ψυχροὺς ... 'of the frigid they speak frigidly, and call e 4 them frigid disputants.' Cf. Aristot. *Rhet.* iii. 3, 1 τὰ ψυχρά, 'faults of taste'; Isocr. *Ad Nicocl.* 21 D εὑρήσεις γὰρ ἐπὶ τὸ πολὺ τοὺς μὲν σεμνυνομένους ψυχροὺς ὄντας. Athen. vi. 40 ἀηδὴς καὶ ψυχρός. Cic. *De clar. Orat.* 178 'lentus in dicendo et paene frigidus.'

λοιδορεῖ, 'you are abusive': λοιδόρει BT, 'go on with your 6 abuse'; but Heindorf's correction has been generally accepted, the middle voice being as usual as the active, and confirmed here by λοιδορεῖσθαι 285 D 5. Cf. *Charm.* 154 A; *Conv.* 213 D.

ἀγριωτέρως ... ἔχειν BT, 'to be rather savage': ἀγροικοτέρως V, 285 'rather rude,' perhaps adopted from 283 E 2 ἀγροικότερον. a 2

δέχεσθαι ἃ λέγουσιν, ἐὰν ἐθέλωσι διδόναι BT. Badham would read 5 δέχεσθαι ἂν ἐθέλωσι διδόναι, so as to express the proverb more neatly. Cf. *Gorg.* 499 C κατὰ τὸν παλαιὸν λόγον τὸ παρὸν εὖ ποιεῖν, καὶ τοῦτο δέχεσθαι τὸ διδόμενον, 'to make the best of what you have, and accept what is offered.' Hdt. ix. 111 ὡς μάθῃς τὰ διδόμενα δέκεσθαι.

μὴ ὀνόματι διαφέρεσθαι, 'not to quarrel about a word,' *sc.* ἐξολωλέναι 283 D.

εἴτε καὶ παρ' ἄλλου του ἐμαθέτην. This seems to be one of many 8 allusions in the dialogue to Protagoras, who is represented as boasting that those who became his pupils would grow better and better every day (*Protag.* 318 A), and that he knew better than all others how to make men virtuous (ibid. 328 A).

285 c NOTES

C 1 ὥσπερ ἐν Καρὶ ἐν ἐμοὶ ἔστω ὁ κίνδυνος. Socrates offers himself as a *vile corpus* for experiment. Cf. *Lach.* 187 B σκοπεῖν χρὴ μὴ οὐκ ἐν τῷ Καρὶ ὑμῖν ὁ κίνδυνος κινδυνεύηται, ἀλλ' ἐν τοῖς υἱέσι τε καὶ ἐν τοῖς τῶν φίλων παισί. The epithet βαρβαροφώνων applied to the Carians by Homer, *Il.* ii. 867 is critically discussed by Strabo 661. The Carians were the first mercenary soldiers, and Carian slaves were numerous: cf. Aristoph. *Aves* 764 εἰ δὲ δοῦλός ἐστι καὶ Κὰρ ὥσπερ Ἐξηκεστίδης, | φυσάτω πάππους παρ' ἡμῖν. There is a still older proverb in Hom *Il.* ix. 378 ἐχθρὰ δέ μοι τοῦ δῶρα, τίω δέ μιν ἐν καρὸς αἴσῃ. But the quantity of καρός forbids our referring it, as the Scholiast does, to the Carians. The meaning is 'pili facio.'

3 ὥσπερ τῇ Μηδείᾳ τῇ Κόλχῳ. The first article is emphatic, 'the famous Medea.' Cf. Ov. *Met.* vii. 164–349, where Medea, after restoring Aeson to youth, persuades the daughters of Pelias to cut their father in pieces and boil him. Apollod. i. 9, 27 καὶ τοῦ πιστεῦσαι χάριν κριὸν μελεΐσασα καὶ καθεψήσασα ἐποίησεν ἄρνα. On a vase in the British Museum, found at Canino in Etruria, the ram restored to youth is seen jumping out of the pot: see Murray's *Greek and Roman Antiq.* OLLA. For the form Κόλχῳ compare the Latin 'venena Colcha' (Hor. *Od.* ii. 13, 8), 'Colchus an Assyrius' (id. *Ars Poet.* 118).

5 εἰ δ', ὅ τι βούλεται. Cf. Alcib. i. 114 B. *Pol.* 432 A εἰ μὲν βούλει, φρονήσει· εἰ δὲ βούλει, ἰσχύῖ, εἰ δέ, καὶ πλήθει. *Sympos.* 212 C εἰ μὲν βούλει, ὡς ἐγκώμιον εἰς Ἔρωτα νόμισον εἰρῆσθαι, εἰ δέ, ὅτι καὶ ὅπῃ χαίρεις ὀνομάζων, τοῦτο ὀνόμαζε. From these passages it is evident that after εἰ δέ we must understand not μή or ἄλλο τι, as proposed by Stephanus and others, but βούλεται. See also *Cratyl.* 407 D; *Legg.* 688 B.

9 δέρειν. Cf. Aristoph. *Nub.* 439:
νῦν οὖν χρήσθων ὅ τι βούλονται·
τουτὶ τό γ' ἐμὸν σῶμ' αὐτοῖσιν
παρέχω τύπτειν, πεινῆν, διψῆν,
αὐχμεῖν, ῥιγῶν, ἀσκὸν δείρειν.

d 1 ἡ τοῦ Μαρσύου. Cf. Hdt. vii. 26 'Here too, in this market-place (Celaenae) is hung up to view the skin of the Silenus Marsyas, which Apollo, as the Phrygian story goes, stripped off and placed there.' Xen. *Anab.* i. 2, 8.

8 ποιεῖ τοὺς λόγους; 'Do you argue upon the supposition that there

NOTES 285 d

is such a thing as contradiction?' Aristot. *Top.* i. 11, 4 gives as an example of a paradoxical opinion ὅτι οὐκ ἔστιν ἀντιλέγειν, καθάπερ ἔφη 'Αντισθένης. Cf. Introd. p. 15; Zeller, *Plato*, note 94.

Οὔκουν σύ γ' ἄν, ἔφη, ἀποδείξαις πώποτε ἀκούσας κτλ. 'You cer- **e 3** tainly, said he, could not prove that you have ever heard,' &c. For the construction of ἀκούσας referring to the subject of ἀποδείξαις cf. Eur. *Orest.* 802 ποῦ γὰρ ὢν δείξω φίλος; *Med.* 548 ἐν τῷδε δείξω πρῶτα μὲν σοφὸς γεγώς. *Bacch.* 47. Plat. *Menex.* 242 E οὗτοι γὰρ ἐνταῦθα ἔδειξαν . . . τούτους νικῶντες ἰδίᾳ.

'Αληθῆ λέγεις, ἔφη. Ctesippus admits that he cannot prove that **5** he has heard : to himself it is proved by his own sense of hearing, but this cannot be demonstrated to another. A principle of wide application : 'No proof can establish the existence of that within a man of which he alone has the final cognisance' (B. F. Westcott). There is no reason therefore for turning ἀληθῆ λέγεις into a question. The sense is vigorously expressed by Jowett: 'Indeed, said Ctesippus; then now you may hear me contradicting Dionysodorus.'

ἀλλὰ ἀκούωμεν νῦν εἴ σοι ἀποδείκνυμι Τ. In B ἀκούω μέν is probably a mere error of transcription. Stallbaum retains the reading of T, and explains it simply and well: 'But let us hear now whether I prove it to you, while Ctesippus contradicts Dionysodorus.' Badham's conjectural emendation, ἀκούων μὲν νυνί σοι ἀποδείκνυμι, 'I am proving to you now that I hear Ctesippus contradicting Dionysodorus,' is very ingenious, and at first sight attractive; but it is open to the same objection that Ctesippus could not prove that he himself heard.

ὑπόσχοις ἂν τούτου λόγον; Cf. *Protag.* 338 D ἐπειδὰν δὲ ἐγὼ **7** ἀποκρίνωμαι ὁπόσ' ἂν οὗτος βούληται ἐρωτᾶν, πάλιν οὗτος ἐμοὶ λόγον ὑποσχέτω ὁμοίως. It is evident from this passage that λόγον ὑπέχειν, like δοῦναι λόγον, means to give a reason in answer to a question, so that 'quaerenti respondere' (Winckelmann) and 'rationem reddere' (Stallbaum) are both implied in the phrase. Cf. *Gorg.* 465 A; Xen. *Mem.* iv. 4, 9; Aristot. *Rhet.* i. 1, 1.

εἰσὶν ἑκάστῳ τῶν ὄντων λόγοι; 'Have all things their proper **9** definitions?' Cf. *Legg.* 895 E 'Ωι δὴ ψυχὴ τοὔνομα, τίς τούτου λόγος; Οὐκοῦν ὡς ἔστιν ἕκαστον . . .; 'Of each therefore as it is, or as it **10** is not?'

EUTHYDEMUS 33 L

286 a NOTES

286 τὸ γὰρ μὴ ὂν οὐδεὶς ἐφάνη λέγων, 'for it was shown that no one
a 2 speaks that which is not.' This refers to 284 C 2 Οὐκ ἄρα τά γε μὴ
ὄντ', ἔφη, λέγει οὐδείς.

5 ⟨τὸν⟩ τοῦ αὐτοῦ πράγματος λόγον ἀμφότεροι λέγοντες, 'if we both
gave the definition of the same thing.' ⟨τόν⟩ omitted in BT, but
added by Heindorf, is adopted by most subsequent editors, except
Stallbaum. The article is required by the previous statement
(285 E 9) that each thing has its proper definition. Cf. *Theaet.*
200 B : 'If a man knows both knowledge and ignorance, does he
think that one of them which he knows is another which he knows?
Or if he knows neither, does he suppose that one which he knows
not is another which he knows not? Or if he knows one and not
the other, does he think that the one which he knows is the one
which he does not know, or that the one which he does not know
is the one which he knows.' In a later passage of *Theaet.* 208 C
knowledge is declared to be the power of 'Definition by the
characteristic difference' (L. Campbell), i.e. λόγον εἰπεῖν, and in the
Euthydemus this is assumed as already settled.

6 λέγοντες V, γνόντες BT. The reading of V corresponds better to
τὸν τοῦ πράγματος λόγον, immediately following.

b 5 ἢ ἐγὼ λέγω . . . 'Or do I describe the thing, and you describe
nothing at all?'

6 ⟨ἂν⟩ ἀντιλέγοι. In BT ἂν is omitted, probably because of the
ἀν- immediately following: ἂν is found in one MS., and is perhaps
rightly adopted, though not indispensable, 'the boundary between
absolute and hypothetical possibility and hypothetical possibility
being naturally uncertain' (Bernhardy, *Gr. Synt.* 411).

9 οὐ γάρ τοι ἀλλὰ τοῦτόν γε, 'for in very truth,' more emphatic than
οὐ γὰρ ἀλλά. Cf. 305 E 3.

c 2 οἱ ἀμφὶ Πρωταγόραν. The doctrine of Protagoras based upon the
assumption that sensation is knowledge is criticized by Plato, *Theaet.*
152–172. See especially 160 C, D : 'Then my perception is true to
me, for it is always inseparable from my own being : and according
to Protagoras I am the judge to myself of what is and of what is
not to me . . . How then, if I never err (ἀψευδὴς ὤν) and never
trip in my conception of things being or becoming, can I fail of
knowing that which I perceive? . . . Then you were quite right
in affirming that knowledge is only perception, and the meaning

34

NOTES   286 c

turns out to be the same, whether with Homer and Heracleitus
and all that company you say that all is motion and flux, or, with
the great sage Protagoras, that man is the measure of all things'
(Jowett in part). This theory (well summarized by L. Campbell,
n. 16) is then criticized by Socrates. Cf. Diog. L. ix. 8, 51 ; Sext.
Emp. *Hypotyp.* A 216.

καὶ οἱ ἔτι παλαιότεροι. Cf. *Theaet.* 152 E ἔστι μὲν γὰρ οὐδέποτ' 3
οὐδέν, ἀεὶ δὲ γίγνεται. καὶ περὶ τούτου πάντες ἑξῆς οἱ σοφοὶ πλὴν Παρ-
μενίδου ξυμφερέσθων, Πρωταγόρας τε καὶ Ἡράκλειτος καὶ Ἐμπεδοκλῆς
κτλ. *Cratyl.* 429 D Ἆρα ὅτι ψευδῆ λέγειν τὸ παράπαν οὐκ ἔστιν, ἆρα
τοῦτό σοι δύναται ὁ λόγος ; συχνοὶ γάρ τινες οἱ λέγοντες, ὦ φίλε Κράτυλε,
καὶ νῦν καὶ πάλαι. This mention of Protagoras in connexion with
Heracleitus points to the fact noticed by Schleiermacher in his
Introduction to the *Theaetetus* (Dobson, p. 91) : 'The dialogue
begins with showing that the Protagorean denial of a general
standard of knowledge and the Heracleitic theory of the flux of all
things, and of *Becoming* alone remaining to the exclusion of all
Being, as well as the principle here tried throughout which sets up
Perception, and Perception alone, for knowledge, do all refer to
one another, and form one system.' Cf. Pater, *Plato*, p. 100.

ἀνατρέπων καὶ αὐτὸς αὑτόν. When Antisthenes invited Plato to hear 4
him lecture περὶ τοῦ μὴ εἶναι ἀντιλέγειν, Plato asked how he could
write about this doctrine, and showed that it could be turned
round and destroyed itself (διδάσκοντος ὅτι περιτρέπεται, Diog. L.
iii. 35). Cf. 288 A 4.

ἄλλο τι ψευδῆ λέγειν οὐκ ἔστιν;—τοῦτο γὰρ δύναται ὁ λόγος· ἢ γάρ; 6
The statement that it is impossible to contradict is here declared
by Socrates to be equivalent to saying, 'It is impossible to speak
falsehood.' The phrase τοῦτο δύναται ὁ λόγος occurs in *Cratyl.*
429 D, quoted above on C 3.

ψευδῆ λέγειν μέν Vat. Θ, Bekker, Badham. 'Vulgarem ordinem, d 1
ψευδῆ μὲν λέγειν, immutandum fuisse nobis plane persuasimus'
(Stallbaum).

τὸ ψεύδεσθαι τῶν πραγμάτων, 'the misrepresentation of things.' 7
The preceding statement concerning ψευδὴς δόξα gives to ψεύδεσθαι
a meaning inclusive of false opinion as well as false statement.
Stallbaum refers to *Apolog.* 22 D καὶ τούτου μὲν οὐκ ἐψεύσθην:
Lysias 156, 2 πολλῶν ἐψεύσθητε τῆς οὐσίας, i. e. 'You were mistaken

35   L 2

about many men's property'; with which compare Antiph. *Or.* v.

11   134, 40 καθ' ὅ τι δ' ἂν ψευσθῆτε τἀληθοῦς, κατὰ τοῦτο ἀπόλλυμαι.

11   Λόγου ἕνεκα, *dicis causa,* 'for form's sake.' Cf. *Lach.* 196 c
ὁρῶμεν μὴ Νικίας οἴεταί τι λέγειν καὶ οὐ λόγου ἕνεκα ταῦτα λέγει. *Crito*
46 D νῦν δὲ κατάδηλος ἄρα ἐγένετο (ὁ λόγος) ὅτι ἄλλως ἕνεκα λόγου
ἐλέγετο.
ἵνα δὴ ἄτοπον λέγῃς, 'in order to state a paradox.'

e 1   Ἀλλὰ σύ, ἔφη, ἔλεγξον, 'Nay, it is for you to refute me.'

5   Οὐδ' ἄρα ἐκέλευον, ἔφη, ἐγὼ νυνδή, ὁ Διονυσόδωρος, ἐξελέγξαι BT.
This reading of the best MSS. has been altered very much for the
worse by recent editors into Οὐδ' ἄρα ἐκέλευεν, ἔφην ἐγώ, νυνδὴ Διονυσόδωρος ἐξελέγξαι. For the order of the words in BT compare
289 C Οὐκ οἶμαι, ἔφη, ἐγώ, ὁ Κλεινίας ὑπολαβών. Translate therefore: 'Neither then did I,' said Dionysodorus, 'bid you just now
to refute me.' νῦν δή refers to E 1 Ἀλλὰ σύ, ἔφη, ἔλεγξον. See also
287 B 2, 297 A 5, and the examples collected by Riddell, *Digest,*
§ 288, of 'Clauses intermingled by Hyperbaton.'

6   ⟨Σὺ δ' ἐκέλευες;⟩ Σὺ δὲ κελεύεις ; Vind. marg., Οὐδὲ κελεύεις B,
Vind., om. T, Stallb.   On the frequent corruption in B of ου for συ
see note on 277 A 6. The question is put by Socrates, who pretends
to be confused and in doubt which of the Sophists had bidden him,
just as in 290 E 7 he pretends not to remember whether Cleinias or
Ctesippus had been speaking. The emphatic position of Σύ shows
that a different person, not Dionysodorus, is now addressed:
'Was it you that were bidding me? For, Euthydemus,' said I,
'I do not at all understand these clever arguments, not even
those that are right, but I have only a dull sort of idea.' The
imperfect ἐκέλευες is better than κελεύεις, as corresponding to
ἐκέλευον in E 5.

287   ἄλλο τι οὐδ' ἐξαμαρτάνειν ἐστιν; 'Is it not impossible even to make
a 2   a mistake?'

8   τίνος διδάσκαλοι ἥκετε; Cf. *Theaet.* 161 C: 'For if truth is only
sensation, and one man's discernment is as good as another's, and
no man has any superior right to determine whether the opinion of
any other is true or false, but each man, as we have several times
repeated, is to himself the sole judge, and everything that he judges
is true and right, why should Protagoras be preferred to the place
of wisdom and instruction, and deserve to be well paid, and we

poor ignoramuses have to go to him, if each one is the measure of
his own wisdom' (Jowett). The same argument stated so sum-
marily in the *Euthydemus* is one of many indications that this
dialogue is later than the *Theaetetus*.

οὕτως εἶ Κρόνος; 'Are you such a dotard?' Cf. Aristoph. *Nub.* b 2
929 Οὐχὶ διδάξεις τοῦτον Κρόνος ὤν. Plut. 581 Κρονικαῖς λήμαις ὄντως
λημῶντες. Diog. L. ii. 111 Εἰσὶ δὲ καὶ ἄλλοι διακηκοότες Εὐβουλίδου,
ἐν οἷς καὶ Ἀπολλώνιος ὁ Κρόνος, οὗ Διόδωρος Ἀμεινίου Ἰασεὺς καὶ αὐτὸς
Κρόνος ἐπίκλην, περὶ οὗ φησι Καλλίμαχος ἐν ἐπιγράμμασιν

Αὐτὸς ὁ Μῶμος
ἔγραφεν ἐν τοίχοις 'ὁ Κρόνος ἐστὶ σοφός.'

νῦν ἀναμιμνήσκει . . . νῦν ἀναμνησθήσει. 'Nescio quomodo (haec) 3
inter se possint iungi, putoque interpolationem statuendam esse'
(Schanz, *N.C.P.* p. 77). In his text Schanz brackets νῦν ἀναμνησθήσει,
but this leaves καὶ εἴ τι πέρυσιν εἶπον in an unusual position.

χαλεποί. The masculine is used as if λόγοις had been used instead 6
of λεγομένοις (Baiter), or with it (Heindorf).

τί, Heindorf's conjecture for ὅ τι, is rejected by Stallbaum, who 9
explains the indirect ὅ τι as in 271 A 6; but in the present passage
τί is more likely to have been changed into ὅ τι, which occurs here
so frequently, than the converse.

ἢ δῆλον ὅτι ὡς. After ὅτι we must mentally repeat λέγεις.

νοεῖ, 'means.' Cf. *Crat.* 407 E τί καὶ νοεῖ τὸ ὄνομα; ἐννοεῖ, the c 1
reading of BT, is apparently not used in this manner: this is the
only passage quoted by L. and Sc. νοεῖ and νοοῖ occur immediately
below. Cf. Stallbaum.

Οὐκ ἔχω ὅ τι χρήσωμαι T: χρήσομαι B, which Stallbaum prefers: 2
but as only a single action is in question, and not a continuance in
the future, the aorist is to be preferred here, as in 306 D, *Gorg.*
466 A, *Phaed.* 95 A.

Ἀλλ' ὃ σὺ λέγεις κτλ. 'Nay, but your phrase,' referring to νοεῖ, 3
as is evident from the following discussion in D 7.

τούτῳ ⟨γ' οὐ⟩ πάνυ χαλεπὸν χρῆσθαι, 'with this it is not at all
difficult to deal.' The whole clause is omitted by Burnet, leaving
the former part of the sentence incomplete and unintelligible.
Badham's ingenious conjecture γ' οὐ for τῷ is accepted by Schanz.
For τούτῳ τῷ Bekker and Stallbaum adopt the Aldine reading τοῖτο
τό, which, like Hermann's τούτῳ τοι, gives an intelligible but less

appropriate meaning: 'It is this phrase of yours (νοεῖ) that *is so difficult* to deal with.' Dionysodorus tries to shift the discussion from his own phrase, οὐχ ἕξεις ὅ τι χρῇ, which he finds too much like οὐκ ἐξελέγξεις, to that of Socrates, νοεῖ τοῦτο τὸ ῥῆμα, which he says 'is *not at all difficult* to deal with,' as he tries to show, D 7.

d 1 οὐδ' ἄν BT : ἄν is omitted by Badham and Schanz, but defended by Ast, *Lex. Plat.*, and Stallbaum, on the ground that the indicative, present, or future may stand in the same sentence with ἄν, provided that ἄν is not joined with the verb, and does not make the whole sentence conditional, but affects only an accessory word or phrase.

e 4 εἰ γὰρ μὴ ἐξήμαρτον. On this passage Lutoslawski remarks (211): 'To the right belief explained in the *Meno* Plato adds in the *Euthydemus* (284 A, 287 E) his explanation of error and wrong belief, whose existence is proved against the Sophists by the hypothetical method taught in the *Meno*.'

288 ἐν ταὐτῷ μένειν. Cf. *Phaed.* 86 E ἐμοὶ γὰρ φαίνεται ἔτι ἐν τῷ αὐτῷ ὁ
a 3 λόγος εἶναι, ' It appears to me that the argument remains just where it was,' i. e. has made no advance. *Theaet.* 200 A οὐκοῦν μακρὰν περιελθόντες πάλιν ἐπὶ τὴν πρώτην πάρεσμεν ἀπορίαν. ibid. C εἰς ταὐτὸν περιτρέχειν μυριάκις οὐδὲν πλέον ποιοῦντες.

4 ὥσπερ τὸ παλαιόν, i. e. in the time of Protagoras and earlier, 286 C 2.

καταβαλὼν πίπτειν. Cf. 286 C 4 τούς τε ἄλλους ἀνατρέπων καὶ αὐτὸς αὑτόν.

ὥστε τοῦτο μὴ πάσχειν . . . ἐξηυρῆσθαι. Cf. 303 E 6 ἐξηύρηται ὥστε.

8 ὦ ἄνδρες Θούριοι εἴτε Χῖοι. Cf. 271 C 3.

b 1 εἴθ' ὁπόθεν καὶ ὅπῃ κτλ., 'or from whatever place and in whatever way you like to be named.'

8 τὸν Αἰγύπτιον σοφιστήν. Cf. Hom. *Od.* iv. 385 ἀθάνατος Πρωτεὺς Αἰγύπτιος, ὅς τε θαλάσσης πάσης βένθεα οἶδε. Plat. *Phaedr.* 275 B 'Ω Σώκρατες, ῥᾳδίως σὺ Αἰγυπτίους καὶ ὁποδαποὺς ἂν ἐθέλῃς λόγοις ποιεῖς. A reminiscence of Plato's recent visit to Egypt.

c 1 Μενέλαον μιμώμεθα. Cf. *Od.* iv. 456:

ἀλλ' ἦ τοι πρώτιστα λέων γένετ' ἠϋγένειος,
αὐτὰρ ἔπειτα δράκων καὶ πάρδαλις ἠδὲ μέγας σῦς·
γίγνετο δ' ὑγρὸν ὕδωρ καὶ δένδρεον ὑψιπέτηλον.
ἡμεῖς δ' ἀστεμφέως ἔχομεν τετληότι θυμῷ.

NOTES   288 c

ἐκφανῆτον ἐφ' ᾧ αὐτὼ σπουδάζετον. Cf. C 5 ἐκφανῆναι, 'to show 2 themselves.' Translate: 'Until they let us see the object about which they are themselves in earnest.' Cf. *Pol.* 497 C δῆλος δὴ οὖν εἰ ὅ τι μετὰ τοῦτο ἐρήσει.

οἶμαι γάρ τι αὐτοῖν πάγκαλον φανεῖσθαι, 'for I think that some- 3 thing very splendid in them will appear.' 'Cf. *Apolog.* 17 A μάλιστα δὲ αὐτῶν ἐν ἐθαύμασα' (Stallb.).

ἐγὼ οὖν μοι δοκῶ. 'I am inclined therefore myself to indicate 5 again the character in which I beseech them to appear.' For ὑφηγήσασθαι Heindorf proposes ὑφηγήσεσθαι, and Schanz changes καί into κἄν, but neither is necessary: 'Vult enim Socrates statim et e vestigio uno aliquo commonstrare exemplo quales sibi illos apparere cupiat : unde recte utitur aoristo, quem etiam libri tuentur omnes' (Stallb.).

ἐάν πως t, πᾶν ὅπως BT: 'Nisi putas critici esse elegantes d 2 lectiones captare recipies quae boni libri tibi praebent' (Schanz, *N. C. P.* p. 78).

συντεταμίνον, 'intent': cf. Xen. *Oecon.* ii. 18 γνώμη συντεταμένη ἐπιμελουμένους.

ἡ δὲ φιλοσοφία κτῆσις ἐπιστήμης. 'While in the *Protagoras* the 8 word "philosophy" was still used in the meaning of love of wisdom (335 D, 342 D), here we see it defined as acquisition of knowledge (288 D), and the dialectician, who had received his first rules in the *Meno*, becomes the highest judge of every particular knowledge (290 C)' (Lutoslawski, p. 210).

ἆρ' οὐ τοῦτο μὲν ἁπλοῦν; Cf. *Pol.* 545 E ἢ τόδε μὲν ἁπλοῦν; 'absque e 1 ulla exceptione validum' (Ast).

εἰ ἐπισταίμεθα γιγνώσκειν περιιόντες, 'if we knew how to go about 2 and learn.'

ἐξηλέγξαμεν, 'we fully proved.' Cf. *Phaedr.* 273 B; Thuc. 5 iii. 64 ἃ δὲ ἡ φύσις ἀεὶ ἐβούλετο, ἐξηλέγχθη ἐς τὸ ἀληθές. But in our present passage the idea of refutation remains, for what is proved is the negative proposition ὅτι οὐδὲν πλέον κτλ. Cf. *Theaet.* 166 C ἐξέλεγχον ὡς οὐχὶ ἴδιαι αἰσθήσεις ἑκάστῳ ἡμῶν γίγνονται.

τὸ πᾶν ἡμῖν χρυσίον γένοιτο, 'all the gold in the world should 6 become ours.'   289

ἄνευ τοῦ ἐπίστασθαι τῇ ἀθανασίᾳ χρῆσθαι. Cf. Lutosl. p. 210: 'Plato b 1

39

is so proud of his acquired certainty of knowledge that he would
not give it up even for immortality, if not accompanied by knowledge how to use it (*Euth.* 289 B).'

2   ἔοικεν ὄφελος οὐδέν. The omission of εἶναι is not unusual: cf.
Polit. 280 B πάλιν οὖν ἔοικεν ἐπανιτέον. *Crat.* 424 A ἤδη ἔοικεν ἐπι-
σκεπτέον.

7   λυροποιοὺς δεῖν εἶναι Heindorf, Badham, Burnet.   For δεῖν we
have δεινούς in BT, δεῖν δεινούς Heusde, δεινοὺς ὄντας Winckelmann,
Schanz.   This last reading gives the sense:—' It is far from being
the case that, if we are clever lyre-makers, we are also in possession
of any such knowledge as this which we are seeking.'   Heindorf's
reading is simpler: ' It is far from being the case that we ought to
be lyre-makers and possessed of any such art as this (lyre-making).'
There is, I think, no force in Winckelmann's assumption that such
an indefinite phrase as τοιαύτης τινός must refer to the same kind
of art here as in B 4.   On the contrary its reference is determined
by the nearer context (λυροποιούς), and confirmed by ἐνταῦθα γάρ
following.

c 3   διῄρηται δὲ τοῦ αὐτοῦ πέρι BV, δέ is omitted in T.   The
omission of the whole clause by Schanz is quite arbitrary and un-
justifiable.   ' The art which makes the lyre is separate from the art
which uses it, but though distinct they refer to the same thing.'

6   Ἀλλὰ πρὸς θεῶν, ἔφην ἐγώ, ' But seriously, said I.'

7   ἣν ἔδει κεκτημένους κτλ., ' which we must acquire in order to be
happy.'   Cf. 282 E 3 ἣν δεῖ λαβόντα εὐδαιμονεῖν.

8   Οὐκ οἶμαι, ἔφη, ἐγώ, ὁ Κλεινίας.   For the like order compare
286 E 5.

d 2   λογοποιούς.   Cf. Ammonius, *De Diff. Voc.* Λογογράφος μέν ἐστιν ὁ
τοὺς δικανικοὺς λόγους γράφων· λογοποιὸς δὲ ὁ λόγους τινὰς καὶ μύθους
συντιθείς.   The two meanings are, in fact, common to both words;
but λογογράφος more frequently means a ᾽chronicler' or ' prose
writer,' as in Thuc. i. 21 οὔτε ὡς ποιηταὶ ὑμνήκασι ... οὔτε ὡς λογο-
γράφοι συνέθεσαν.   The λογοποιός, or λόγων ποιητής, is distinguished
from the ῥήτωρ who delivered the speech, Isocr. *Adv. Soph.* 17
τοὺς δὲ καταδεεστέραν τὴν φύσιν ἔχοντας ἀγωνιστὰς μὲν ἀγαθοὺς ἢ λόγων
ποιητὰς οὐκ ἂν ἀποτελέσειεν.

4   ἀλλὰ καὶ ... ἀδύνατοι D 5, omitted by Winckelmann and Schanz
against the authority of the MSS.

θεσπεσία τις, 'inspired as it were.' So in *Theaet.* 151 B, Prodicus e 4 and others are spoken of as σοφοῖς τε καὶ θεσπεσίοις ἀνδράσι. κήλησίς τε καὶ παραμυθία τυγχάνει οὖσα, 'a charming and soothing.' 290 In *Protag.* 315 A the great Sophist is described as κηλῶν τῇ φωνῇ a 4 ὥσπερ Ὀρφεύς. Cf. *Pol.* 358 B ὥσπερ ὄφις κληθῆναι. *Phaedr.* 261 A τὸ μὲν ὅλον ἡ ῥητορικὴ ἂν εἴη τέχνη ψυχαγωγία τις διὰ λόγων, 271 C Ἐπειδὴ λόγου δύναμις τυγχάνει ψυχαγωγία οὖσα, a passage of which there may be a reminiscence in the use of the same phrase τυγχάνει οὖσα.

ἐμὲ οἶμαι ηὑρηκέναι. The personal pronoun marks the antithesis : 9 Cleinias having confessed his ignorance, Socrates exclaims : 'I think *I* have found it.' Cf. Hom. *Il.* xiii. 269 οὐδὲ γὰρ οὐδ' ἐμέ φημι λελασμένον ἔμμεναι ἀλκῆς. *Symp.* 175 C, *Pol.* 400 C.

Οὐδεμία, ἔφη, τῆς θηρευτικῆς αὐτῆς ἐπὶ πλέον ἐστίν. For αὐτῆς, BT, b 7 many changes have been proposed : ' δύναμις Heindorf, ἁπάσης Ast, ἄσκησις Orelli, ἱκανότης Vermehren, αὐτή Vahlen : post αὐτῆς supplevit χρεία vel ὠφέλεια Badham, οὐδέν pro οὐδεμία scripsit Thompson ad *Phaedr.* 128' (Schanz). Schanz himself marks αὐτῆς † as corrupt, but Routh, Winckelmann, Stallbaum, and Burnet rightly leave it untouched. Ficinus gives a mere paraphrase : 'Nullus sane venationis opus ulterius porrigit quam,' &c. Routh's translation is much better : 'Nulla *pars*, inquit, ipsius artis venatoriae latius patet, quam ut,' &c. : but he gives no explanation of the construction, which is in fact quite simple. Οὐδεμία agrees with τέχνη understood from the preceding context : τῆς θηρευτικῆς is a substantive, as in *Polit.* 289 A γεωργικῇ δὲ καὶ θηρευτικῇ καὶ γυμναστικῇ καὶ ἰατρικῇ καὶ μαγειρικῇ πᾶν ὑποτιθέντες ὀρθότερον ἀποδώσομεν ἢ τῇ πολιτικῇ. Thus αὐτῆς marks the distinction between ' actual' hunting, and the metaphorical hunting of the geometers, astronomers, and dialecticians.

οὐ γὰρ ποιοῦσι τὰ διαγράμματα, 'for they are not the makers of c 2 the geometrical figures.' This is explained by the passage in *Meno* 82 B, where Socrates shows that the uneducated slave has in himself the ideas of the geometrical figures.

τὰ ὄντα ἀνευρίσκουσι, 'they discover the existing realities.' Cf. 3 *Pol.* 527 B τοῦ γὰρ ἀεὶ ὄντος ἡ γεωμετρικὴ γνῶσίς ἐστιν.

τοῖς διαλεκτικοῖς. Lutoslawski, p. 331, argues that ' διαλεκτική 5 meaning metaphysical science (is) never used before Plato, and by

41

Plato first in *Rep.* vii, cf. *Phaedr.* 276 E; διαλεκτικός meaning, not as in the *Cratylus, Euthydemus*, and in Xenophon, one who knows how to ask and answer questions, but the philosopher able to discover unity in the variety of particulars, *Phaedr.* 266 B.' But in this passage τοῖς διαλεκτικοῖς must indicate in the higher sense the metaphysicians to whom the geometers hand over their hypotheses to be traced up to first principles. In the full description of Plato's 'dialectic' *Pol.* 531 B–536 B compare with our present passage especially 533 B, C: 'And the remaining arts which, as we said, have some small apprehension of true Being, such as geometry and the arts connected with it, we find that though they dream about real Being, they are unable to behold it in a waking state, so long as they leave the hypotheses which they use unexamined, because they are unable to explain the reason of them . . . Therefore the dialectic method alone proceeds in this way,—it carries up its hypotheses to the first principle of all, in order to establish them firmly.' Cf. Dr. H. Jackson's excellent articles on the *Republic* in *The Journal of Philology*, vol. x. p. 143, and Lutoslawski, p. 302.

d 4   τοῖς ὀρτυγοτρόφοις, 'the quail-breeders,' who bred and trained the birds to fight. Cf. Ov. *Amor.* ii. 6, 27 'Ecce coturnices inter sua praelia vivunt.'

e 7   'Ἀλλ' ἄρα, ὦ πρὸς Διός; 'But then, I wonder, was it Ctesippus?' Socrates pretends to have forgotten : for a similar ironical profession of doubt see 286 E 5, note.

291   Ποῖος Κτήσιππος ; 'Ctesippus indeed?' In this idiomatic use of
a 1   ποῖος the interrogation is equivalent to an indignant denial. Cf. 304 E Ποῖον, ἔφη, χαρίεν, ὦ μακάριε ;

4   μή τις τῶν κρειττόνων; 'Was it some superior being that was there and spoke thus?' Crito perhaps means Socrates himself. 'Vides ad Deum auctorem solita ironia . . . eum referre ea quae ipse dialectica quasi obstetricia arte in iuvene egregiae indolis effecerat: vide *Theaet.* 150 C, D, E.'

6   τῶν κρειττόνων μέντοι τις ἐμοὶ δοκεῖ. 'It was indeed some superior being, it seems to me, and very superior.'

b 1   Πόθεν . . . ηὕρομεν; 'Find it, my good fellow? Nay, our case was quite ridiculous.' Cf. A 1 Ποῖος Κτήσιππος ; *Pol.* 330 A Ποῖ' ἐπεκτησάμην ;

2   κορύδους, 'crested larks.' Schol. in loc. Κόρυδοι ὄρνιθες ὄρτυξιν

42

NOTES   291 b

ὅμοιοι, οὓς ἔνιοι μὲν κορυδάλλους φασί, Γῆς καὶ Ἀθηνᾶς ἱεροί. Cf.
Aristoph. *Aves* 471:

  οὐδ' Αἴσωπον πεπάτηκας,
  ὃς ἔφασκε λέγων κορυδὸν πάντων πρώτην ὄρνιθα γενέσθαι,
  προτέραν τῆς γῆς.

Plutarch, *Mor.* 507 E Κόρυδος ὦπται πετόμενος κράνος ἔχων χρυσοῦν
καὶ δόρυ. Chrysost. *Orat.* ix. 141 D οἱ δὲ κόρυθοι πόσῳ τινὶ θᾶττον
ὑμῶν διέρχονται τὸ στάδιον;
ὑπεξέφευγον, 'kept slipping away from us.'   b 3
τὰ μὲν οὖν πολλά, 'the long story.'   4
τὴν βασιλικὴν . . . τέχνην.   On the βασιλικὴ τέχνη cf. Xen. *Mem.* 5
iv. 2, 11. Stallbaum, *Disp.* 31, points out that the whole argument about 'the regal art' of statesmanship is intended to refute
the doctrine of Protagoras, who limited the idea of virtue to
prudence in domestic affairs and ability to speak and act for the
best in affairs of state: cf. *Protag.* 318 E–328 D, *Meno* 91 A.
ἀτεχνῶς κατὰ τὸ Αἰσχύλου ἰαμβεῖον. Cf. Aesch. *Sept. c. Theb.* 1 d 1
Κάδμου πολῖται, χρὴ λέγειν τὰ καίρια | ὅστις φυλάσσει πρᾶγος ἐν πρύμνῃ
πόλεως | οἴακα νωμῶν. On the use of ἀτεχνῶς in quoting proverbial
sayings cf. 292 E 3, 303 E 1.
τὶ ἡμῖν ἀπεργάζεται ἔργον, 'opus aliquod efficit an non?' (Ficinus). 7
The indefinite τί is shown to be right by the form of the answer,
πάντως δήπου, 'something most surely.' Schanz, *N. C. P.* p. 80,
defends the separation of τί from ἔργον by referring to *Symp.* 194 D
εἴ τι ἴσως οἷοιο αἰσχρὸν ποιεῖν: 174 E καί τι ἔφη αὐτόθι γελοῖον παθεῖν.
ὑγίειαν ⟨ἂν⟩ φαίης. Ast added ⟨ἂν⟩, which may easily have e 7
dropped out after ὑγίειαν, as before ἀντιλέγοι 286 B 5; but see the
note there.
τί ἔργον ἀπεργάζεται; ἔργον B Vind., om. T Burnet. Cf. *Charm.* 292
165 D τὴν ὑγίειαν καλὸν ἡμῖν ἔργον ἀπεργάζεται. *Tim.* 30 B ὅπως ὅτι a 1
κάλλιστον εἴη . . . ἔργον ἀπειργασμένος. *Symp.* 178 D, *Legg.* 801 E,
Pol. 353 B, 553 C, &c.
ἀπήγγειλας, 'as you report the discussion': on this case of the c 3
aorist referring to what has taken place *just immediately before*,
compare the similar use of ἐπήνεσα, ἥσθην, ἐδεξάμην, ἀπέπτυσα,
ἔγνων, &c.
ἢ ἄλλους ἀγαθοὺς ποιήσομεν; 'Shall we say it is that by which we d 5
shall make others good?'

43

e 2 ἠτιμάσαμεν BT Vind. 'We discredited.' The correction in t
ἀπεδοκιμάσαμεν is only an explanatory gloss.

ἀτεχνῶς τὸ λεγόμενον, 'there comes in exactly the proverb
"Corinthus son of Zeus".' The Scholiast on the passage relates
that when Corinth had sent ambassadors to Megara to complain
of their revolt, one argument advanced was that the mythical
founder 'Corinthus son of Zeus' would be aggrieved if they failed
to exact condign punishment. The proverb came to be used of
boastful repetitions of the same story. Cf. Paus. ii. 1, 1 Διὸς δὲ
εἶναι Κόρινθον οὐδένα οἶδα εἰπόντα πω σπουδῇ πλὴν Κορινθίων τῶν
πολλῶν. Cf. Pind. Nem. vii. 104:

ταὐτὰ δὲ τρὶς τετράκι τ' ἀμπολεῖν
ἀπορία τελέθει, τέκνοισιν ἅτε μαψυλάκας, Διὸς Κόρινθος.

Plutarch, Mor. 1072 B πολὺς οὖν ὁ Διὸς Κόρινθος ἐπὶ τῶν λόγων αὐτῶν
ἀφίκται. On ἀτεχνῶς cf. 291 D, note.

5 ποιήσειε BT, ποιήσει Heindorf, Winckelmann, Badham, Schanz,
Burnet. Stallbaum rightly defends the optative, referring to Hermann, Viger De Idiot. 491. Cf. Aesch. Choeph. 594 ἀλλ' ὑπέρ-
τολμον ἀνδρὸς φρόνημα τίς λέγοι; When the optative is used in
this potential sense it is not easy to determine in what cases the
particle ἄν may or may not be omitted. 'For the boundary
between the conditional and unconditional possibility must naturally
be very wavering and uncertain' (Bernhardy, Gk. Synt. 410). In
the dramatists the omission is not uncommon: cf. Eur. Hippol.
1186 καὶ θᾶσσον ἢ λέγοι τις ἐξηρτυμένας. Iph. in Aul. 417 μήτηρ δ'
ὁμαρτεῖ σῆς Κλυταιμνήστρας δέμας | καὶ παῖς Ὀρέστης, ὥστε τερφθείης
ἰδών. In prose writers the omission occurs chiefly, if not solely, in
questions as here, cf. Plat. Legg. 894 C τῶν δὴ δέκα μάλιστα ἡμῖν
κινήσεων τίνα προκρίναιμεν ...; Lach. 190 B 4 ἡμᾶς τῷδε παρακαλεῖτον
εἰς συμβουλήν, τίνα τρόπον τοῖς ὑέσιν αὐτῶν ἀρετὴ ... ἀμείνους ποιήσειε ;
See also Dinarch. c. Demosth. 98 ; Lycurg. c. Leocrat. 168 ; Plut.
Mor. 75 E.

293 πᾶσαν ἤδη φωνὴν ἠφίειν. Cf. Eur. Med. 278 ἐχθροὶ γὰρ ἐξιᾶσι
a 1 πάντα δὴ κάλων. Schol. ἀπὸ μεταφορᾶς τῶν οὐριοδρομούντων καὶ χαλών-
των πρὸς τὸ πνεῦμα τοὺς ἀρτέμονας. Cf. Aristoph. Eq. 756 νῦν δή
σε πάντα δεῖ κάλων ἐξιέναι. Plat. Pol. 475 καὶ ἑνὶ λόγῳ προφάσεις
προφασίζεσθέ τε καὶ πάσας φωνὰς ἀφίετε.

2 ὥσπερ Διοσκόρω, 'apogr. Marcianum 184' (Schanz) ; διοσκούρων

NOTES 293 a

BT. 'Recte Stephanus et Bekkerus Διοσκόρω . . . Nihil durius quam ἐπικαλούμενος sine accusativo positum; neque σῶσαι aliunde quam a δεόμενος pendere potest' (Badham). Cf. Rutherford, *The New Phrynichus* 310 'Διόσκουροι, ὀρθότερον Διόσκοροι. γελάσει οὖν τοὺς σὺν τῷ υ λέγοντας. Lobeck's note on this article is in his best style : " Nimirum natura ita comparatum est ut dualis numeri longe maior sit usus, apud veteres praesertim, quam plurativi nominis. Διοσκόρω Eur. *Or.* 465; Arist. *Pax* 285; *Eccles.* 1069, &c." ' The mention of the Dioscuri (*nautis* ' optatos Tyndaridas,' Propert. i. 17, 18) shows the origin of the preceding phrase πάσας φωνὰς ἀφιέναι.

τῆς τρικυμίας τοῦ λόγου. Cf. Aesch. *Prom. V.* 1036 κακῶν 3 τρικυμίᾳ.

τίς ποτ' ἐστὶν ἡ ἐπιστήμη. Cf. *Charm.* 174 A τίς αὐτὸν τῶν ἐπιστη- 4 μῶν ποιεῖ εὐδαίμονα; ἢ ἅπασαι ὁμοίως ;

οἷόν τέ τι τῶν ὄντων. 'Do you then think it possible for any being b 9 not to be this very thing which it is?

τούτου γε αὐτοῦ, 'just of this thing itself.' Socrates tries to limit c 3 the proposition to some particular case, as again in c 6 ἐκείνου γε.

τυγχάνεις ὤν . . . , 'you actually are, and, at the same time in the 8 same relation, are not the very same that you are.'

κατὰ ταὐτά, i.e. in relation to knowledge. d 1

εἶεν, 'be it so.' Cf. Ruhnk. *Tim. Lex.* Εἶεν· συγκατάθεσις μὲν τῶν 3 εἰρημένων, συναφὴ δὲ πρὸς τὰ μέλλοντα. The Scholiast on Plat. *Polit.* 257 A renders it by Ἄγε δή : and the Scholiast on Eur. *Phoen.* 856 εἶεν· διηρημένως ἀναγνωστέον. ἔστι δὲ ἐπίρρημα.

καλὰ δὴ πάντα λέγεις BT. Scholiast, Καλὰ δὴ πάντ' ἄγεις, ἀντὶ τοῦ ἀγγέλλεις· ἐπὶ τῶν αἴσια ἀναγγελλόντων. πολλάκις δὲ λέγεται καὶ κατ' εἰρωνείαν. Ἀριστοφάνης Γεωργοῖς καὶ Πλάτων Εὐθυδήμῳ. Whether ἄγεις be a right reading or not, the Scholiast's interpretation of the passage is perfectly clear from what follows, and is admirably suited to the passage. Socrates having been declared by the Sophist to know all things pretends to accept the statement as 'good news entirely.' The words καλὰ πάντα had already become proverbial: cf. Theogn. 283 ἡγεῖσθαί θ' ὡς καλὰ πάντα τιθεῖ. Hdt. i. 32 πάντα καλὰ ἔχοντα. Plutarch, *Mor.* 236 B τῶν πολιτῶν πυνθανομένων αὐτοῦ Ποῖά τινα ἐν Ἀθήναις, Πάντα, εἶπε, καλά· εἰρωνευόμενος καὶ παριστὰς ὅτι πάντα παρὰ τοῖς Ἀθηναίοις καλὰ νομίζεται, αἰσχρὸν δὲ

45

293 d   NOTES

οὐδέν. Winckelmann quotes examples of a similar usage from Plato, *Polit.* 273 B, 284 A, *Phileb.* 26 A, *Legg.* 783 E. The conjecture of Abresch. καλὰ δὴ παταγεῖς, adopted by Stallbaum, Badham, and Schanz, has no support from MSS., nor from any passage in which παταγεῖν is so used, the usual phrase being φθέγγεσθαι, as in *Theaet.* 179 D τὴν φερομένην ταύτην οὐσίαν διακρούοντα εἴτε ὑγιὲς εἴτε σαθρὸν φθέγγεται. The reading of BT is rightly retained by Burnet. The quotation of the passage in Hesych. καλὰ δὴ παταγεῖς· καλὰ λαλεῖς is regarded by Heindorf as a corruption of καλὰ δὴ πάντ' ἄγεις.

5   ὡς δή, 'since forsooth.' Stallbaum refers to the same ironical use of ὡς δή in *Pol.* 337 C Εἶεν, ἔφη· ὡς δὴ ὅμοιον τοῦτο ἐκείνῳ; *Gorg.* 486 E, 492 B, *Protag.* 542 C, in all which passages the ironical sense is evident.

8   ἆρα οὕτως λέγεις; 'Is that your argument, and that your wise invention?'

e 1 αὐτὸς σαυτόν γε δὴ ἐξελέγχεις. 'Yes, surely you are refuting yourself.'

2   Τί δέ, . . . σὺ οὐ πέπονθας κτλ. 'What then, are not you in this same plight? For whatever I might suffer in company with you and our dear friend Dionysodorus here, I certainly should not be at all aggrieved.' On φίλης κεφαλῆς cf. Hom. *Il.* viii. 281 Τεῦκρε, φίλη κεφαλή. *Phaedr.* 264 A Φαῖδρε, φίλη κεφαλή. *Gorg.* 513 C.

294 καὶ σύ γε πρός. 'Yes, and you too.' On this absolute use of πρός
a 2 see *Protag.* 321 D πρὸς δὲ καὶ αἱ Διὸς φυλακαὶ φοβεραὶ ἦσαν. *Gorg.* 469 B καὶ ἐλεεινόν γε πρός. In 298 D καὶ πρὸς . . . is corrupt.

9   Ἀλλὰ τί; 'But what then?' The complete question represented elliptically by τί may ask either for a reason, 'Why?', or, as here, for an inference, 'What then?' Cf. *Phaed.* 89 B, *Euthyphro* 14 D, *Pol.* 357 D ; Aristoph. *Ran.* 489, and see Riddell, *Digest,* § 20 ; Jelf, *Gk. Gr.* 880, Obs. 2.

b 2 μόλις ὑμᾶς προυκαλεσάμην, 'I could hardly incite you.' Schanz suspects a corruption in σπουδάζειν.

6   νευρορραφεῖν, 'to do stitching,' as a part of 'shoemaking,' σκυτοτομεῖν (σκυτική), distinct from καττύειν 'to sole': cf. Xen. *Cyr.* viii. 2, 4 ἔστι δὲ ἔνθα καὶ ὑποδήματα ὁ μὲν νευρορραφῶν μόνον τρέφεται, ὁ δὲ σχίζων.

8   τοὺς ἀστέρας ὁπόσοι εἰσί, καὶ τὴν ἄμμον; Cf. Hdt. i. 47 Οἶδα δ' ἐγὼ

46

ψάμμου τ' ἀριθμὸν καὶ μέτρα θαλάσσης. Pind. *Ol.* ii. 98 ψάμμος
ἀριθμὸν περιπέφευγεν. Euseb. *Praep. Ev.* 212, 230.

ὁπόσους ὀδόντας ἔχει. Cf. Aristoph. *Plut.* 1057 πόσους ἔχεις C 4
ὀδόντας. Aristot. *Rhet.* iii. 5, 4 τύχοι γὰρ ἄν τις μᾶλλον ἐν τοῖς
ἀρτιασμοῖς ἄρτια ἢ περισσὰ εἰπὼν μᾶλλον ἢ πόσα ἔχει. Lysias, *Fr.*
2, 8 ῥᾷον αὐτῆς τοὺς ὀδόντας ἀριθμεῖν ἢ τοὺς τῆς χειρὸς δακτύλους. This
last is the game to which Ctesippus alludes, the modern 'Mora,' or
'How many fingers do I hold up?' Aristotle says that 'Even or
odd' ('Ludere par impar') is easier.

μηδαμῶς, 'do not say so.' Cf. *Phaedr.* 234 E, *Menex.* 236 C.   7

φαίνησθε γνόντες, 'be found to have known by my counting.'   9

πάνυ ἀπαρακαλύπτως, 'Ctesippus without any reserve whatever d 3
went on asking anything and everything, at last even the most
indecent things,—did they know them?'

ἀνδρειότατα ὁμόσε ᾔτην, 'most valiantly encountered his questions.' 5
Cf. *Pol.* 610 C ἐὰν δέ γέ τις . . . ὁμόσε τῷ λόγῳ τολμᾷ ἰέναι. *Euthyphr.*
3 C. Hom. *Il.* xiii. 337 ὡς ἄρα τῶν ὁμόσ' ἦλθε μάχη. Eustathius
remarks that the use of the phrase in Attic writers was taken from
this passage of Homer. Cf. Ruhnk. *Tim. Lex.* Ὁμόσε. On the
form ᾔτην cf. Schanz, *Praefatio in Euthyd.* § 15.

οἱ κάπροι . . . ὁμόσε ὠθούμενοι. Cf. Xen. *Cyr.* i. 4, 11 οἱ δὲ κάπροι, 6
ὥσπερ τοὺς ἄνδρας φασὶ τοὺς ἀνδρείους, ὁμόσε ἐφέροντο.

[τὸν Εὐθύδημον]. Either this name, or ὁ Διονυσόδωρος, must be 8
omitted, as is proved by ἥκεις following; and τηλικοῦτος ὤν applies
better to Dionysodorus as being the elder.

ἐς μαχαίρας γε κυβιστᾶν. Cf. Xen. *Conviv.* ii. 11 μέτα δὲ τοῦτο e 2
κύκλος εἰσηνέχθη περίμεστος ξιφῶν ὀρθῶν. εἰς οὖν ταῦτα ἡ ὀρχηστρὶς
ἐκυβίστα τε καὶ ἐξεκυβίστα ὑπὲρ αὐτῶν (Routh). Plat. *Sympos.* 190 A
καὶ ὁπότε ταχὺ ὁρμήσειεν θεῖν, ὥσπερ οἱ κυβιστῶντες εἰς ὀρθὸν τὰ σκέλη
περιφερόμενοι κυβιστῶσι κύκλῳ. See the illustration in Smith's *Dict.
Class. Antiq.* SALTATIO, p. 106.

ἐπὶ τροχοῦ δινεῖσθαι. Routh finds a description of this gymnastic 3
feat in Xen. *Conviv.* ii. 22 ὅτι δ' ἡ παῖς εἰς τοὔπισθεν καμπτομένη
τροχοὺς ἐμιμεῖτο, ἐκεῖνος ταῦτα εἰς τὸ ἔμπροσθεν ἐπικύπτων μιμεῖσθαι
τροχοὺς ἐπειρᾶτο. But ἐπὶ τροχοῦ δινεῖσθαι can only mean 'to be
whirled round upon a wheel,' and this meaning is found in a later
passage of Xen. *Conviv.* vii. 3 δοκεῖ οὖν μοι τὸ μὲν εἰς μαχαίρας
κυβιστᾶν κινδύνου ἐπίδειγμα εἶναι, ὃ συμποσίῳ οὐδὲν προσήκει. καὶ μὴν

294 e   NOTES

τό γε ἐπὶ τοῦ τροχοῦ ἅμα περιδινουμένου γράφειν τε καὶ ἀναγιγνώσκειν
θαῦμα μὲν ἴσως τί ἐστιν, ἡδονὴν δὲ οὐδὲ ταῦτα δύναμαι γνῶναι τίν' ἂν
παράσχοι.

3 οὕτω πόρρω σοφίας ἥκεις; The separation of this from the former
part of the sentence is rightly removed by Winckelmann, Badham,
and Burnet. οὔπω inserted before οὕτω by Schanz is quite unnecessary. 'Surely, said I, you do not also know how to turn a
somersault into the midst of swords, or to be whirled round on
a wheel at your time of life, having attained to such skill as that?'

9 εὐθὺς γενόμενοι, 'from the moment of your birth.'

11 Ἐφάτην ἅμα ἀμφοτέρω. 'They both affirmed it together.' Schanz
adds a second πάντα before ἐφάτην without authority.

295 Πλήν γ' ὅτι, ⟨ἦν δ'⟩ ἐγώ..., 'Yes (I cannot believe), except that
a 3 you are likely to be wise. ἦν δ' omitted in the MSS. was added
by Stephanus from Cornarius. Schanz thinks ἀπιστῶ should be
inserted after ἐγώ: but 'I do not believe that you are likely to
be wise' is very unlike the ironical courtesy of Socrates. A better
word than ἀπιστῶ would be οἶμαι or something similar. Then
πλήν γ' ὅτι ἐγὼ ⟨οἶμαι⟩ κτλ., 'Yes, except in so far as I think you
are likely to be wise.' Either ἐγώ must be omitted or a verb
supplied.

6 ἥδιστα ταῦτα ἐξελέγχομαι, 'I am delighted to be refuted on these
points.'

8 ἕρμαιον. Cf. 273 E 2.

b 9 ἀλλὰ μὴ... A certain correction of ἀλλὰ μὴν..., adopted by
all editors, except Winckelmann, whose attempt to explain ἀλλὰ
μήν is not satisfactory.

c 1 Ὑπολαμβάνεις, 'of course you understand something (as the
meaning) of what I say.'

4 ἄλλη ἐρωτᾷς διανοούμενος, 'ask a question intending it in one way,
and I take it in another way.'

6 μηδὲν πρὸς ἔπος, 'nothing to the point.' Cf. Philol. 18 τὸ τί πρὸς
ἔπος αὖ ταῦτ' ἐστίν; The phrase became proverbial, as in Lucian,
Philopseud. 29 Οὐδὲν πρὸς ἔπος ταῦτα, φασίν. A similar phrase is
οὐδὲν πρὸς λόγον, Philol. 33 B, 42 E (Heindorf).

7 Ἔμοιγε κτλ. 'It will satisfy me, but not you, I imagine.' For
a like arrogant speech cf. 296 B Οὔκουν ἡμᾶς γ', ἔφη, ἀλλ' εἴπερ, σέ.

10 Οὐκ ἀποκρινεῖ. The future was rightly restored by Bekker, as

48

repeating scornfully Socrates' refusal to answer. 'You will not answer what you understand from time to time (to be meant), because you are continually talking nonsense, and are too much of a dotard.'

διαστέλλοντι τὰ λεγόμενα. Cf. Aristot. *Soph. El.* xvii. 15 Ἐν μὲν οὖν d 1 τοῖς κυρίως λεγομένοις ὀνόμασιν ἀνάγκη ἀποκρίνεσθαι ἢ ἁπλῶς ἢ διαιρούμενον, 'When words are used in their proper sense, we must answer either simply "yes" or "no," or by drawing a distinction.' ibid. Δῆλον οὖν ὡς ἐν οἷς ἀσαφὲς τὸ προτεινόμενον οὐ συγχωρητέον ἁπλῶς.

θηρεῦσαι τὰ ὀνόματα περιστήσας, 'to entrap me in his verbal toils.' 2 διενοούμην B Vind., 'I had determined,' better than διενοούμην T. 5

Οὗτος αὖ, ἔφη, προσαποκρίνεται. 'Here again the fellow answers 296 more than is asked.' a 1

Ἀεί, ὅταν ἐπίστωμαι. Socrates foresees the fallacy involved in 7 Ἀεί meaning either 'at all times' absolutely or 'at each time.'

παύσει παραφθεγγόμενος; 'again will you not cease from super- 8 fluous qualifications?' In Plutarch, *Mor.* 169 D παραφθέγγεσθαι is 'to speak aside,' and in Polybius xviii. 15. 13 'obiter dicere.'

σφήλῃ BT Vind.; the old reading σφάλῃ was altered by Heindorf 9 to σφαλεῖ, but there is no reason for rejecting σφήλῃ.

Τοῦτ' ἐκεῖνο, 'There it is again! The same superfluous qualifica- b 7 tion.'

μηδὲ ἕν ... ἀφέλῃς. The Sophist arrogantly tells Socrates that he 9 need not withdraw his qualification, meaning himself to ignore it entirely, as he does in his next question.

δύναιο ἂν ἅπαντα ἐπίστασθαι ...; The question is framed on the c 1 assumption that Socrates had admitted ἅπαντα ἐπίσταμαι, and the qualification ἃ γ' ἐπίσταμαι is disregarded.

εἰ μὴ πάντα ἐπίσταιο. The word used at the beginning of the argument was πάντα, but Socrates in his answer B 5 had said ἅπαντα, seemingly without intending to make a distinction between these two words. But in fact πάντα means 'all severally' (καθ' ἓν ἕκαστον 294 D 2), while ἅπαντα (= ἅμα πάντα 296 C 10) means 'all together.' The Sophist takes advantage of the distinction to frame a question which can only be answered without qualification (ἁπλῶς); and the answer τέρας γὰρ ἂν εἴη is equivalent to a simple 'No.'

ἅπαντα γὰρ ὁμολογεῖς ἐπίστασθαι. The Sophist is exultant: he 4 seizes upon ἅπαντα (B 5) and entirely ignores the limitation. His argument would run thus in a formal syllogism :

> You cannot know ἅπαντα without knowing πάντα :
> You admit that you know ἅπαντα :
> Therefore you know πάντα.

6 Ἔοικα . . . ἐπίσταμαι. 'So it seems, said I, since the limitation "what things I know" has not any force, but I know all things.' The last clause is still dependent on ἐπειδήπερ.

9 εἴτε ὅταν ἐπίστῃ εἴτε ὅπως βούλει. Again the Sophist declares his contempt for all limitations such as A 7 ἀεί, ὅταν ἐπίστωμαι.

10 καὶ ἅμα πάντα. Cf. B 3 ἀεὶ δ' ἐπιστάμενος . . . πάντα; When ἀεὶ πάντα is taken with the absolute sense of ἀεί, it necessarily implies ἅμα πάντα. This absolute ἀεί he next proceeds to develop.

d 1 ὅτ' ἐγίγνου καὶ ὅτ' ἐφύου, 'at the time of your birth, and at that of your begetting.' The climax requires this sense of ἐφύου, which might otherwise mean 'growing up' (Jowett).

3 [αὐτὸs] ἀεί BT. αὐτός is condemned by all editors, but no satisfactory correction has been found: αὖ Schanz, αὖθις Ast, εὐθύς Heindorf, αὖθις or εὐθύς Stallbaum, ἐσαεί for αὐτὸς ἀεί Badham. Possibly αὐτός, which is certainly superfluous, may be only an erroneous repetition from αὐτὸς γενέσθαι just above. Without it the sense is quite clear.

5 ὦ πολυτίμητε Εὐθύδημε. He addresses the Sophist as a god: cf. 273 E σφὼ ὥσπερ θεὼ προσαγορεύω. Aristoph. *Acharn.* 807 ὦ πολυτίμηθ' Ἡράκλεις. *Vesp.* 1001 ὦ πολυτίμητοι θεοί.

7 συμβουληθείη, 'should be willing to help': cf. *Legg.* 718 B συμβουληθέντων θεῶν.

e 1 ἀμφισβητοίην . . . ὅπως ἐγὼ οὐ πάντα ἐπίσταμαι. 'As to other points I know not how I could argue with men of such prodigious wisdom as you that I do not know all things.' Cf. *Charm.* 169 E Οὐ τοῦτο . . . ἀμφισβητῶ, ὡς οὐχ . . . αὐτὸς αὐτὸν γνώσεται. *Parmen.* 135 A ἀμφισβητεῖν ὡς οὐκ ἔστι ταῦτα. *Pol.* 476 D.

2 τερατώδεσιν. On Plato's frequent use of adjectives in -ώδης and εἰδῆς see Lutoslawski, p. 113.

297 Διαφθείρεις, ἔφη, τὸν λόγον, ὁ Εὐθύδημος. On the separation of the
a 5 nominative from ἔφη compare 286 E, note. Euthydemus is represented as sharper than his elder brother, and so is made the chief speaker throughout.

NOTES 297 b

*Ἔασον, ὠγαθέ ... καὶ μή μοι φθονήσῃς τοῦ μαθήματος. Cf. *Sympos.* b 4 223 A ἀλλ' ἔασον, ὦ δαιμόνιε, καὶ μὴ φθονήσῃς τῷ μειρακίῳ ἐπ' ἐμοῦ ἐπαινεθῆναι.

Φεύγεις, 'You are running away.' 7

ἥττων γάρ εἰμι καὶ τοῦ ἑτέρου ὑμῶν, 'for I am weaker than either 9 one of you.' Cf. *Theaet.* 185 A οὐδ' αὖ διὰ τοῦ ἑτέρου περὶ ἀμφοτέρων αἰσθάνοι' ἄν. *Gorg.* 475 A ἢ τῷ ἑτέρῳ τούτοιν ἢ ἀμφοτέροις ὑπερβάλλων.

πολλοῦ δέω μὴ οὐ δύο γε φεύγειν, 'I do not hesitate to run away 10 from two.'

τοῦ Ἡρακλέους. Cf. *Phaed.* 89 C πρὸς δύο λέγεται οὐδ' ὁ Ἡρακλῆς C 1 οἷός τε εἶναι. Ἀλλὰ καὶ ἐμέ, ἔφη, τὸν Ἰόλεων παρακαλεῖ, ἕως ἔτι φῶς ἐστιν. The Scholiast on the *Phaedo* gives several explanations of the proverb, of which the most generally accepted is quoted from Herodorus and Hellanicus, that 'when Hercules was killing the Hydra, Juno set a crab upon him; and being unable to fight against two he called for Iolaus as his ally, and hence the proverbial saying.' Cf. *Legg.* 919 B ὀρθὸν μὲν δὴ πάλαι τε εἰρημένον, ὡς πρὸς δύο μάχεσθαι καὶ ἐναντία χαλεπόν. Cf. Apollod. ii. 5, 2.

τῇ τε ὕδρᾳ διαμάχεσθαι, σοφιστρίᾳ οὔσῃ, 'to fight it out both with the Hydra, who was a lady-sophist, and by virtue of her wisdom, if any one cut off one head of the argument, sent up many instead of the one.' σοφιστρία is found only here, being specially coined for the occasion. Cf. Schanz, *N.C.P.* p. 82 : 'Porson ap. Dobree Adn. ad Aristoph. *Plut.* 971 "Vox συκοφαντρία videtur esse ab Aristophane ficta ut σοφιστρία a Platone, *Euthyd.* p. 297 C."' The second Plutus was acted in the Archonship of Antipater 388 B.C. Plato therefore formed his new word in imitation of the recent coinage of Aristophanes.

νεωστί μοι δοκεῖν καταπεπλευκότι. After μοι B inserts τινι, an evident 5 repetition of τινι immediately above. Dionysodorus, the crab, and his brother had but recently arrived, as is clear from the opening of the dialogue.

ἐκ τοῦ ἐπ' ἀριστερά. Cf. 271 B 6 ὁ δὲ παρ' ἐμὲ καθήμενος ἐξ ἀριστερᾶς 6 ... Διονυσόδωρος.

λέγων καὶ δάκνων. Cf. Apollod. ibid. ἐβοήθει δὲ καρκίνος τῇ ὕδρᾳ ὑπερμεγέθης δάκνων τὸν πόδα.

βοηθὸν ἐπεκαλέσατο. Apollod. ibid. ἐπεκαλέσατο καὶ αὐτὸς βοηθὸν 7

51 M 2

297 c   NOTES

τὸν Ἰόλαον. Apollodorus (*circ.* B. C. 140) seems to have followed Plato's description very closely.

d 1   ὁ δ' ἐμὸς Ἰόλεως [Πατροκλῆς] εἰ ἔλθοι. Patrocles was the nephew (ἀδελφιδοῦς) of Socrates, being the son of his half-brother Chaeredemus (E 7). But the insertion of his name here is probably due to a marginal gloss. ὁ δ' ἐμὸς Ἰόλεως means little more than 'my helper': 'Iolaum pro *auxiliatore* vulgo accipi ostendit Erasmus *Chiliades*, p. 93' (Routh). The author of the gloss failed to see in the words πλέον ἂν θάτερον ποιήσειεν the allusion to Ctesippus and his fierce retorts upon the Sophists.

ἔλθοι. Heindorf thinks that this cannot refer to Ctesippus who was present without some such addition as εἰς βοήθειαν or βοηθήσων. But this idea is already implied in ὁ ἐμὸς Ἰόλεως, 'my helper'; and ἐλθεῖν is used in the same indefinite way without any addition in *Protag.* 310 C 5, 335 C 5.

3   ὁπότε σοι ταῦτα ὕμνηται, 'whenever you have finished this song.' Ὑμνεῖν, like the Latin *cantare* and our English 'canting,' is often used in the sense of 'harping upon' a thing. Cf. *Pol.* i. 329 B καὶ ἐπὶ τούτῳ δὴ τὸ γῆρας ὑμνοῦσιν, ὅσων κακῶν σφίσιν αἴτιον. *Pol.* viii. 549 E ὅσα καὶ οἷα φιλοῦσιν αἱ γυναῖκες περὶ τῶν τοιούτων ὑμνεῖν. v. Ruhnk. *Tim. Lex.*

e 2   παραπλήσιον μὲν τοὔνομα Ἰφικλῆς. But παραπλήσιος is preferred by Schanz, as at one time by Heindorf. The neuter is the reading of B T, but the construction is doubtful, for it is not clear, as Heindorf once thought, that because we find ἀνὴρ ὄνομα Ἰφικλῆς we may also write παραπλήσιον τοὔνομα Ἰφικλῆς. An example of such usage is wanted.

6   οὐχ ὁμοπάτριός γε. Socrates tries to add the proper limitation to the undistributed term ἀδελφός, as again 298 A 2 τοῦ πατρός: Τοὐμοῦ γ', ἔφην, ἔφη.

8   Πατὴρ δὲ ἦν, ἔφη. Dionysodorus, without noticing the objection of Socrates, passes at once to another question.

298   Ἀρ' οὖν πατὴρ ἦν ἕτερος ὢν πατρός; See the note on B 2 ἕτερος ὢν
a 2   πατρὸς οὐ πατήρ ἐστιν.

3   τῷ λίθῳ, 'the (proverbial) stone': see the next note.

4   μὴ φανῶ ὑπὸ σοῦ ὁ αὐτός. To be like a stone was a common expression of contempt. Cf. *Gorg.* 494 A τὸ ὥσπερ λίθον ζῆν ... μήτε χαίροντα μήτε λυπούμενον: ibid. B Χαραδριοῦ τινα αὖ σὺ βίον λέγεις,

52

ἀλλ' οὐ νεκροῦ οὐδὲ λίθου. *Sympos.* 198 c μὴ ... αὐτόν με λίθον τῇ ἀφωνίᾳ ποιήσειε. The Sophist chose λίθος cunningly, as Socrates would gladly admit that he was not a stone. Cf. *Soph. El.* iv. 528.

Οὐκοῦν ... ἕτερος ὢν πατρὸς οὐκ ἂν πατὴρ εἴη, T. ἂν πατήρ ἐστιν B. 8 Schanz writes οὔκουν, omits οὐκ ἄν, and reads ἐστιν. These many changes are quite unnecessary.

ἕτερος ὢν πατρὸς οὐ πατήρ ἐστιν. 'Fallacia est *Accidentis*' (Routh). b 2 Cf. Aristot. *Soph. El.* v. 'Paralogisms which arise from accident are when anything is asserted to be equally true of the subject (τῷ πράγματι) and of its accident (τῷ συμβεβηκότι). For since the same subject has many accidents, it is not necessary that the same should all be present to the predicates and to the subject of which they are predicated; for in this case all things would be the same, as the Sophists say. Such a fallacy is the following: If Coriscus is different from a man, he is different from himself, for he is a man. Or, if he is other than Socrates, and Socrates is (a) man, you have acknowledged, say they, that he is other than man, because it happens that he is other than one who is (a) man.'

The passage in the *Euthydemus* put into a syllogism would run thus:

Chaeredemus is not Sophroniscus:
Sophroniscus is a father:
∴ Chaeredemus is not a father.

There is evidently an illicit process of the minor, 'father' being particular in the premiss but universal in the conclusion.

On this 'fallacia accidentis' see Mansel, *Artis Logicae Rudimenta*, Append. 136. Diog. Laert. iii. 33, 53 Δύο δὲ τῆς ἐπαγωγῆς εἰσι τρόποι, ὅ τε κατ' ἐναντίωσιν, καὶ ὁ ἐκ τῆς ἀκολουθίας. ὁ μὲν οὖν κατ' ἐναντίωσίν ἐστιν ἐξ οὗ τῷ ἐρωτωμένῳ περὶ πᾶσαν ἀπόκρισιν ἀκολουθήσει τὸ ἐναντίον οἷον, Ὁ ἐμὸς πατὴρ τοῦ σοῦ πατρὸς ἤτοι ἕτερός ἐστιν ἢ ὁ αὐτός· εἰ μὲν οὖν ἕτερός ἐστι τοῦ ἐμοῦ πατρὸς ὁ σὸς πατήρ, πατρὸς ἕτερος ὢν οὐκ ἂν εἴη πατήρ. εἰ δὲ ὁ αὐτός ἐστι τῷ ἐμῷ πατρί, ὁ ἐμὸς ἂν εἴη πατήρ.

οὐ ταὐτὰ ταῦτα πέπονθεν; 'And is not your father in the same 5 plight?'

Οὐκ ἂν συμβουλοίμην, 'I should not wish that,' or more plainly, 7 'I should be sorry if he were.'

53

298 c   NOTES

c 5 μὴ γάρ . . . συνάπτεις. For the construction cf. *Alcib.* ii. 139 D
ἀλλ' ὅρα . . . μὴ οὐχ οὕτω ταῦτ' ἔχει. *Laches* 196 C ἀλλ' ὁρῶμεν μὴ
Νικίας οἴεταί τι λέγειν. *Theaet.* 145 B ἀλλ' ὅρα μὴ παίζων ἔλεγεν. In
this sense, 'whether,' μή may also be used without ὅρα or any
similar verb: cf. *Protag.* 312 A 'Αλλ' ἆρα μὴ οὐχ ὑπολαμβάνεις,
'Perhaps then you do not suppose.' So, in our present passage,
'Perhaps, as the proverb is, you are not joining like with like,' i. e.
the cases which you compare are not similar. See Riddell, *Digest
of Idioms*, § 138.

6 οὐ λίνον λίνῳ συνάπτεις. Cf. Aristot. *Phys. Auscult.* iii. 6, 12 Οὐ
γὰρ λίνον λίνῳ συνάπτειν ἔστι τῷ ἅπαντι καὶ ὅλῳ τὸ ἄπειρον. Simplicius
ad Aristot. locum οὐ τὰ συγκλώθεσθαι πεφυκότα συγκλώθειν (Heindorf).

d 4 κωβιῶν .. Cf. Athen. 106 E Θύννοισι τευθίς, κωβιοῖσι κωρίδες,
'With tunnies cuttle-fish, with gudgeons shrimps.' For κωβίων T,
the more usual word βοΐδίων has been substituted in B.

5 ⟨Κάπρος⟩ Badham, Καὶ πρὸς BTV. 'Quod καὶ πρὸς in κάπρος
invitis omnibus libris mutavi, audacius sane factum est ; sed quum
ex altera parte sordes et tenebras conspicis ex altera lucem et
nitorem, difficile est religionis non aliquando oblivisci' (Badham).

e 4 πατὴρ ὢν σός ἐστιν, ὥστε σὸς πατὴρ γίγνεται. 'Fallacia haec est
quae vocatur *compositionis*, i. e. cum coniunctim accipiuntur, quae
erant accipienda divisim' (Routh). Cf. Aristot. *Soph. El.* xxiv,
where as examples we find ἆρ' ὁ ἀνδριὰς σόν ἐστιν ἔργον, ἢ σὸς ὁ
κύων πατήρ ; and the solution οὐδ', εἰ τοῦτ' ἐστὶν ἐμόν, ἔστι δὲ ἔργον,
ἐμόν ἐστιν ἔργον, ἀλλ' ἢ κτῆμα ἢ πρᾶγμα ἢ ἄλλο τι. See note on
298 B 2.

299 πατέρα τύπτοιμι BT, πατέρ' ἂν τύπτοιμι Sauppe, Burnet. δικαιό-
a 1 τερον ἄν Ast, Schanz. But ἄν is not necessary : see 292 E 5 ποιήσειε,
note.

2 ὅ τι μαθών, 'that he was so foolish as to beget such wise sons.'
Cf. 283 E.

ἀλλ' ἦ που, ironical. 'But I suppose the father of you two and
of the puppies has gained many good things from this wisdom
of yours.' Cf. Soph. *Ajax* 1008 ἦ πού με Τελαμών, σὸς πατὴρ ἐμός
θ' ἅμα, | δέξαιτ' ἂν εὐπρόσωπος ἵλεώς τ' ἴσως.

b 4 Σὺ ἄριστα εἴσει, 'You will know best,' i. e. when you have heard
what I am going to say.

54

NOTES   299 b

τοῦτο ⟨τὸ⟩ ἀγαθόν. 'Articulum τό e cod. *Par.* addidi' (Heindorf). 7
τό is omitted in BT Vind., having probably dropped out after the
preceding το.

καὶ καλῶς ἐκεῖ ἔξει, 'in that case it will be well.' 'Cf. *Theaet.*
172 B ἀλλ' ἐκεῖ, οὗ λέγω, ἐν τοῖς δικαίοις' (Badham). Schanz reads
ἐκεῖνος, and Heindorf thinks that ἐκεῖ is an interpolation arising out
of the following ἔξει.

τρίψας ἐγκεράσῃ ἐλλεβόρου ἅμαξαν, 'should pound and infuse a 8
wagon-load of hellebore.' Cf. Theophrast. *Hist. Plant.* ix. 10, 2
μίσγεται δὲ πρὸς τὴν πόσιν ὅπως εὐεμὲς ᾖ τὸ τῆς ἐλλεβορίνης σπέρμα.
Cf. Menand. *Arreph.* Fr. v. Ἑλλέβορον ἤδη πώποτ' ἔπιες, Σωσία ;
πάλιν πάλιν νῦν πίθι· μαίνει γὰρ κακῶς. Cf. Hor. *Sat.* ii. 3,
82, &c.

ὁ ἀνδριὰς ὁ ἐν Δελφοῖς. Pausanias (Lib. x.) gives an almost c 1
countless list of statues at Delphi, but does not mention any one of
unusual size. Probably the statue here meant was that of Apollo
himself, as ' the Greeks who fought against the king of the Persians
erected a brazen Zeus at Olympia, and an Apollo at Delphi, after
the battles of Artemisium and Salamis' (Paus. 832).

τὸν Γηρυόνην. Cf. *Legg.* 795 C Γηρυόνου δέ γε εἴ τις φύσιν ἔχων 5
ἢ καὶ τὴν Βριάρεω φύοιτο, ταῖς ἑκατὸν χερσὶν ἑκατὸν δεῖ βέλη ῥίπτειν
δυνατὸν εἶναι. Hesiod. *Theog.* 287 Χρυσάωρ δ' ἔτεκε τρικάρηνον
Γηρυονῆα μιχθεὶς Καλλιρόῃ κούρῃ κλυτοῦ Ὠκεάνιιο. Cf. Apollod.
ii. 5, 10.

Βριάρεων. Cf. Apollod. i. 1, 1 : Hes. *Theog.* 149 Κόττος τε Βριάρεώς 6
τε Γύης θ', ὑπερήφανα τέκνα | τῶν ἑκατὸν μὲν χεῖρες ἀπ' ὤμων ἀΐσσοντο |
ἄπλατοι, κεφαλαὶ δὲ ἑκάστῳ πεντήκοντα.

καὶ τόνδε τὸν ἑταῖρον. This clause is rejected by Schanz, ap- 7
parently without sufficient reason.

τὰ πρότερον ἀποκεκριμένα. The previous answers of Ctesippus d 1
had reference to the advantage, in some cases, of having many
shields and spears.

The following argument is intended to ridicule the greed for
money which is so severely satirized by Aristophanes in the
Plutus, which was acted in its second form, as we now have it
in 388 B.C.

⟨χρῆναι ἀεί⟩ Badham. 'Librarius quum ad loci rationem minus 4
attenderet XPHNAIAEI in XPHMATAEI corrupit' (Badham).

55

e 4 Σκυθῶν ... οἳ χρυσίον τε ἐν τοῖς κρανίοις ἔχουσιν. Cf. Hdt. iv. 65 (Rawlinson): 'The skulls of their enemies, not indeed of all, but of those whom they most detest, they treat as follows. Having sawn off the portion below the eyebrows, and cleaned out the inside, they cover the outside with leather. When a man is poor, this is all that he does; but if he is rich, he also lines the inside with gold: in either case the skull is used as a drinking-cup. They do the same with the skulls of their own kith and kin if they have been at feud with them, and have vanquished them in the presence of the king. When strangers whom they deem of any account come to visit them, these skulls are handed round,' &c. Cf. Strabo 300.

5 τοῖς ἑαυτῶν. Ctesippus meets the Sophists with their own weapons: as Dionysodorus had argued (298 E 4) πατὴρ ὢν σός ἐστιν, ὥστε σὸς πατὴρ γίγνεται ὁ κύων, so Ctesippus calls the skulls which the Scythians had taken 'their own,' and so 'they drink out of their own gilded skulls,' and 'hold their own head in their hands and see inside it.'

300 τὰ δυνατὰ ὁρᾶν. The phrase has two meanings, corresponding
a 2 to the active and passive senses of δυνατός: (1) ἃ δύναται ὁρᾶν, (2) ἃ δύναταί τις ὁρᾶν. The former is common and needs no illustration: for the latter sense cf. Aesch. Agam. 97 ὅ τι καὶ δυνατὸν καὶ θέμις αἰνεῖν. Xen. Anab. iv. 1, 24 δυνατὴν καὶ ὑποζυγίοις πορεύεσθαι ὁδόν. The fallacy therefore may be regarded as belonging either to the class παρὰ τὴν ὁμωνυμίαν or παρὰ τὴν ἀμφιβολίαν, on which see Aristot. Soph. El. iv. 526 and 527: as an example of the latter Aristotle gives ἆρα ὃ ὁρᾷ τις τοῦτο ὁρᾷ; ὁρᾷ δὲ τὸν κίονα, ὥστε ὁρᾷ ὁ κίων.

3 Κἀγώ, scilicet ὁρῶ τὰ δυνατὰ ὁρᾶν. The Sophist seems to have acted like Antisthenes when he turned out the rags of his cloak for Socrates to see, Diog. Laert. vi. 8.

5 Τί δέ; ... Μηδέν. 'But what can they see?' Nothing. Cf. Riddell, Digest of Idioms, § 135 'Μή. (a) In indicative sentences expressing a negative supposition. Theaet. 192 E Σωκράτης ἐπιγιγνώσκει Θεόδωρον καὶ Θεαίτητον, ὁρᾷ δὲ μηδέτερον, μηδὲ ἄλλη αἴσθησις αὐτῷ πάρεστι περὶ αὐτῶν.' I have completed the quotation.

6 οὕτως ἡδὺς εἶ, 'sweet innocent as you are.' Cf. Gorg. 491 D,

NOTES 300 a

Pol. 337 D, Ruhnk. *Tim. Lex.* Ἡδύς· εὐήθης καὶ ἄφρων. Suidas: Ἡδύς· εὐήθης, ἐκάλουν δὲ οὗτω καὶ τοὺς ὑπομώρους.

οὐ καθεύδων ἐπικεκοιμῆσθαι, 'to have fallen asleep with your eyes **7** open.' Cf. Lucian, *Alex.* 255 λαμβάνων γὰρ τὰ βιβλία ἐπεκοιμᾶτο, ὡς ἔφασκεν, αὐτοῖς.

σιγῶντα λέγειν, 'a speaking of the silent.' Cf. Aristot. *Soph. El.* **b 1** iv. 528 Παρὰ τὴν ἀμφιβολίαν οἱ τοιοίδε λόγοι . . . ἆρ' ἔστι σιγῶντα λέγειν; διττὸν γὰρ καὶ τὸ σιγῶντα λέγειν, τό τε τὸν λέγοντα σιγᾶν καὶ τὸ τὰ λεγόμενα. ibid. x. 558 διὸ ἢ ἐν τῷ συλλογισμῷ ἔσται τὸ αἴτιον, ἢ ἐν τῇ ἀντιφάσει (προσκεῖσθαι γὰρ δεῖ τὴν ἀντίφασιν), ὅτε δ' ἐν ἀμφοῖν, ἐὰν ᾖ φαινόμενος ἔλεγχος. ἔστι δὲ ὁ μὲν τοῦ σιγῶντα λέγειν ἐν τῇ ἀντιφάσει, οὐκ ἐν τῷ συλλογισμῷ.

φθεγγόμενα . . . λέγεται, 'the irons, if anybody touch them, are **5** spoken of as roaring and crying aloud.' For λέγεται, BT, Ast conjectured λέγει. But the passive is right in answer to οὐ σιγῶντα λέγεις;

τοῦτο μὲν ὑπὸ σοφίας ἔλαθες οὐδὲν εἰπών, 'in this your wisdom has **7** made you unwittingly talk nonsense.'

λέγοντα σιγᾶν, 'to be silent in speaking.' **8**

ὑπεραγωνιᾶν, 'to be over anxious on account of the boy.' Cf. **c 1** *Charm.* 162 C I Καὶ ὁ Κριτίας δῆλος μὲν ἦν καὶ πάλαι ἀγωνιῶν καὶ φιλοτίμως πρός τε τὸν Χαρμίδην καὶ πρὸς τοὺς παρόντας ἔχων.

τὰ λέγοντα, a necessary emendation of τὰ λεγόμενα BT, adopted **4** by all editors (except Winckelmann) before Schanz, who bracketed τὰ λεγόμενα.

τά γε δήπου λέγοντα. Euthydemus himself tries to limit the **6** universal term τὰ πάντα by a distinction such as he would not allow Socrates to use, 295 B 4, 296 A I οὐ γὰρ ἔγωγε ἐρωτῶ ὅτῳ, ἀλλ' εἰ ἐπίστασαί τῳ.

μέγα πάνυ ἀνακαγχάσας, 'with a loud roar of laughter.' Cf. *Pol.* **d 3** 337 A καὶ ὃς ἀκούσας ἀνεκάγχασέ τε μάλα σαρδάνιον. See 276 D note.

ἐξημφοτέρικεν τὸν λόγον. For the explanation of this phrase **4** Winckelmann rightly refers to *Pol.* 479 C τοῖς ἐν ταῖς ἑστιάσεσιν, ἔφη, ἐπαμφοτερίζουσιν ἔοικε καὶ τῷ τῶν παίδων αἰνίγματι τῷ περὶ τοῦ εὐνούχου τῆς βολῆς περὶ τῆς νυκτερίδος, ᾧ καὶ ἐφ' οὗ αὐτὸν αὐτὴν αἰνίττονται βαλεῖν. The riddle itself is preserved by the Scholiast on that passage.

57

300 d NOTES

Κλεάρχου γρῖφος
αἰνός τίς ἐστιν ὡς ἀνήρ τε κοὐκ ἀνὴρ
ὄρνιθα κ' οὐκ ὄρνιθ' ἰδών τε κοὐκ ἰδὼν
ἐπὶ ξύλου τε κοὐ ξύλου καθημένην
λίθῳ βαλών τε κοὐ λίθῳ διώλεσεν.
Νυκτερίδα ὁ εὐνοῦχος νάρθηκι κισήρει.

The point of comparison is that one who 'is and is not a man
strikes that which 'is and is not a bird,' &c. Upon this Plato by
the mouth of Glaucon remarks that we cannot form a positive
conception of such things either as being or not-being (καὶ οὔτε
εἶναι οὔτε μὴ εἶναι οὐδὲν αὐτῶν δυνατὸν παγίως νοῆσαι). Winckelmann
also refers (*Proleg.* xxiii. note b) to an anecdote about Menedemus
in Diog. Laert. ii. 135 Ἀλεξίνου ποτὲ ἐρωτήσαντος εἰ πέπαυται τὸν πατέρα
τύπτων, Ἀλλ' οὔτ' ἔτυπτον, φάναι, οὔτε πέπαυμαι. Πάλιν τ' ἐκείνου
λέγοντος ὡς ἐχρῆν εἰπόντα ναί ἢ οὔ λῦσαι τὴν ἀμφιβολίαν, Γελοῖον, εἶπε,
τι ἰς ὑμετέροις νόμοις ἀκολουθεῖν, ἐξὸν ἐν πύλαις ἀντιβῆναι.

Our Sophists in the *Euthydemus* had insisted on the same rule
that the answer must be given categorically 'Yes' or 'No'; and
Ctesippus shrewdly turns their own chief weapon against them:
'That is not what I ask, but "Do all things keep silence or speak?"'
This is exactly the 'Fallacia plurium interrogationum, quando plures
quaestiones velut una proponuntur' (Aldrich ap. Mansel, *Artis
Logicae Rudimenta*, App. 139, Whateley, *Elements of Logic*, Bk.
iii. 9). Cf. Aristot. *Soph. El.* v. 11 ἢ πάλιν, ὧν τὰ μέν ἐστιν ἀγαθὰ
τὰ δὲ οὐκ ἀγαθά, πάντα ἀγαθὰ ἢ οὐκ ἀγαθά; ὁπότερον γὰρ ἂν φῇ, ἔστι
μὲν ὡς ἔλεγχον ἢ ψεῦδος φαινόμενον δόξειεν ἂν ποιεῖν· τὸ γὰρ φάναι
τῶν μὴ ἀγαθῶν τι εἶναι ἀγαθὸν ἢ τῶν ἀγαθῶν τι μὴ ἀγαθὸν ψεῦδος. ibid.
xxx. Πρὸς δὲ τοὺς τὰ πλείω ἐρωτήματα ἐν ποιοῦντας εὐθὺς ἐν ἀρχῇ
διοριστέον· ἐρώτησις γὰρ μία, πρὸς ἣν μία ἀπόκρισίς ἐστιν ὥστε οὔτε
πλείω καθ' ἑνὸς οὔτε ἓν κατὰ πολλῶν, ἀλλ' ἓν καθ' ἑνὸς φατέον ἢ
ἀποφατέον.

In the present case, however, where both sides of the dilemma
are to be denied, Dionysodorus might have escaped, if instead of
answering 'Yes' or 'No' he had been allowed and contented to
answer simply Οὐδέτερον; but 'by adding ἀμφότερα he has ruined
his argument' (ἐξημφοτέρικεν τὸν λόγον).

5   ἀπόλωλέ τε καὶ ἥττηται BT, 'he is beaten and done for. 'Pro-
didit' (Ficinus), ἀπολώλεκε (Heindorf). 'Quid reponendum sit

58

non exputo' (Badham). The objection that the weaker word comes first is hardly a sufficient reason for tampering with the text of BT. πλεῖον ἢ δεκαπλάσιος. 'Aristid. *Orat. Sacr.* i. 494 Ἤδη μέν τις καὶ 6 ἄλλος χρηστοῦ τινος αὐτῷ συμβάντος καὶ βουλόμενος ἐνδείξασθαι τὴν ἡδονὴν εἶπεν ὡς ἄρα εἴη πλείων ἢ διπλάσιος γεγονώς' (Heindorf). ὁ δέ μοι ΒΤ, γρ. ὁ δ' ἐδόκει μοι ἅτε Τ, ὁ δ' οἶμαι Badham, Schanz. 7 The reading of BT ὁ δέ μοι πανοῦργος ὤν, ὁ Κτήσιππος, has been rightly retained by Bekker, Winckelmann, Stallbaum, and Hermann : μοι is what is called the *dativus commodi*, frequently used to express the interest or opinion of the person speaking (Jelf, *Gk. Gr.* 600, Obs. 2): if any change were to be made, the best would be μοι δοκεῖ (Burnet), used parenthetically : 'And he, methinks, rogue that he was, I mean Ctesippus, had overheard this very trick from these men themselves, for there are no other men living that have such wisdom. But cf. *Sophist.* 216 D τοῦ μέντοι ξένου ἡμῖν ἡδέως ἂν πυνθανοίμην.

παρηκηκόει. Cf. Aristoph. *Ran.* 750 καὶ παρακούειν δεσποτῶν ἅττ' 8 ἂν λαλῶσι (Stallbaum).

'Αρα ἕτερα ὄντα τοῦ καλοῦ; 'Were they other than the beautiful?' 301 'In these words I see not merely, with Steinhart, "a close a 1 approximation to the doctrine of ideas," but the actual enunciation of this doctrine' (Zeller, *Plato* 126, note). Stallbaum more correctly sees here only the *logical* doctrine of universals as held by Socrates, upon which Plato afterwards founded his *metaphysical* doctrine of 'Ideas.' Cf. *Meno* 73 D εἴπερ ἕν γέ τι ζητεῖς κατὰ πάντων. 74 A πολλὰς αὖ ηὑρήκαμεν ἀρετὰς μίαν ζητοῦντες . . . τὴν δὲ μίαν, ἣ διὰ πάντων τούτων ἐστίν, οὐ δυνάμεθα ἀνευρεῖν. *Parmen.* 130 B. Aristot. *Metaph.* i. 6, 2, and see note on 301 A 4 πάρεστιν, κτλ.

ἐν παντὶ ἐγενόμην ὑπὸ ἀπορίας, 'was at my wit's end for want of an 2 answer.' Cf. Wyttenbach, Plut. *Mor., De Sera Num. Vind.* 568 A 'ἐν παντὶ γενέσθαι κακῷ διὰ φόβον. Satis erat ἐν παντὶ γενέσθαι ; ut postrema ab annotatore quodam addita videantur. 'Εν παντὶ εἶναι est Attica locutio, quae notat *in maximo timore esse.* . . . Plato tamen *Pol.* 579 B usus est pleniore forma ἐν παντὶ κακοῦ εἴη.' Cf. Stallbaum ad Plat. *Sympos.* 194 A εὖ καὶ μάλ' ἂν φόβοιο καὶ ἐν παντὶ εἴης. Xen. *Hell.* v. 4, 29 ἐν παντὶ ἦσαν.

ὅτι ἔγρυξα, 'for putting in my grunt': cf. Aristoph. *Plut.* 598 3 ἀλλὰ φθείρου καὶ μὴ γρύξῃς ἔτι μηδ' ὁτιοῦν.

4   πάρεστιν μέντοι ἑκάστῳ αὐτῶν κάλλος τι.   Lutoslawski argues (p. 212, note) that the use of πάρεστιν in this passage does not correspond to the terminology of ideas in Plato. But on the many various terms including παρεῖναι and παρουσία, by which Plato expresses the relation between the universal ideas and the particulars of experience, see Jowett and Campbell, *Rep.* ii. 309, and *Classical Rev.* March, 1904, p. 122.

5   ἐὰν οὖν, ἔφη, παραγένηταί σοι βοῦς. 'Est fallacia Homonymiae: sita est enim ambiguitas in vocibus παραγίγνομαι et πάρειμι; nam diverso sensu παραγίγνονται alicui bos et pulcritudo' (Routh).

8   Ἀλλὰ τίνα τρόπον . . . , 'But in what way must one thing be present to another, in order that this other may be other (than it was)?' For example, how must beauty be present to a stone that it may be beautiful? See the full discussion of this question in *Lys.* 217 D, and cf. *Meno* 71 A ἀρετὴν γοῦν εἴτε διδακτὸν εἴθ᾽ ὅτῳ τρόπῳ παραγίγνεται εἰδέναι.

b 1   τοῖν ἀνδροῖν τὴν σοφίαν ἐπεχείρουν μιμεῖσθαι. The Sophist had used the predicate ἕτερον in a different sense from that which it bore in τὸ ἕτερον, where it indicates merely the numerical distinction of individuals. Socrates does what the Sophists had often done before, he changes the meaning of the predicate ἕτερον, pretending to understand it in the same sense as in the subject τὸ ἕτερον.

3   Πῶς γὰρ οὐκ ἀπορῶ . . . ὃ μὴ ἔστι; 'Of course I am at a loss about a thing that does not exist.' Cf. Zeller, *Socrates* 277 'He (Stilpo) rejected, as did Antisthenes, every combination of subject and predicate, since the conception of the one is different from the conception of the other, and two things with different conceptions can never be declared to be the same.' ibid. (note) 'Since the conception of Σωκράτης μουσικός is a different one from Σωκράτης λευκός, the one according to Megarian hypothesis must be a different person from the other.'

6   Ἐὰν ἔμοιγε, ἔφη, δοκῇ, 'Yes, if it seems so to me.' This is the doctrine of Protagoras that 'man is the measure of all things,' i.e. 'what a thing seems to a man that it is to him.' Cf. 301 E 6; Zeller, *Outlines*, p. 92.

c 1   ἀπορῆσαι, ὡς οὐ τὸ ἕτερον ἕτερόν ἐστιν, 'would have doubted that the other is other.'

2   τοῦτο μὲν ἑκὼν παρῆκας. 'This point you purposely omitted, since

in all the rest, like workmen whose business it is to finish each his proper work, you also seem to me to finish in very beautiful style the practice of discussion.'

τίνα χαλκεύειν προσήκει, 'whom it befits to forge copper.' 'Dicit 7 τίνα non τίνι, ut statim ambiguitas sermonis nascatur' (Heindorf).

τί δέ, κεραμεύειν; 'Well again, whom to make pots?' The 8 alteration of τί BT into τίνα, with some inferior MSS., is unnecessary.

τὰ μικρὰ κρέα ... ὀπτᾶν, 'and cut up and boil and roast the small 9 pieces.' Badham reads τὰ κρέα σμικρὰ κατακόψαντα, 'to cut up the flesh into small pieces': but τὰ μικρὰ κρέα depends on the principal verbs ἕψειν καὶ ὀπτᾶν as much if not more than on κατακόψαντα.

κολοφῶνα ἐπιτιθείς. Cf. Strabo 643 Ἐκτήσαντο δέ ποτε καὶ ναυτικὴν e 1 ἀξιόλογον δύναμιν Κολοφώνιοι καὶ ἱππικήν, ἐν ᾗ τοσοῦτον διέφερον τῶν ἄλλων ὥσθ' ὅπου ποτὲ ἐν τοῖς δυσκαταλύτοις πολέμοις τὸ ἱππικὸν τῶν Κολοφωνίων ἐπικουρήσειε λύεσθαι τὸν πόλεμον· ἀφ' οὗ καὶ τὴν παροιμίαν ἐκδοθῆναι τὴν λέγουσαν "τὸν Κολοφῶνα ἐπέθηκεν," ὅταν τέλος ἐπιτεθῇ βέβαιον τῷ πράγματι.

ἐπιτιθεῖς Schanz : ἐπιτιθεὶς B, ἐπιτίθης T. Cf. Rutherford, New Phrynichus, ccxx. 'The authority of Porson (ad Eur. Or. 141) has induced many scholars to prefer ἵης and τίθης to ἱεῖς and τιθεῖς. Brunck, on Aristoph. Lys. 895 and Soph. Phil. 992, took the opposite view to that of Porson, and in this case the verdict of the great English critic must be reversed. The authority of the MSS. is wholly on the side of Brunck. Thus in Aristoph. Lys. 895 the Ravenna exhibits διατιθεῖς, and on Eq. 717 ἐντιθεῖς.' In Soph. Philoct. 992 Jebb reads τίθης against the authority of the MSS.

ἐπιγνοίης ἂν αὐτήν...; 'Should you recognize it?' 4

ἀπὸ σοῦ γὰρ δεῖ ἄρχεσθαι, τελευτᾶν δ' εἰς Εὐθύδημον. An imitation 8 of the common mode of beginning an address to a deity. Cf. Theocr. xvii. 1 Ἐκ Διὸς ἀρχώμεσθα, καὶ ἐς Δία λήγετε, Μοῖσαι. Theogn. Gnom. Ὦ ἄνα, Λητοῦς υἱέ, Διὸς τόκος, οὔποτε σεῖο λήσομαι ἀρχόμενος, οὐδ' ἀποπαυόμενος. Hom. Hymn. ad Dionys. 17, Arati Phaen. 1, Virg. Ecl. iii. 59. The same mode of expression is used in Hom. Il. ix. 97 by Nestor in addressing Agamemnon: ἐν σοὶ μὲν λήξω, σέο δ' ἄρξομαι.

οἷον βοῦς καὶ πρόβατον, ἆρ' ἂν ἡγοῖο ταῦτα σὰ εἶναι. On this use 302 of the nominative to introduce an object without regard to the a 1

302 a   NOTES

construction that follows see Bernhardy, *Gr. Synt.* p. 68; Jelf, § 477;
Kühner-Blass, § 356, 2.

5 ἀνακύψοιτο τῶν ἐρωτημάτων Β, ἀνακύψοι τὸ τῶν ἐρ. Τ. 'I knew
that some fine result would pop up from their questions.' For the
future middle see Aristoph. *Av.* 147 ἀνακύψεται κλητῆρ' ἄγουσ' ἔωθεν
ἡ Σαλαμινία.

b 3 εἰρωνικῶς πάνυ ἐπισχών, 'after pausing with a very ironical air.'
Cf. *Symp.* 218 D ἀκούσας μάλα εἰρωνικῶς καὶ σφόδρα ἑαυτῷ εἰωθότως.
Cratyl. 384 A οὔτε ἀποσαφεῖ οὐδέν, εἰρωνεύεταί τε πρός με, προσποιού-
μενός τι αὐτὸς ἐν ἑαυτῷ διανοεῖσθαι.

6 ἄπορόν τινα στροφὴν ἔφευγον, 'I tried to escape by some desperate
dodge, and began at once to twist about as if caught in a net.' Cf.
Pol. 405 C πάσας μὲν στροφὰς στρέφεσθαι.

7 Οὐκ ἔστιν. Socrates tries to elude the coming attack of Dionysodorus by what he himself describes as ἄπυρόν τινα στροφήν, 'a
helpless kind of twist.' The title Ζεὺς Πατρῷος was used in two
senses, (1) as he was the ancestor of an individual or of a race,
(2) as he was the guardian of piety towards parents. For (1) cf.
Plat. *Pol.* 391 E (with Adam's note)

            Οἱ θεῶν ἀγχίσποροι
        οἱ Ζηνὸς ἐγγύς, ὧν κατ' Ἰδαῖον πάγον
        Διὸς πατρῴου βωμός ἐστ' ἐν αἰθέρι.

Soph. *Trach.* 287 εὖτ' ἂν ἀγνὰ θύματα ῥέξῃ πατρῴῳ Ζηνί. ibid. 754
ἔνθα πατρῴῳ Διὶ βώμους ὁρίζει τεμενίαν τε φυλλάδα. As Tantalus and
Heracles both were sons of Zeus, the title πατρῷος is rightly used
in reference to them in sense (1). (2) Aristoph. *Nub.* 1468:

        ΣΤΡ. Ναί, Ναί, καταιδέσθητι πατρῷον Δία.
        ΦΕΙΔ. Ἰδού γε Δία πατρῷον, ὡς ἀρχαῖος εἶ.

Eur. *El.* 675 ὦ Ζεῦ πατρῷε, where Zeus is invoked by Orestes 'as
the god who avenges the outraged name of *Father*' (Paley). Plat.
Legg. 881 D ἀρᾶ ἐνεχέσθω Διὸς ὁμογνίου καὶ πατρῴου κατὰ νόμον.
Observe also that neither Tantalus, Heracles, nor Orestes was an
Athenian, so that the Tragedians in these passages do not contradict what Plato says here. Thus Socrates imitates the logical
tricks of the Sophists by denying in one sense what was true in
another. Cf. Lobeck, *Aglaoph.* p. 770.

c 2 Ἔα, . . . εὐφήμει τε, 'Ah! said I, speak reverently, and do not
harshly lecture me too soon.' Cf. Aesch. *Prom.* 688 ἔα, ἔα, ἄπεχε.

βωμοὶ καὶ ἱερὰ οἰκεῖα καὶ πατρῷα, 'altars and sacred rites domes- 4
tic, ancestral, and all the rest of such things that the other
Athenians have.'

Ζεὺς ὁ πατρῷος; BT. 'Have not the other Athenians Zeus as their 6
ancestral god?' Schanz rejects the article unnecessarily in his
text, having previously proposed ὁ Ζεὺς ὁ πατρῷος.

αὕτη ἡ ἐπωνυμία, 'this ancestral title.' 7

Ἀπόλλων πατρῷος. Cf. Harpocrat. s. v. τὸν δὲ Ἀπόλλωνα κοινῶς d 1
πατρῷον τιμῶσιν Ἀθηναῖοι ἀπὸ Ἴωνος· τούτου γὰρ οἰκήσαντος τὴν
Ἀττικήν, ὡς Ἀριστοτέλης φησί, τοὺς Ἀθηναίους Ἴωνας κληθῆναι καὶ
Ἀπόλλω πατρῷον αὐτοῖς ὀνομασθῆναι. The quotation from Aristotle
was probably from the opening, now lost, of his treatise On the
Constitution of Athens: see Kenyon, p. 171. Cf. Demosth. In
Eubulidem 1315 παιδίον ὄντα με εὐθέως ἦγον εἰς τοὺς φράτορας, εἰς
Ἀπόλλωνος πατρῴου ἦγον, εἰς τἆλλα ἱερά. De Corona 274 καὶ τὸν
Ἀπόλλω τὸν Πύθιον, ὃς Πατρῷός ἐστι τῇ πόλει. Cf. Plut. Alcib. 2
Αὐλείτωσαν οὖν, ἔφη, Θηβαίων παῖδες· οὐ γὰρ ἴσασιν διαλέγεσθαι· ἡμῖν
δὲ τοῖς Ἀθηναίοις, ὡς οἱ πατέρες λέγουσιν, Ἀρχηγέτις Ἀθηνᾶ καὶ Πατρῷος
Ἀπόλλων ἐστίν, ὧν ἡ μὲν ἔρριψε τὸν αὐλόν, ὁ δὲ καὶ τὸν αὐλητὴν ἐξέδειρε.

διὰ τὴν τοῦ Ἴωνος γένεσιν. Ion, son of Apollo and Creusa, was
represented to Xanthus by the oracle as being his own son by
Creusa. The story is told in Eur. Ion 64-75.

ἕρκειος, 'defender of the house.' 'Harpocrat. Ἕρκειος Ζεύς, ᾧ 2
βωμὸς ἐντὸς ἕρκους ἐν τῇ αὐλῇ ἵδρυται· τὸν γὰρ περίβολον ἕρκος ἔλεγον.
Ὅτι δὲ τούτοις μετῆν τῆς πολιτείας οἷς εἴη Ζεὺς Ἕρκειος δεδήλωκε καὶ
Ὑπερείδης' (Heindorf). Cf. Aristot. De Rep. Athen. [col. 28] ἐπερωτῶ-
σιν δ' ὅταν δοκιμάζωσιν, πρῶτον μὲν τίς σοι πατὴρ καὶ πόθεν τῶν δήμων, καὶ
τίς πατρὸς πατήρ, καὶ τίς μήτηρ, καὶ τίς μητρὸς πατὴρ καὶ πόθεν τῶν δήμων·
μετὰ δὲ ταῦτα εἰ ἔστιν αὐτῷ Ἀπόλλων πατρῷος καὶ Ζεὺς ἕρκειος, καὶ ποῦ
ταῦτα τὰ ἱερά ἐστιν. The ἱερά seem to have been movable shrines.

φράτριος. A φρατρία was a third part (τριττύς Demosth. 184) of
one of the four ancient tribes into which Attica was divided either
by Aegeus and his three brothers, sons of Pandion (Soph. Fr. 19,
Strabo 392), or according to a different tradition by Ion (Strabo 383).
Schol. in Plat. Axioch. 371 'Γεννήτῃ] Ἀριστοτέλης φησί, τοῦ ὅλου
πλήθους διῃρημένου Ἀθήνησιν εἴς τε τοὺς γεωργοὺς καὶ τοὺς δημιουργούς,
φυλὰς αὐτῶν εἶναι τέσσαρας, τῶν δὲ φυλῶν ἑκάστης μοίρας εἶναι τρεῖς,
ἃς τριττύας τε καλοῦσι καὶ φρατρίας, ἑκάστης δὲ τούτων τριάκοντα εἶναι

302 d

NOTES

γένη, τὸ δὲ γένος ἐκ τριάκοντα ἕκαστον ἀνδρῶν συνεστάναι. τούτους δὲ τοὺς εἰς τὰ γένη τεταγμένους γεννήτας καλοῦσιν.' Cf. Aristot. *De Rep. Athen.* (Kenyon) 21, ibid. Append. Fr. 347.

3 Ἀθηναία φρατρία. Under this title Athena was worshipped together with Zeus at the Ἀπατούρια, an annual festival of the phratriae, Xen. *Hell.* i. 7, 8 ἐν οἷς οἵ τε πατέρες καὶ οἱ συγγενεῖς σύνεισι σφίσιν αὐτοῖς. Cf. Hdt. i. 147.

8 τί γὰρ πάθω; 'For what can become of me?' Cf. Eur. *Phoen.* 895 τὸ μέλλον εἰ χρὴ πείσομαι· τί γὰρ πάθω; *Androm.* 513, with Paley's note, Hom. *Od.* v. 465 ὤ μοι ἐγώ, τί πάθω; τί νύ μοι μήκιστα γένηται ; e 5 θῦσαι ⟨δὴ⟩ Schanz, θῦσαι ἂν BT. ἄν, which was omitted by Stephanus and Heindorf, was brought back by Winckelmann and Stallbaum, but changed by Schanz into δή. The uncial ΔΗ is very easily mistaken for ΑΝ.

303 Πυππὰξ ὦ Ἡράκλεις, ἔφη, καλοῦ λόγου. 'Bravo, by Heracles ! a 6 what a fine argument.' Cf. Cratin. Δραπ. Fr. 7 οἵδε πυππάζουσι περιτρέχοντες. Aristoph. *Eq.* 680 οἱ δ᾽ ὑπερεπήνουν ὑπερεπύππαζόν τέ με. Schol. in *Euthyd.* τὸ νῦν βομβὰξ λεγόμενον πύπαξ ἔλεγον, ὡς καὶ Λυκόφρων ᾠήθη. οὐκ ἔστι δέ· τὸ μὲν γὰρ πύπαξ τίθεται καὶ ἐπὶ σχετλιασμοῦ καὶ ἐγκωμίου τὸ δὲ βομβὰξ οὐκέτι.

7 ὁ Πυππάξ. Dionysodorus turns the adverb into a proper name.

9 ἀφίσταμαι, 'I withdraw,' 'I give up.' 'Sic iam Pindar, *Ol.* i. 82 sq. elegantissimo asyndeto dixit ἐμοὶ δ᾽ ἄπορα γαστρίμαργον μακάρων τιν᾽ εἰπεῖν· ἀφίσταμαι' (Winckelmann).

b 2 καὶ γελῶντες Badham. καὶ γελῶντε B, γελῶντε T. 'Incredibile est neminem adhuc ad vulgatam lectionem offendisse, quae ipsos Sophistas sibi plaudentes induceret, idque adeo vehementer ut paene deficerent. Unum superest verae lectionis vestigium quod in Clarkiano καὶ γελῶντε scriptum est' (Badham). ibid. in App. Crit. 'καὶ e Clarkiano restitui, et dualem in pluralem ter mutavi.'

3 ὀλίγου παρετάθησαν, 'were almost killed with laughing, and clapping, and rejoicing.' Cf. *Lys.* 204 C παραταθήσεται ὑπὸ σοῦ ἀκούων θαμὰ λέγοντος. *Symp.* 207 B τῷ λιμῷ παρατεινόμενα. Xen. *Mem.* iii. 13, 6 παρετάθη μακρὰν ὁδὸν πορευθείς.

ἐπὶ μὲν γὰρ τοῖς ἔμπροσθεν ἐφ᾽ ἑκάστοις πᾶσι. 'Over the former victories the admirers of Euthydemus alone shouted gloriously over each and all.' 'Iungendum haud dubie ἐφ᾽ ἑκάστοις πᾶσι, quod nescio cur Winckelmannus recte fieri posse negaverit. Nam ἕκαστα

64

πάντα sunt *singula quaeque* ' (Stallbaum). On Plato's use of πᾶς or its compounds with ἕκαστος see Walbe *ap.* Lutoslawski, p. 126. καὶ οἱ κίονες. Cf. *Pol.* 492 B πρὸς δ' αὐτοῖς αἵ τε πέτραι καὶ ὁ τόπος, 5 ἐν ᾧ ἂν ὦσιν, ἐπηχοῦντες διπλάσιον θόρυβον παρέχωσι τοῦ ψόγου καὶ ἐπαίνου. ' Acerba irrisio inest in Socratis verbis ' (Schanz, *N. C. P.* p. 84).

παντάπασι καταδουλωθεὶς κτλ., 'being altogether overpowered by c 2 their wisdom I took to praising and extolling them.'

*Ὦ μακάριοι σφώ, 'O happy pair, what wonderful genius, that you 4 have brought so great a subject to perfection so readily and in so short a time !'

ἐν δὲ τοῖς καὶ τοῦτο μεγαλοπρεπέστερον BT, 'but among them just 7 this is especially magnificent.' ' Utrum μεγαλοπρεπέστατον ?' STEPH. ' Ita verterat ante Stephanum Cornarius. Sed comparativus mihi magis placet, dum sonat *quiddam plus quam solito magnificum* ' (Routh). The change to μεγαλοπρεπέστατον was very easily suggested by the well-known use of ἐν τοῖς with a superlative, to which it gives additional emphasis (Thuc. iii. 81 ἐν τοῖς πρώτη ἐγένετο : Jelf, *Gk. Gr.* § 140, 4 ; Donaldson, *Gk. Gr.* § 416 (cc)). But as in that idiom the two words seem never to be separated not even so slightly as here (ἐν δὲ τοῖς), it is safer to regard τοῖς simply as the demonstrative looking back to πολλὰ . . . καλά, and used here instead of τούτοις because of τοῦτο immediately following. The comparative is maintained by Winckelmann and by Bernhardy, *Gr. Synt.* 436, who refers to this passage, and apparently by Ficinus, ' in quibus id praecipue magnificum est.'

τῶν πολλῶν ἀνθρώπων κτλ., 'for the mass of mankind and for 8 men of importance indeed and of great repute you care nothing at all.' Both words, σεμνῶν and δή, are constantly used in irony. For δοκούντων εἶναί τι cf. *Gorg.* 472 A. S. Paul, *Gal.* ii. 6.

πάνυ μὲν ἂν ὀλίγοι ἀγαπῷεν ἄνθρωποι ὅμοιοι ὑμῖν, 'very few would be d 2 satisfied, and those men like yourselves.'

οὕτω νοοῦσιν αὐτούς B Vind., 'have such a notion of them,' 'so 3 conceive of them ': cf. *Pol.* 508 D Οὕτω τοίνυν καὶ τὸ τῆς ψυχῆς νόει, ' thus conceive of the soul also ': *Phaedr.* 246 C οὔτε ἰδόντες οὔτε ἱκανῶς νοήσαντες θεόν. The various reading οὕτως ἀγνοοῦσιν T has given rise to many needless conjectures.

δημοτικόν τι καὶ πρᾷον, 'a popular and kindly feature.' πρᾷον 6

303 d   NOTES

refers to their closing their own mouths as well as those of others.
Winckelmann refers to Plutarch, *Mor.* 148 D καὶ τὸν πατέρα τοῖς
πολίταις πρᾳότερον ἄρχοντα παρέχει καὶ δημοτικώτερον.

7 ὁπόταν φῆτε μήτε καλὸν εἶναι μηδὲν μήτε ἀγαθὸν πρᾶγμα κτλ.
'Whenever you deny that anything is either beautiful or good':
i.e. when you say that there is no unity of substance and attribute,
or of subject and predicate. Cf. *Sophist.* 251 C χαίρουσιν οὐκ ἐῶντες
ἀγαθὸν λέγειν ἄνθρωπον, ἀλλὰ τὸ μὲν ἀγαθὸν ἀγαθόν, τὸν δὲ ἄνθρωπον
ἄνθρωπον. The motive was to avoid admitting that the same thing
could be both one and many. See the passages quoted in the
Introduction, p. 40.

e 1 ἀτεχνῶς μὲν τῷ ὄντι συρράπτετε κτλ., 'you do in fact simply sew
up men's mouths, just as you say.'

3 πάνυ χαρίεν τέ ἐστιν κτλ., 'is a most charming result, and does
away with the invidiousness of your arguments.'

5 ταῦτα οὕτως ἔχει ὑμῖν καὶ τεχνικῶς ἐξηύρηται, ὥστε κτλ. BT. Two
constructions are in this reading combined, οὕτως ἔχει ὥστε and
ἐξηύρηται ὥστε. Cf. 288 A καὶ ὥστε τοῦτο μὴ πάσχειν οὐδ' ὑπὸ τῆς
ὑμετέρας πω τέχνης ἐξηυρῆσθαι. For ἔχει Schanz reads εὖ, Badham
εὖ ἔχει.

6 ὥστ' ⟨ἐν⟩ πάνυ ὀλίγῳ χρόνῳ. ὥστε BT. 'De Platonis more
scribendum suspicor ὥστ' ἐν πάνυ ὀλίγῳ χρόνῳ, ut § 74 (303 C 5) ἐν
ὀλίγῳ χρόνῳ, § 3 (272 B 3), *Soph.* 234 A, . . . *Apol. Socr.* 19 A, . . .
24 A, 37 B, *Criton* 52 E, et sexcenta alia loca' (Heindorf).

7 ἔγνων ἔγωγε. 'Haec cum antecedentibus coniungunt *Ald.* et
Basilienses. Melius opinor diviserunt interpretes et Stephanus;
et mihi quidem proprium suum in arte sophistica profectum signi-
ficare videtur Socrates' (Routh). Winckelmann, Badham, and
Schanz connect ἔγνων ἔγωγε with the preceding sentence, and, I
think, rightly: 'But the grandest thing, that this system is so
arranged by you and so skilfully invented that any one in the
world can learn it in a very short time—this I myself learnt by
observing how quickly Ctesippus was able to imitate you offhand.'

καὶ τῷ Κτησίππῳ. For this use of καί see Riddell, *Digest of
Idioms*, § 132 on 'Καί expletive, preceding and indicating the emphatic word.'

304 τοῦτο μὲν οὖν τοῦ πράγματος σφῶν, 'This part then of your business
a 1 is excellent in regard to its rapid transmission, but not expedient

66

for discussion in public.' The addition in T of τὸ σοφόν after σφῶν may possibly, as Stallbaum suggests, have arisen from σφῶν itself. αὐτὼ πρὸς ἀλλήλω μόνω. Cf. Cobet, *Var. Lect.* III 'Alterum indicium eiusdem interpolationis (μόνω) est in Platonis *Euthydemo* p. 504 A . . . ubi si μόνω in margine apponetur, pristinam sedem et iustam receperit.' Recent editors rightly retain μόνω, as adding force to αὐτώ, according to a very common usage : cf. *Gorg.* 500 B; *Theaet.* 202 A; *Legg.* 667 B.

τὸ γὰρ σπάνιον . . . τίμιον. Cf. Plut. *Mor.* 826 C τὸ τίμιον ἐν τῷ b 3 σπανίῳ τιθέμενον.

ἄγετε . . . ὅπως . . . παραδέξεσθον. After ἄγετε, which involves the 4 notion of exhorting or inciting, ὅπως with the future indicative has its original meaning ὅτῳ τρόπῳ, *quo pacto* as below B 7 σκόπει οὖν ὅπως συμφοιτήσεις : cf. Xen. *Cyr.* i. 2, 3 οἱ Περσικοὶ νόμοι ἐπιμέλονται ὅπως τὴν ἀρχὴν μὴ τοιοῦτοι ἔσονται οἱ πολῖται. Jelf, *Gk. Gr.* 811.

τοῦ χρηματίζεσθαι BT. If we retain this reading of the MSS. c 4 we must, with Winckelmann and others, make a parenthesis of ὃ δὲ καὶ σοὶ . . . οὐδέν, which for convenience of translation we may transpose to the end : 'and (they say) that no limit of capacity or age excludes any one whatever from easily acquiring their wisdom, and what it most concerns you to hear, they say that there is nothing to hinder a man from money-making.' If we adopt the conjectural emendation of Stephanus τὸ χρηματίζεσθαι, or that of Routh, ⟨τὸ⟩ τοῦ χρηματίζεσθαι, the construction is even simpler : 'and (they say) that they exclude no kind of capacity or age, and, what it most concerns you to hear, that not even attention to business at all hinders any one whatever from easily acquiring their wisdom.' Crito seems to have been very keen about his profits from agriculture : cf. 291 E ἡ ὑμετέρα τέχνη ἡ γεωργία.

μανθάνοιμι B, μάθοιμι T. The present is the better tense, as the 7 learning would not be confined to one single act.

κινδυνεύω . . . εἶναι, 'Yet I fear that I too am not one of those who are like Euthydemus, but of those others of whom you were yourself speaking just now, those who would rather be refuted than refute others by such arguments.'

ἃ γ' ἤκουον, 'what was said to me just now.' The use of the d 3 imperfect is like that of ἔλεγες just above.

⟨ἴσθ'⟩ ὅτι Heindorf, οἶσθ' ὅτι BT. The change from either to 4

304 d   NOTES

the other by a simple itacism is so easy that Plato's usage is the best criterion, and this is strongly in favour of ἴσθ᾽ ὅτι, which also gives the more suitable sense: cf. *Phaedr.* 243 D; *Gorg.* 453 A; *Theaet.* 145 B; *Parmen.* 135 D; *Pol.* 328 D; *Euthyd.* 284 E. 'You must know that one of those who were coming away from you came up to me as I was walking about.'

5   τούτων τις τῶν ... δεινῶν. As a litigant at Athens was obliged to plead his own cause, a practice was adopted by Antiphon, Aeschines, Isocrates and other rhetoricians of writing speeches to be recited in court by their clients. On the supposed reference here to Isocrates see Introduction, p. 18.

7   ἀκροᾷ, 'listen to the teaching.' Φυσικαὶ ἀκροάσεις is the title of Aristotle's lectures on Physics. Cf. *Menex.* 236 A ᾽Ασπασίας ... ἠκροώμην περαινούσης ἐπιτάφιον λόγον.

8   οὐ γὰρ οἷός τ᾽ ἦ προσστὰς κατακούειν, 'for I was not able to hear clearly, though I stood close up.' προστάς BT, 'though I stood forward.'

e 1   ἵνα ἤκουσας. After an historic tense (ἄξιόν γ᾽ ἦν ἀκοῦσαι) indicating an unfulfilled circumstance ἵνα, like ὡς and ὅπως, is used with a past indicative to declare what would have, but has not, taken place: ' in which case' (or 'that') you might have heard.' Cf. *Protag.* 335 C ἀλλὰ σὲ ἐχρῆν ἡμῖν συγχωρεῖν τὸν ἀμφότερα δυνάμενον, ἵνα συνουσία ἐγίγνετο. *Crito* 44 D; *Meno* 89 5; Soph. *Oed. R.* 1386 :

εἰ τῆς ἀκουούσης ἔτ᾽ ἦν
πηγῆς δι᾽ ὤτων φραγμός, οὐκ ἂν ἐσχόμην
τὸ μὴ ᾽ποκλεῖσαι τοὐμὸν ἄθλιον δέμας,
ἵν᾽ ἦ τυφλός τε καὶ κλύων μηδέν.

Eur. *Hippol.* 645.

οἱ νῦν σοφώτατοί εἰσι τῶν περὶ τοὺς τοιούτους λόγους. This, like τῶνδε τῶν σοφῶν D 7, is ironical.

3   Τί οὖν ἐφαίνοντό σοι; If ἐφαίνοντο refers to the Sophists, the answer is framed as if Crito had asked Τί οὖν ἐφαίνετό σοι ἃ οὗτοι ἔλεγον; Τί δὲ ἄλλο ... ἢ οἷά περ κτλ. But Schanz (*N. C. P.* p. 86) prefers to supply οἱ τοιοῦτοι λόγοι.

5   (οὑτωσὶ γάρ πως καὶ εἶπεν τοῖς ὀνόμασι). 'For it was just so that he spoke word for word,' Lat. *verbum e verbo.* Cf. *Phaedr.* 234 C οὐχ ὑπερφυῶς τά τε ἄλλα καὶ τοῖς ὀνόμασιν εἰρῆσθαι; *Phaedo* 71 B κἂν εἰ μὴ χρώμεθα τοῖς ὀνόμασιν ἐνιαχοῖ, 'if we do not use the exact terms

in some places.' 'I am quoting, says Crito to Socrates, the very words this person used. . . . This is an intimation that some one in particular is meant, and that the reader is expected to recognize the author by his style' (Thompson, *Phaedr.* p. 181). Cf. Introduction, p. 18.

'Ἀλλὰ μέντοι κτλ. 'But surely philosophy is a fine sort of thing.' 6 Ποῖον, ἔφη, χαρίεν; 'Fine indeed? said he.' Cf. 291 A Ποῖος 7 Κτήσιππος;

ὦ μακάριε, 'my blessed fellow,' a polite mode of expressing strong disagreement : 'mein Lieber,' vel 'Bester' (Ast). 305 οὐδενὸς μὲν οὖν ἄξιον, 'Nay rather, good for nothing.' a 1 ἑαυτὸν παρέχειν, 'to lend himself' as a tool. Cf. *Euthyphr.* 3 D 3 σὺ μὲν δοκεῖς σπάνιον σεαυτὸν παρέχειν. *Meno* 95 A παρέχειν αὑτοὺς διδασκάλους τοῖς νέοις.

παντὸς δὲ ῥήματος ἀντέχονται, 'lay hold of every word.' 'Cuivis 4 vocabulo adhaerent' (Winckelm.). 'Arripiunt et tuentur quidquid in solum venit' (Heind.). 'Clark. Vatic. pro ῥήματος nobis tradiderunt χρήματος, quod, cum effundat bonum sensum, restituendum est : scriptor enim universe dicit : "aggrediuntur rem quamlibet"' (Schanz, *N. C. P.* p. 86). On ῥῆμα see Lutosl. p. 430.

ἀλλὰ γάρ, 'But the fact is'; cf. Riddell, *Digest*, 182. 6

τὸ πρᾶγμα αὐτὸ καὶ οἱ ἄνθρωποι. The distinction between philosophical discussion in itself and the men who make a bad use of it is introduced for the sake of what follows, τὸ πρᾶγμα ἐδόκει οὐκ ὀρθῶς ψέγειν.

οἱ τοιοῦτοι ἄνδρες, 'Wonderful fellows are the men of this class,' b 4 i. e. such as the critic you mention, ἀνὴρ οἰόμενος πάνυ εἶναι σοφός.

ὅ τι μέλλω ἐρεῖν, 'what I am to say.' Cf. *Gorg.* 455 B ἐγὼ μὲν γάρ 5 τοι οὐδ' αὐτός πω δύναμαι κατανοῆσαι ὅ τι λέγω. In μέλλω the notion of what is about to be done is combined with that of what ought to be done : cf. *Polit.* 291 C εἰ μέλλομεν ἰδεῖν ἐναργῶς.

ῥήτωρ τις. The title 'rhetor' or 'orator' is thus appropriated to 7 those who actually speak in the law-courts or assemblies of the δῆμος, in distinction from those who composed speeches for others to deliver. Cf. Xen. *Mem.* ii. 6, 15 Ἑώρων γάρ, ἔφη ὁ Κριτόβουλος, ῥήτοράς τε φαύλους ἀγαθοῖς δημηγόροις φίλους ὄντας. The more powerful of the δημηγόροι were called δημαγωγοί: cf. Schömann, *de Com. Athen.* p. 109; Valckenar. *Diatrib. de Aristob.* xxiii. 251 sq.

τῶν τοὺς τοιούτους εἰσπεμπόντων, 'One of those who equip and send into court the former class of men, one who makes the speeches with which the orators (οἱ ῥήτορες) do battle.' Stallbaum would omit οἱ ῥήτορες, supposing that the title could not be applied to litigants who used speeches written for them by others. But the reading of the MSS. is retained by Schanz, and rightly defended by Winckelmann, *Proleg.* xxxvii. note a, on the ground that ῥήτωρ is applied to the actual speaker as such, however his speech may have been prepared. Cf. *Apolog.* 18 A, where ῥήτορος refers to Socrates himself, though it was the first time he had ever appeared to address a court. On the ῥήτορες as a professional class see Riddell, *Apolog.* p. x. note.

C 2 ἐπὶ δικαστήριον ἀναβεβηκέναι. The same phrase occurs *Apolog.* 17 D 'The preposition has the notion of "presenting oneself to the court." Cf. Isaeus, *Fr.* vii. I. l. 15 λέγειν ἐπὶ δικαστηρίου. The ἀναβέβημα refers to the βῆμα' (Riddell). ibid. Introd. xv. 'The raised platform, called βῆμα, served for accuser and accused in turn as well as for their witnesses.'

5 Ἤδη μανθάνω· περὶ τούτων. In the older editions these words were connected, but Routh first corrected the punctuation. For a similar use of μανθάνω cf. *Rep.* 524 D μανθάνω τοίνυν ἤδη, ἔφη, καὶ δοκεῖ μοι οὕτω. The absence of any conjunction (asyndeton) before περὶ τούτων is quite in keeping with the rather excited and rapid speech of Socrates (Stallbaum): 'these are the men of whom I was myself going to speak just now.'

6 οὓς ἔφη Πρόδικος μεθόρια κτλ., 'whom Prodicus called borderers between a philosopher and a statesman.' I have not found any other reference to this saying. On Prodicus cf. 277 E 4, note, and on μεθόρια compare the two passages from which 'we obtain a complete notion of what Isocrates meant by "philosophy," a combination of the accomplishments of the ῥήτωρ and the πολιτικός' (Thompson, *Phaedr.* Append. ii. 172). Isocr. *Antid.* 196 οἱ δὲ περὶ τὴν φιλοσοφίαν ὄντες τὰς ἰδέας ἁπάσας αἷς ὁ λόγος τυγχάνει χρώμενος διεξέρχονται τοῖς μαθηταῖς. ibid. 290 σοφοὺς μὲν νομίζω τοὺς ταῖς δόξαις ἐπιτυγχάνειν ὡς ἐπὶ τὸ πολὺ τοῦ βελτίστου δυναμένους, φιλοσόφους δὲ τοὺς ἐν τούτοις διατρίβοντας, ἐξ ὧν τάχιστα λήψονται τὴν τοιαύτην φρόνησιν. On the question whether Isocrates is here meant see the Introduction, p. 19.

8 πρὸς δὲ τῷ εἶναι καὶ δοκεῖν, 'and (think themselves) not only to be

but also to be so regarded among very many, so that there are none but the philosophers to stand in the way of their universal reputation.' The reading of the chief MSS. τὸ εἶναι must either be altered, as by Stallbaum, to the dative, or altogether omitted, as by Schanz. In this latter case τὸ εἶναι must be regarded as a marginal gloss intended to form a construction for πρός, the absolute use of which was not understood: cf. Hom. *Il.* v. 307 θλάσσε δέ οἱ κοτύλην, πρὸς δ' ἄμφω ῥῆξε τένοντε. Hdt. i. 71 πρὸς δὲ οὐκ οἴνῳ διαχρέονται. Eur. *Hel.* 110 καὶ πρός γ᾽ Ἀχαιοί.

εὐδοκιμεῖν ἐμποδὼν σφίσιν εἶναι. Verbs or phrases expressing 9 hindrance are followed by an infinitive either with or without μή or τοῦ, which Stephanus added in this place. Heindorf refers to Plat. *Pol.* 407 C ὥστε, ὅπῃ αὕτη, ἀρετῇ ἀσκεῖσθαι καὶ δοκιμάζεσθαι πάντῃ ἐμπόδιος. Thuc. i. 16 ἐπεγίγνετο ... κωλύματα μὴ αὐξηθῆναι.

τοὺς περὶ φιλοσοφίαν ἀνθρώπους. The addition of ἀνθρώπους, which d 1 is otherwise unnecessary, is intended to express contempt. Cf. *Phaedr.* 268 C εἴποιεν ἄν, οἶμαι, ὅτι μαίνεται ἄνθρωπος. *Gorg.* 518 C διακόνους μοι λέγεις καὶ ἐπιθυμιῶν παρασκευαστὰς ἀνθρώπους, ' a parcel of fellows, ministers and caterers to men's appetites' (Cope).

ἐὰν τούτους εἰς δόξαν καταστήσωσιν μηδενὸς δοκεῖν ἀξίους εἶναι, ' if 2 they reduce these to the reputation of being good for nothing.' For the pleonasm δόξαν . . . δοκεῖν cf. Crito 44 C καίτοι τίς ἂν αἰσχίων εἴη ταύτης δόξα ἢ δοκεῖν χρήματα περὶ πλείονος ποιεῖσθαι ἢ φίλους; ibid. 53 B.

ἀναμφισβητήτως . . . σοφίας πέρι, ' they will at once indisputably 3 carry off the victory in regard to reputation for wisdom.'

εἶναι . . . σφᾶς σοφωτάτους T. For the accusative, instead of the 5 more usual nominative with the infinitive, see 290 A 9, note: both here and there the addition of the personal pronoun is emphatic. In our present passage the MSS. vary, B having σφᾶς σοφώτατοι, from which Schanz adopts σφεῖς σοφώτατοι.

ἐν δὲ τοῖς ἰδίοις λόγοις ὅταν ἀποληφθῶσιν, ' when they are caught in private conversations.' Cf. *Pol.* 499 A ἐν δίκαις καὶ ἐν ἰδίαις συνουσίαις. I do not understand why Schanz prefers ἀπολειφθῶσιν to the well authenticated ἀποληφθῶσιν BT, for which cf. *Gorg.* 522 A ἐν τούτῳ τῷ κακῷ ἀποληφθέντα.

κολούεσθαι, ' are cut short ': Schol. κολούεσθαι ἐλαττοῦσθαι, ἐμποδί- 7 ζεσθαι. Cf. *Apol.* 39 D μὴ τοὺς ἄλλους κολούειν, ἀλλ᾽ ἑαυτὸν παρασκευάζειν ὅπως ἔσται ὡς βέλτιστος. The loose rhetoric which was uninterrupted in a forensic speech was easily refuted by the sharp dialectic of the Sophists: cf. 305 E ἐκτὸς δὲ ὄντες κινδύνων καὶ ἀγώνων.

πάνυ εἰκότως, 'quite naturally': Stallbaum spoils the rhythm of the sentence by his punctuation πάνυ· εἰκότως, both here and 287 B. In Plato and in other authors far most frequently πάνυ precedes the word which it strengthens, as below πάνυ ἐξ εἰκότος λόγου.

8   μετρίως μὲν γὰρ φιλοσοφίας ἔχειν, 'for they think that they are moderately acquainted with philosophy.' Cf. Gorg. 484 C φιλοσοφία γάρ τοί ἐστιν, ὦ Σώκρατες, χαρίεν, ἄν τις αὐτοῦ μετρίως ἅψηται ἐν τῇ ἡλικίᾳ. ibid. 487 C. 'The middle position, which Isocrates himself aimed at, is shown to be untenable' (Zeller, Plato, p. 132). In these words 'we are inevitably reminded of the description of Isocrates in the Phaedrus as one in whose genius ἔνεστί τις φιλοσοφία' (Thompson, Phaedrus, Append. ii. 181).

e 2 καρποῦσθαι τὴν σοφίαν. The finishing touch in the picture (ἐκτὸς δὲ ... σοφίαν) agrees perfectly with the account of himself and his own way of life, which is given by Isocrates with no little self-gratulation in the Antidosis (Thompson, ibid.).

3   οὐ γάρ τοι ἀλλά, 'for it cannot be denied that.' Cf. 286 C, note.

5   ὄντως Ven. 184, οὕτως BT Vind. Cf. Routh: 'ὄντως. Non liquet fortasse quid legerit Ficinus, qui vertit ut dicis.' 'Videlicet grammatici vel scribae ignorarunt usum illum loquendi, quo ὄντως et τῷ ὄντι in dictorum usurpatur confirmatione, ideoque in eius locum otiosum illud atque languidum οὕτως suffecerunt. V. ad Lach. 196 D' (Stallbaum).

εὐπρέπειαν μᾶλλον ἢ ἀλήθειαν, 'plausibility rather than truth': cf. Phaedo 92 C μετὰ εἰκότος τινὸς καὶ εὐπρεπείας.

306   ὅσα μεταξύ τινοιν δυοῖν κτλ., 'all other things that are halfway
a 2   between some two and partake of both, if compounded of evil and good, are made better than the one and worse than the other, but if of two things good for different objects, they are inferior to both in reference to any object for which either of those component parts is useful.' This notion is not contrary to Plato's conviction that true statesmanship must be based upon a sound philosophy: cf. Gorg. 581 D.

NOTES 306 a

ὅσα δὲ ἐκ δυοῖν κακοῖν κτλ., 'but all intermediate compounds of 6
two evil things not having the same object, these and these only
are better than either of those things of both of which they
participate.'

μετέχουσιν BT : Hirschig's conjecture μετέχει, adopted by Schanz, b 2
is unnecessary. The thought is really directed, both at first and
throughout, not to things neuter but to men, as immediately appears
from the next sentence.

ἡ πολιτικὴ πρᾶξις, 'the business of statesmanship.' Cf. Gorg.
484 D ἐπειδὰν οὖν ἔλθωσιν εἴς τινα ἰδίαν ἢ πολιτικὴν πρᾶξιν.

οὗτοι δ' ἀμφοτέρων μετέχοντες. Stallbaum takes ἀμφοτέρων as 3
masculine, i. e. τῶν φιλοσόφων καὶ τῶν πολιτικῶν : but the close
relation to ἑκατέρα shows that it should be referred rather to
ἡ φιλοσοφία and ἡ πολιτικὴ πρᾶξις. Cf. Aristot. Eth. Nic. x. 9, 18 τὰ
δὲ πολιτικὰ ἐπαγγέλλονται μὲν διδάσκειν οἱ σοφισταί κτλ.

ἀμφοτέρων γάρ εἰσι φαυλότεροι. Stallbaum's explanation of ἀμ- 4
φοτέρων is properly applicable to this second occurrence of the
word.

οὕτως ἄν τι λέγοιεν ἀληθές, 'in this case there would be some 6
truth in what they say.' If philosophy and statesmanship are both
bad, those who have but a little of each are better than those who
have much of either.

πρὸς ἑκάτερον, πρὸς ὃ ἥ τε πολιτικὴ κτλ., 'for either object, for c 3
which statesmanship on the one hand and philosophy on the other
are important.' The conjunctions τε καί are here used disjunctively:
cf. Xen. Hier. i. 2 πῇ διαφέρει ὁ τυραννικός τε καὶ ὁ ἰδιωτικὸς βίος.
Plat. Laws 831 D; Jelf, Gk. Gr. 758, 1 ; Donaldson, Gk. Gr. § 554.

συγγιγνώσκειν . . . αὐτοῖς . . . τῆς ἐπιθυμίας. This use of the 6
genitive after συγγιγνώσκειν appears to be very rare. The accusative occurs in Eur. Androm. 840 συγγνώσεταί σοι τήνδ' ἁμαρτίαν
πόσις.

πάντα γὰρ ἄνδρα χρὴ ἀγαπᾶν, 'we ought to be satisfied with any 8
man.' Cf. Cratyl. 391 C τὰ δὲ τῇ τοιαύτῃ ἀληθείᾳ ῥηθέντα ἀγαπῴην ὡς
του ἄξια.

ἐχόμενον φρονήσεως, 'bordering on good sense': cf. Pol. 496 A
οὐδὲν γνήσιον οὐδὲ ἄξιον οὐδὲ φρονήσεως ἀληθινῆς ἐχόμενον. 'Isocrates
calls his own philosophy a φρόνησις in Antid. § 290' (Thompson,
ibid. 182).

73

d 2 περὶ τῶν υἱέων. Cf. Diog. Laert. ii. 13 καὶ οἱ παῖδες δὲ αὐτοῦ (*Critonis*) διήκουσαν Σωκράτους, Κριτόβουλος, Ἑρμογένης, Ἐπιγένης, Κτήσιππος, quorum e numero eximendos esse et Hermogenem et Ctesippum vel hic Platonis locus declarat' (Heindorf).

υἱέων B, υἱῶν Schanz (1880). In the Appendix to the *Phaedrus* (1882) Schanz writes: 'In hoc dialogo semper est υἱός in BT, et semper νῦν δή.'

5 Κριτόβουλος. Cf. *Apol.* 38 B Πλάτων δὲ ὅδε, ὦ ἄνδρες Ἀθηναῖοι, καὶ Κρίτων καὶ Κριτόβουλος καὶ Ἀπολλόδωρος κελεύουσί με τριάκοντα μνῶν τιμήσασθαι, αὐτοὶ δ' ἐγγυᾶσθαι.

ἡλικίαν ἔχει, 'is grown up.' This description of his age agrees with the fact of his offering bail for the fine which Socrates proposes to pay. Cf. *Men.* 89 B ἀλλ' ἐπειδὴ ἀφίκοιντο εἰς τὴν ἡλικίαν, χρήσιμοι γίγνονται ταῖς πόλεσιν. *Charm.* 154 A οὔπω ἐν ἡλικίᾳ ἦν. *Lys.* 209 A.

ὅστις αὐτὸν ὀνήσει, 'who will be of use to him,' i. e. as a teacher.

7 ὥστ' ἐμοὶ ... B, ὥστέ μοι T. Cf. 278 C 7, note.

e 2 αὐτῶν δὲ περὶ παιδείας. The position of αὐτῶν makes it emphatic, 'to take no care of the boys themselves in the matter of education.'

4 καί μοι δοκεῖ. Schanz does not attempt to apply the rule about ἐμοί, 278 C 7, because there is no possibility here of making μοι δοκεῖ a parenthesis. Why should it be made formally in the other passages?

5 πάνυ ἀλλόκοτος, 'quite unfit for the task.' Cf. Ruhnk. *Tim. Lex.* 'Phrynichus Προπαρασκ. Σοφιστ. MS. Ἀλλόκοτος σημαίνει μὲν κυρίως τὸ παρηλλαγμένον τῆς καθεστώσης διαίτης καὶ τρόπου; κτλ.'

307 ὥς γε πρὸς σὲ τἀληθῆ εἰρῆσθαι, 'to tell you the truth between our-
a 1 selves.' Cf. *Pol.* 595 B ὡς μὲν πρὸς ἡμᾶς εἰρῆσθαι, οὐ γάρ μου κατερεῖτε, 'speaking as between ourselves, for you will not tell of me.'

b 1 ἕκαστον τὸ ἔργον BT: 'τῶν ἔργων Aristides, probavit Heindorf' (Schanz). Cf. *Phaedr.* 274 E περὶ ἑκάστης τῆς τέχνης.

8 αὐτὸ τὸ πρᾶγμα, 'the thing itself,' i.e. philosophy.

c 3 τὸ λεγόμενον δὴ τοῦτο. Cf. *Laws* 804 D τὸ λεγόμενον, πάντ' ἄνδρα καὶ παῖδα ... παιδευτέον ἐξ ἀνάγκης. *Pol.* 372 B κατακλινέντες ἐπὶ στιβάδων ἐστρωμένων μίλακί τε καὶ μυρρίναις, εὐωχήσονται αὐτοί τε καὶ τὰ παιδία.

I. INDEX OF GREEK WORDS

75

I. INDEX OF GREEK WORDS

I. INDEX OF GREEK WORDS

I. INDEX OF GREEK WORDS

κελεύω 286 E.
κεραμεύς 301 C.
κεφαλαῖον 280 B, 281 D.
κεφαλή 283 E, 293 E.
κήλησις 290 A.
κιθαριστής 272 C.
κινδυνεύω 304 C.
κίων 303 B.
κολούεσθαι 305 D.
κολοφών 301 E.
κόρυδος 291 B.
κράνιον 299 E.
κρέας 301 C.
κρείττονες 291 A.
κρόνος 287 B.
κυβιστάω 294 E.
κυνάριον 298 D.
κυνηγέτης 290 B.
κωβιός 298 D.
κωλύω 272 D.

λαβύρινθος 291 B.
λανθάνω 300 B.
λεγόμενον (τό) 292 E, 293 D.
λίθος 298 A.
λίνον λίνῳ 298 C.
λογιστικός 290 C.
λογοποιικός 289 C.
λογοποιός 289 D.
λόγος ('definitio') 285 E, 286 A.
λόγου ἕνεκα 286 D.
λοιδορεῖσθαι 284 E.
λοιδορία 288 B.
λυροποιός 289 B.

μάγειρος 301 D.
μαθητής 273 A.
μαθών (ὅ τι μ.) 299 A.
μακάριος 293 B, 305 A.
μανθάνω 276 B, C.
μάχαιρα 294 E.
μέγας (=χαλεπός) 275 D.
„ βασιλεύς 274 A.
μειράκιον 273 B.
μεθόριον 305 C.
μέλλω 305 C.
μένειν (ἐν ταὐτῷ) 288 A.

μέντοι 273 C.
μεταξύ 306 A.
μετέχω 271 B, 306 B.
μετρίως 305 D.
Μνήμη 275 D.
μοι δοκεῖν 273 A, 278 C, 297 C,
   298 A, 300 D.
μόλις 294 B.

νεανίσκος 273 A.
νεμεσητός 282 B.
νευρορραφεῖν 294 B.
νοεῖν 287 D, 303 D.

ὃ δέ 271 C.
ὀδούς 294 C.
οἰκεῖος 301 E.
οἷος (εἰς τι) 272 A.
οἷον 302 A.
ὀλίγου 303 B.
ὁμομήτριος 297 E.
ὁμοπάτριος 297 E.
ὁμόσε (ᾔτην) 294 D.
ὀνίνημι 306 D.
ὄνομα 304 E.
ὄντα (τὰ μή) 284 C, 286 A.
ὄντως (v. l. οὕτως).
ὁπλομάχης 299 C.
ὁπότερος 271 A.
ὁρᾶν (δυνατά) 300 A.
ὀρθότης 277 E.
ὀρθῶς 280 E, 281 A.
ὀρτυγοθήρης 290 D.
ὀρτυγοτρόφος 290 D.
ὀρχεῖσθαι 277 E, 294 E.
ὅς (=οἷος) 283 D.
ὅσον μή 273 A.
ὅ τι (v. l. τί) 287 B.
ὅ τι μαθών 283 E, 299 A.
οὔπω . . . καί 273 A, 277 B.
οὗτος (=ἐκεῖνος) 271 B.
ὄψις 271 B.
ὀψοποιός 290 B.

παγκρατιαστής 271 C.
παγκρατιαστικός 272 A.
παῖσαι 278 C.

78

I. INDEX OF GREEK WORDS

πάλαισμα 277 D.
πάμμαχος 271 C.
πανοῦργος 300 D.
πάνσοφος (πάσσοφος) 271 C.
πάντα καλά 293 D.
πάνυ (εἰκότως) 287 B, 300 C, 305 D.
παραγίγνεσθαι 301 A.
παραδίδωμι 272 B, 285 C, 292 A, C.
παρακαθέζομαι 273 B.
παρακελευστικός 283 B.
παρακούω 300 D.
παραμυθία 290 A.
παραμύθιον 272 B.
παραπλήσιος 297 E.
παρατείνω 303 B.
παραφθέγγομαι 296 A.
παράφθεγμα 296 B.
παρεῖναι 301 A.
πάρεργον 273 D.
παρέχειν 305 A.
πᾶς (ἐν παντί) 301 A.
πᾶς ἕκαστος 303 B.
πάσσοφος 271 C.
πάσχω 302 D.
πατρῷος 302 B.
πένης 281 C.
περί (seq. dat.) 275 B.
περιάπτω 272 C.
περιεστήκει (sic) 271 A.
περιέρχομαι 273 A.
περιστάνω 295 D.
περιπατεῖν 273 A.
πέρυσιν 272 B.
ποδαπός 271 C.
πόθεν 291 B.
ποῖος 291 A.
πολιτική 291 C.
πολιτικός 305 C, D.
πολλοῦ (δέω μὴ οὐ) 297 B.
πολυτίμητος 296 D.
πόρρω σοφίας 294 E.
ποτόν 280 C.
πρᾶξις 306 B.
πράττειν (dupl. sensu) 278 E,
281 C.
πρόγονος 302 D.
προΐστασθαι 304 D.

προπέρυσιν 272 B.
πρός (sine casu) 294 A, 298 D
note, 305 C note.
πρὸς ἔπος 295 C.
προσαποκρίνομαι 296 A.
προσκύπτω 275 E.
προσπαίζω 283 B.
προτρεπτικός 278 C, 282 D.
προφερής 271 B.
πρύμνη 291 D.
Πυππάξ 303 A.

ῥήτωρ 284 B, 305 B.

σεμνός 279 A, 303 C.
σημεῖον 272 E.
σιγῶντα λέγειν 300 B.
σκέψις 282 C.
σκληρός 271 B.
σκολύθρια 278 B.
σκυτοτομική 292 C.
σοφιστής 271 C, 288 B.
σοφιστρία 297 C.
σπάνιος (τίμιος) 304 B.
σπουδάζω 273 D.
στρατηγική 291 C.
στρέφω 302 B, (διπλᾶ) 276 D.
στροφή 302 B.
συγγίγνεσθαι 306 D.
συγγιγνώσκω 306 C.
συγγράφεσθαι 272 A.
συμβαίνω 281 E.
συμβούλομαι 296 D, 298 B.
συμμαθητής 272 C.
συμφοιτάω 272 D, 304 B.
συμφοιτητής 272 C.
συνάπτω 298 C.
συνομολογεῖσθαι 280 B.
συντείνομαι 288 D.
συρράπτω 303 E.
σφεῖς 305 D.

ταλαίπωρος 302 B.
τάξις 273 C.
τάχα (cum ἴσως) 272 C.
τεκμαίρομαι 289 B.
τεκτονική 292 C.

79

I. INDEX OF GREEK WORDS

II. INDEX OF PROPER NAMES

OXFORD
PRINTED AT THE CLARENDON PRESS
BY HORACE HART, M.A.
PRINTER TO THE UNIVERSITY

For EU product safety concerns, contact us at Calle de José Abascal, 56–1°,
28003 Madrid, Spain or eugpsr@cambridge.org.